THE BRITISH

OAK

THE BRITISH

OAK

ARCHIE MILES

For my three beautiful women:
Jannie, my love and inspiration,
and our daughters Rowan Beth
and Eleanor Holly.

This is Elly's acorn, drawn when
she was eight years old.

CONSTABLE

First published in Great Britain in 2013 by Constable, an imprint of Constable & Robinson Ltd
This edition published in 2016 by Constable

A CIP catalogue record for this book
is available from the British Library.

ISBN: 978-1-47212-375-6

Printed and bound in China by C&C Offset Co Ltd

Designed by Peter Dawson and Louise Evans: www.gradedesign.com

Constable
An imprint of
Little, Brown Book Group
Carmelite House
50 Victoria Embankment
London EC4Y 0DZ

An Hachette UK Company
www.hachette.co.uk

www.littlebrown.co.uk

OPPOSITE: Oaks in Ickworth
Park, Suffolk.

TREE PROFILES

CONTENTS

LOCATION MAP OF BRITISH OAKS, DEER PARKS, WOODS AND FORESTS

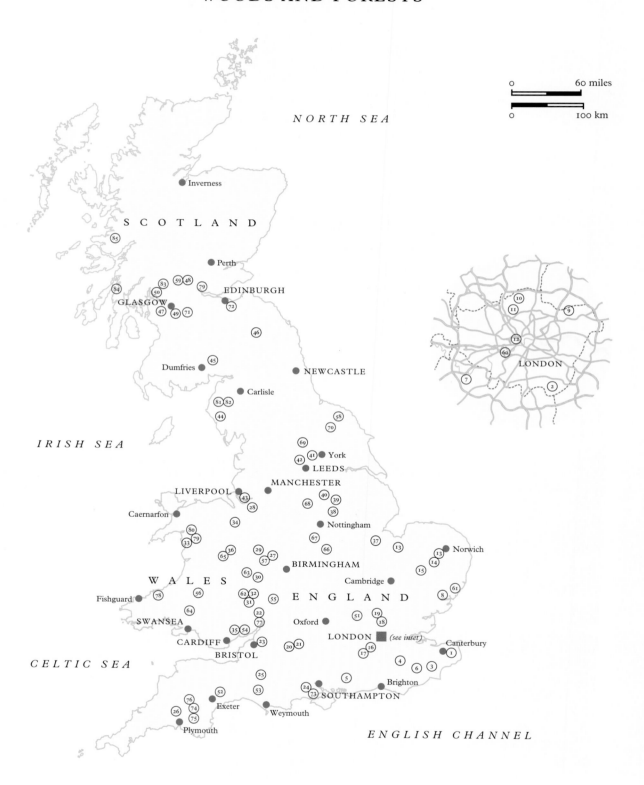

TREE PROFILES

Please refer to the Gazetteer (p.294) for more information.

1 Majesty and the Fredville Oaks
2 The Wilberforce Oak
3 The Bonington Law Day Oak
4 Sir Philip Sidney's Oak
5 Queen Elizabeth's Oak, Cowdray Park
6 Queen Elizabeth's Oak, Northiam
7 The Crouch Oak
8 Old Knobbley
9 The Fairlop Oak
10 The Chandos, or Minchenden Oak
11 Turpin's Oak
12 The Elfin Oak
13 Kett's Oak
14 The Winfarthing Oak
15 The Tea Party Oak
16 Windsor Great Park Oaks
17 Herne's Oak
18 Goff's Oak
19 Panshanger Oak
20, 21 Oaks of Savernake
22 The Newland Oak
23 Gog and Magog Oaks
24 The Knightwood Oak
25 The Silton Oak
26 The Meavy Oak
27 The Boscobel Oak
28 The Marton Oak
29 Owen Glendower's Oak
30 The Gospel Oak at Grendon Bishop
31 Jack of Kent's Oak
32 The Monarch
33 The Nannau Oak
34 The Pontfadog Oak
35 The Golynos Oak
36 The Buttington Oak
37 The Bowthorpe Oak
38, 39, 40 The Oaks of Sherwood
41 The Cowthorpe Oak
42 The Shire Oak, or Skyrack
43 The Allerton Oak
44 The Henry VI Oak
45 The Lochwood Oaks
46 The Capon Tree
47 The Wallace Oaks
48 The Poker Tree
49 The Covenanters' Oak
50 The Strathleven House Oak, or the Bruce Tree

PLACES OF INTEREST

Please refer to the Index (p.298) for more information on the following oaks, parks, woods and forests.

EXTRAORDINARY OAKS

51 Ashridge Estate, oak and ash, Tring, Hertfordshire
52 Remedy Oak, Wimborne, Dorset
53 Billy Wilkins, Melbury Park (private), Dorset
54 Caeryder Oak, Llanhennock, Monmouthshire
55 White-leaved Oak, Malvern Hills, Worcestershire
56 Rhandirmwyn Oak, Carmarthenshire
57 De Coubertin Oak, Much Wenlock, Shropshire
58 Medusa Oak, Ingleby Greenhow, North Yorkshire
59 Inchmahome Oak, Lake of Menteith, Stirling

DEER PARKS

60 Richmond Park, Surrey
61 Staverton Park, Suffolk
62 Moccas Park (restricted), Herefordshire
63 Croft Castle, Herefordshire
64 Dinefwr, Llandeilo, Carmarthenshire
65 Powis Castle Estate (private), Powys
66 Bradgate Park, Leicestershire
67 Calke Abbey, Derbyshire
68 Chatsworth (restricted), Derbyshire
69 Ripley Castle, North Yorkshire
70 Duncomb Park (restricted), North Yorkshire
71 Cadzow Oaks, South Lanarkshire
72 Dalkeith Park, Midlothian

WOODS AND FORESTS

73 New Forest, Hampshire
74 Wistman's Wood, Dartmoor
75 Piles Copse, Dartmoor
76 Black Tor Copse, Dartmoor
77 Forest of Dean, Gloucestershire
78 Pengelli Forest, Ceredigion
79 Coed Ganllwyd, Gwynedd
80 Coed y Rhygen (restricted), Gwynedd
81 Keskadale Oaks, Cumbria
82 Birkrigg, Cumbria
83 Loch Lomond, Stirling/Argyll & Bute
84 Taynish Peninsula, Argyll & Bute
85 Ariundle, Loch Sunart, Highland

MAP **9**

INTRODUCTION

OPPOSITE: Autumnal oak in Taynish woods. Not a spectacular tree in itself, but part of a wonderful mosaic of colours and textures, laden with mosses and lichens, and truly evocative of these west-coast Atlantic oak woods.

My family has a smallholding of almost four acres around the Herefordshire farmstead that we came to twenty-three years ago. Most of the land is given over to an old orchard with dozens of gnarled and aged fruit trees – mainly cider apples. At the bottom of the orchard stand four mighty oaks; English oaks as it happens. When we bought the farm I couldn't quite believe that these were our trees, but then I feel no covetousness, much more a sense of guardianship. These are maiden trees with girths of around 12 feet, and by my best guess must have been planted about 200 years ago. Standing proudly and evenly spaced along the boundary hedgerow, one instinctively knows these are not random seedling upstarts. Whoever planted these oaks planted them with a purpose in mind. They were not pollarded or coppiced, so mature timber must have been the aim. Was there a new house or barn in the offing? Were the trees intended to be sold for ship or boat building one day? We will never know, but whoever that planter was, he had faith in the future for his oaks, yet at the same time he knew that he would never profit by them. A prudent planter, perhaps he had benefitted from the oaks sewn by his forefathers. Either way he had the vision to plant for several generations well beyond his own lifespan.

I frequently walk down to these four old friends to see how they are getting along. One has its roots hanging precariously over the deep-cut lane up to the house. It's a lane with hedgerows of medieval origin, and must have long been a hollow way. This oak has adapted and thrust its roots far into the orchard, developed massive buttresses in the bank and probably driven more roots well below the old lane, long before any twentieth-century roadmen slapped tarmac on the muddy, rutted track. Occasionally I have to peg back the ivy, which races greedily up the rough bark, finding easy purchase until it begins to festoon the boughs, blocking out the light, holding rainwater and detritus in the crooks of the branches, adding weight and windsail worries to the crown. The ivy is hacked off, but I know it will be back to assail the trees once again. A little is okay, as this provides an autumn source of nectar, as well as habitat for small mammals and birds. An infestation, however, can create problems.

If I were to take a dispassionate view of our oaks, it would be to say that they are now probably in their prime, ideal subjects for felling and conversion. Surely their stately forms, their beauty in the landscape makes them sacrosanct? What

would we do with them anyway? Four oaks won't build a house. Sell them? What price could repay their place in our landscape? I have seen the setting sun burnish the autumn gold; kicked through the drifts of leaves, inhaling the departing year; captured the rime-ringed, semi-skeletal leaves, rigid in the brittle grass, and been uplifted every spring when the soft emerald-shiny leaves unfurl again. Indecision will eventually see these four friends falter, fail, and crumble back to the mould from whence they came. The man who planted them all those years ago would probably deride my soft-hearted way of thinking, my lack of commercial acumen. 'It's fine timber,' he'd say, 'chop them down and sell them.' It's a conundrum, but I have no wish to be the one who makes such a decision.

I hatched a plan for a book about the British Oak several years ago (I could say, beneath these very oaks, which has a certain romance); one of those projects that simmers quietly on the back burner until one finds a publisher with a similar vision. So, when I set out to produce this book, it should all have been so easy, so straightforward, after all I'd done so much of the groundwork. It was only when the necessity to proceed and produce began to grapple with my tight timeframe that I came to understand exactly what I'd taken on. I soon realized that fitting everything I'd ever known about the oak tree into one volume was going to be quite a challenge – if only because of all the material I knew I would have to leave out.

For much of the last twenty years I have spent my time becoming intimately acquainted with some of the largest and most ancient oak trees throughout Britain. At this stage many of them feel like old friends. I visit them on a regular basis, to see how they're managing; fearful for them as they creep imperceptibly slowly into their dotage, stag-heading themselves, shedding a bough here and there, and hollowing and rotting back to the earth that first fuelled the acorn so many centuries before. These are often trees of humungous proportions – attaining girths in excess of 40 feet and living maybe 1,200 or 1,300 years (some would say more). Every one of these ancient oaks is unique.

The first strand of the book is an overview of some of our most famous oak trees. Some are famous for their remarkable age and stature, others for the part they have played in Britain's history and culture, and some for their place in the landscape. Researching and developing all of their individual stories has been a joy. In fact, meeting the people who either own or tend to these grand old trees today has been illuminating and heart-warming. As with my own oak trees, their relationships are intimate: These trees are often part of the family, and on the tragic occasions when one is lost, a deep sense of bereavement follows. Everyone is keen to do the best they can for their oaks, and express concern about how to manage them and keep them thriving for as long as possible. The simplest solution, in most cases, is to do as little as possible. Ancient oaks of 700 or 800 years and more have been getting along very well for an incredibly long time – usually without the aid of props or chains. The only management issue might be whether or not to pollard, and thus re-employ the regime that has already kept them with us so long.

The question most people ask me is whether I can tell them how old their oaks might be. It's very difficult to say, for not only are most ancient oaks hollow, which means that no annual ring count could ever be taken, but the older the trees become, the slower they grow (sometimes maybe only 3 or 4 inches in a century). Dendrologist John White came up with a computation for aging oaks, but stresses that there are many variables within his figures. It is plain to see that large woodland oaks have grown at about half the speed of open-grown trees, so a woodland oak of around 12 feet, 6 inches could be 450 years old, while its open-grown counterpart at this size is only 200 years old. When establishing the age of the very biggest trees, those with girths of 30 feet and more, one starts estimating at about 700 years old and moves upward in relatively small increments in size, yet considerable leaps in age. A true 1,000-year-old oak tree will be at least 38 feet around, while the champions in this book, those with a massive 42-foot girth, could be in excess of 1,300 years old. Even so, this is an inexact science. Many different factors affect tree growth. The older the tree, the more likely it is to have had a chequered past. Quite often trees are pollarded for a time, and then after a certain point the regime is abandoned. Changes in nearby watercourses, excessive land drainage or climatic periods of drought can also affect growth. Open-growing trees could have begun their lives 500 years earlier as woodland trees, or vice versa. Old maps sometimes fill in the lost years and help to clarify computations. Ultimately, when I'm put on the spot I make an educated guess, and with the very oldest oaks that's all any of us can do. Still, the mysteries that surround many ancient trees are what help to make them so entrancing.

Most of the trees in this book still exist. A few are long deceased, sometimes as long as two centuries ago, but I have included them here because they were once famous, either through their enormity or the wealth of anecdote that they provide. Choosing fifty trees was a trial in itself (I would have happily chosen a hundred, but editors being editors…). Of course, some splendid oaks just didn't make the cut, but I have tried to represent as varied a cross-section as possible, to illustrate the diversity of their roles and locations.

Among the oaks represented here are trees that hold veteran status, and those that hold ancient status. Many people, including myself, believe the two descriptions are interchangeable, but if one has to distinguish between them, then the very largest, perhaps in excess of 30 feet in girth, are usually considered ancient, while those between 20 and 30 feet in girth can be regarded as veterans. So, all famous oaks in this book are veterans, but only the uber-veterans are ancient.

Although there are two native species of oak – *Quercus robur*, the English oak, and *Quercus petraea*, the sessile oak – there are also so many hybrids and intermediate forms that for the purpose of this book I treat the oak in all its guises as one generic tree. In some cases, such as establishing record-breakers, or developing the right kind of timber for shipbuilding, the delineation between the two species has been significant, but in the vast majority of cases, the difference is unimportant and irrelevant.

The second strand of the book provides an overview of the many different aspects of oak in our culture, society, and economy. Shipbuilding and timber-framed buildings have been the foundations of Britain's stability, success, and growth as a nation, with 'hearts of oak' at the very core. However, the uses of oak have extended far beyond construction: bark for tanning, acorns to feed pigs (and people), charcoal for the iron-ore smelters, staves for the coopers, baskets, dyes, medicines, furniture, and even the shavings to smoke kippers – oak has long been the universal provider. Its utilitarian properties may have made it indispensible, but over and above, the oak has acquired a certain mystique and a spiritual significance that has left its mark since the time of the Druids. The oak has entered the language through place names, peoples' names, and been widely adopted as a symbol of national pride, of valour, strength, dependability. Oak is entrenched in our folklore and superstitions. Poets, naturalists, and diarists have been moved by oaks. Artists in diverse disciplines have depicted the oak, its leaves, and its acorns. By touching on the multifarious aspects of the oak tree in Britain, I hope to raise awareness about a tree that most of us simply take for granted. In so doing, I hope readers are stimulated to look afresh at the oak, to realize its importance to the British treescape, its cultural and historical legacy, and appreciate it for the truly remarkable tree that it is.

Just like the man who planted the four oaks at the end of our orchard, and remembering the wise words of John Evelyn, who exhorted the nation to plant more oaks way back in 1662, we should keep planting more oaks and tending them for the generations who come after us. We have a young oak in our garden, an upstart acorn far from the shadow of any of our other oaks, so perhaps buried by a jay or squirrel several years ago. At about 8 feet high it's doing well, although nothing like the four sentinels down the orchard, and yet still I cherish it.

THE RISE OF OAK

Travel almost anywhere in Britain and the ubiquitous oak will never be far away, whether it be upland or lowland forest, hedgerow, parkland, or simply a statuesque single tree in the middle of a field. The oak has become so familiar that one could show the characteristic lobed shape of the oak leaf to almost anyone with barely any knowledge of trees, and the overwhelming odds are that they would instantly be able to identify our National Tree.

OPPOSITE: A fine pair of oaks in spring.

IT SEEMS STRANGE TO THINK that there was once a time when the oak tree didn't grow in Britain. Like every living thing on the planet, it has had to thrust its way through millions of years of evolution to become what A. G. Tansley called 'the commonest woodland type of natural and semi-natural deciduous British woodland'.

THE OAK IN BRITAIN

Fossil evidence shows that the oak genus has been around for 60 million years, evolving as just one group of the flowering plants known as angiosperms (plants with seeds inside a seed coating and/or fruit). Some of the oak species that we recognize today first appeared about 14 million years ago.

Core samples taken from ice and the ocean bed that date back about 2 million years reveal great climatic fluctuations, with the coldest period of the last Ice Age peaking around 25,000 years ago. It's pretty certain that most plants and all large trees would have disappeared from Britain during the last Ice Age. The retreat of the ice sheets and the warming climate that started to occur 12,000 years ago signalled the start of a tree migration northwards, from southern Europe into Britain. Dwarf willows and birches might have hung on through the Ice Age in southern England, but otherwise they would have been the first to return, followed by birch, aspen, juniper, and pine.

Around 9,500 years ago, the first oaks began to grab a toehold in the south-west. Equally, pollen records taken from East Anglia and dating back 9,000 years, indicate that oak was also approaching from the east. At the same time

ABOVE: These stumps on the beach near Borth, known as the Petrified Forest, are the remains of a forest which was submerged some 8,000 years ago as the ice melted and the seas rose after the last Ice Age. Oak as well as birch, hazel and pine have been identified.

hazel, a tree that would later come to accompany oak in so much of Britain's woodland, was arriving from the west. By 8,000 years ago, oak had spread throughout most of Britain, although it would take another 2,000 years for it to reach up into Scotland.

As temperatures rose, ice melted, and the rising sea levels submerged vast forests beneath what is now the North Sea some 7,500 years ago. The many very large pieces of oak that have been dredged up from the seabed confirm this trajectory. Woods to the west were also submerged beneath the Irish Sea – vestiges of which may be seen today as the numerous 'petrified forests' along the Welsh coast. The land bridge to Europe was also submerged at this time, drawing a close to the northward migration of trees and plants into Britain.

By 6,000 years ago, Britain had reached a 'climatic optimum', the warmest period in post-glacial history, and oak with hazel had become a dominant woodland type through the West Country, most of Wales, and from the Midlands all the way up to central Scotland. Observations of historical oak cover reveal that post-glacial climate fluctuations caused it to come and go from various places. The great oak forests that now lie beneath the Fenland peat of East Anglia, for example, have failed to rise again in the last 5,000 years.

THE ENGLISH AND SESSILE OAKS

There are about 600 species in the genus *Quercus*, but only two of the 72 species of white oaks from the subgenus *Quercus* are native to Britain, including common, English, or pedunculate oak (*Quercus robur*), and sessile or Durmast oak

(*Quercus petraea*). Both trees have a huge native range that stretches throughout Europe to the Caucasus and northward into Scandinavia, although sessile oak does reach slightly further east and north. I will use the names 'English' and 'sessile' in this book.

The physical differences between the two oaks are subtle, and a plethora of intermediate forms and hybrids often confuses identification. English oak is normally a rugged, spreading tree with a zigzag pattern in its branching (creating the knees and crooks much favoured by shipbuilders of old). It often grows to about 100 feet in height. The English oak has acorns on stems, usually an inch or two long, and leaves with little or no stems. There is often a little 'ear' or auricle at either side of the leaf base, but not always. The sessile oak tends to be a taller tree, occasionally reaching 130 feet (the current national champion is a tree at Stourhead in Wiltshire that was measured at 132 feet 6 inches). With somewhat straighter boughs, the sessile oak often adopts a more upswept profile than the English oak. Its easiest identifying characteristics are the acorn and leaf stems. The stemless acorns of the sessile oak are located hard up against the twig, while the leaves have short petioles (stems), usually about a quarter to half an inch long. However, as previously mentioned, the broad range of intermediate forms of oak can often make the English and sessile oaks hard to identify.

Until the late-eighteenth century, *Quercus robur* was the name attributed to both species. In 1755, the botanist Carl Linnaeus had delineated two separate species, but it wasn't until Thomas Martyn's 1792 *Flora Rustica* that they are defined in the form with which we are familiar today: *Quercus robur* and *Quercus sessilis* (later *sessiliflora*, and currently *petraea*). *Quercus* is derived from the Celtic 'quer' and 'cuez', meaning 'fine tree'. *Robur* is Latin for strong, and *petraea* is derived from the Greek 'petra', or rock (the oak that favours stony or rocky ground). Pedunculate indicates a tree with acorns on stalks (or peduncles). Sessile, from the Latin '*sessilis*', indicates stalkless acorns (fit for sitting upon). The Anglo-Saxon name for the oak was 'ak', 'ac' or 'aik' (Scots), thus the popular misconception 'aik-corn' – the grain or seed of the oak. In truth, acorn derives from Old English 'aecern' – signifying a berry or fruit.

It is difficult to be specific about the relative advances of the two species into Britain, since this information is reliant on pollen records taken from core samples extracted from peat bogs or lake sediments, and the pollen of both oak species looks identical. Pollen analysis, along with radio-carbon dating have been invaluable techniques for mapping the progress of tree colonization through Britain after the last Ice Age, helping to build up a picture of tree cover. However, there are caveats that must be considered. Windblown pollen can travel great distances on the wind or when settling on moving water, thus sometimes locating it a long way from the parent tree. Some species also produce greater quantities of pollen than others, while some pollen does not preserve well. In addition, insect-pollinated trees will always be under-represented.

It is generally thought that English oak was the first species to move in, since sessile oak tends to prefer slightly warmer conditions. Perhaps this is reflected by the somewhat bizarre presence of three English oak woods on top of Dartmoor,

in what is predominantly a sessile oak province. The two oaks have established their natural ranges right across Britain, although on balance the English oak is essentially the lowland tree of the deep loams and boulder clays of the south and east, while the sessile oak favours the lighter sandy soils and gravels (often of a more acidic nature) that are predominantly from the west coast, north-west England, and Scotland. In effect, both species have colonies throughout Britain, as well as hybrids of the two and, more commonly, an infinite range of intermediate forms.

ABOVE: Longhorn cattle in a wooded area of Windsor Great Park are being used to try and recreate the pattern of historic wood-pasture.

Today much of the integration of the two oaks has caused some blurring of their natural ranges. This is largely the result of selective planting, as well as the importation of alien stock from mainland Europe, particularly over the last three hundred years, when English oak was perceived to be superior-quality timber for construction and shipbuilding.

THE HISTORY OF THE BRITISH OAK

The prehistoric natural range of oak woodland, complete with its complementary colonies of other tree and plant species, has been well mapped in recent years. That being said, the exact spatial presence and density of British woodland in the pre-Neolithic eras is still very much under debate. Exactly what did the landscape look like before man made his impact? The popular theory for a long time was that an almost blanket forest covering virtually the whole of lowland Britain existed until about 5,500 years ago, when Neolithic peoples arrived and began their slash-and-burn clearances, using primitive axes to fell trees in order to cultivate the land and graze their livestock. There are several problems with this particular theory. It's a slow and laborious job felling large trees with flint axes, and broadleaf trees don't burn that well, so there are limitations to the predicted scale of woodland versus open spaces.

Another credible, more recent theory proposes that much of pre-Neolithic Britain was savanna-like land or wood-pasture, in which large tracts of grassland were dotted with numerous small woodlands. Dutch forest ecologist Frans Vera believes that large wild herbivores were the force that shaped the landscape. These beasts created a hugely fragmented distribution of small woodlands in a constant state of flux: scrub vegetation would protect young trees, which eventually grew large enough to shade out the scrub. This allowed the grazers in, which browsed off any natural regeneration. Eventually the large trees matured, died, and fell, letting in the light and thus returning the land to grassland. Critics have challenged Vera's theory on several fronts, including those who question the applicability of Vera's European model to Britain. There were, first of all, far fewer large herbivores in Britain. Other factors that have weighed in on the debate involve the presence and effectiveness of the carnivores, the pollen

THE OAK.

evidence of various flowering plants and grasses, and the type of landscapes their presence indicates – grassland or woodland. The debate between these two theories rattles on with evidence to support various aspects of both.

What is most certain is that from the Neolithic period onwards woods, their trees, and their products were absolutely fundamental for human existence, and oak figured prominently. People built shelters and houses for themselves, ceremonial structures such as wood henges, and constructed wooden causeways used to cross the marshier regions to get around. They also made huge dug-out canoes (several of which have been excavated along the east coast), they built enclosures for their livestock, and stockades around their communities. They warmed themselves and cooked with fires, they made charcoal to smelt ore, made weapons and tools, and they used tan bark to cure leather. The Anglo-Saxon Chronicles record that oak woods were chiefly valued for their acorns, for the fattening of swine, 'but in years of great scarcity, were eaten by man'. Excavated remains of many ancient sites have confirmed how pivotal oak would have been to human life: From remnants in post holes, boats, components of the ancient trackways, the stunning wood henge off the Norfolk coast, which was moved amid much controversy in 1999, to the contents of charcoal hearths and rubbish pits.

Since the Bronze Age, through the Iron Age, and on to the Roman occupation, these oak woods became increasingly valued and exploited for their renewable produce, partly for construction timber, but more so for wood fuel, tan bark for curing leather, and charcoal for smelting various ores, copper, tin, and notably iron. The Domesday Book, the earliest comprehensive survey ever carried out in Britain, reaffirms the importance of acorns, and values woods, particularly in eastern England, by the number of hogs they would fatten. Tansley lists several of the most important wooded forests at the time of the Norman Conquest in which oak was the principal tree: The Kent and Sussex Weald (the Roman forest of Anderida; Anglo-Saxon Andrede's Weald), Windsor Forest, Forest of Essex, Forest of Arden, Wychwood, Forest of Dean, Wyre Forest, and Sherwood Forest. Remnants of most of these still exist, and the Weald is still one of Britain's most densely wooded regions in which oak remains a prominent element, and where its charcoal was once used in copious quantities by the Romans to fuel their bloomeries.

PLANTING AND MANAGING OAK WOODS

The Domesday Book offers little exact detail of woodlands, but does indicate that about 15 per cent of the land was tree-covered. This compares to about 12 per cent today, although more than half of that is coniferous plantations. Oliver Rackham tells us that, 'by 1250 woods in England were fully developed. They had names, ownerships, boundaries and regular management, which were to remain for the next 700 years'. In the reign of Henry VIII, the first concerns about a scarcity of oak timber were aired by Thomas Tusser, who, writing in 1562, complained that 'men were more studious to cut down than to plant trees'. Tusser urged planters of oak to proceed with care:

BELOW: A superb portrait of
John Evelyn by F. Bartolozzi
from the 1ˢᵗ Hunter edition of
Silva, 1776.

Sow acorns, ye owners that timber do love;
Sow hay and rie with them, the better to prove:
If cattle or coney may enter the crop,
Young oak is in danger of losing his top.

There are a tiny handful of references to monastic tree planting as far back as
the thirteenth century, but it wasn't until the sixteenth century that Holinshed's
Chronicles (1577) notes that 'plantations of trees began to be made for the purpose
of utility'. In 1580 Queen Elizabeth, acutely aware of the need for quality timber
for the navy, assented to Lord Burghley's order to empale 13 acres of Cranbourne
Walk, in Windsor Great Park, and sow it with acorns – the first record of a pure
oak plantation. It would be fascinating to know if and when these oaks were ever
harvested, and whether they did end up in the naval shipyards. Oaks still grow
on the site, but are thought to be too young to derive from this original generation
of planting.

Unfortunately, by the mid-seventeenth century, a lot of oak woodland had
been degraded due to poor management. Excess felling and plundering with
little restorative planting, as well as increased grazing, curtailed natural
regeneration and contributed to the poor condition of oak woods. Charles I was
perhaps the chief villain to blame, for his constant 'necessities … induced him
to make ruinous grants of the royal woods to any person who would supply him
with money'. Matters didn't improve for woods throughout the Civil Wars, and
only in 1669, when Charles II set an example by passing an order to plant 300
acres of the New Forest with oaks, did a culture of planting slowly begin to take
hold. Only the demand for coppice wood had kept
many woods functioning prior to the Restoration,
and that demand was consistently high until the
latter part of the nineteenth century.

JOANNES EVELYN ARM?

The year 1662 had proved to be something of a
watershed year for the British oak tree. This was the
year that John Evelyn grasped the nettle to address the
nation in his speech to the Royal Society. Bemoaning
the parlous state of the nation's woods, he begins:

*Since there is nothing which seems more fatally to threaten
a weakening, if not a dissolution, of the strength of this
famous and flourishing nation, than the sensible and
notorious decay of her wooden walls, when, either through
time, negligence, or other accident, the present navy shall
be worn out and impaired; it has been a very worthy and
seasonable advertisement in the honourable the principal
Officers and Commissioners, what they have lately suggested
to this illustrious Society for the timely prevention and
redress of this intolerable defect. For it has not been the late
increase of shipping alone, the multiplication of glass-works,
iron-furnaces, and the like, from whence this impolitic*

*diminution of our timber has proceeded; but from the disproportionate spreading
of tillage, caused through that prodigious havoc made by such as lately professing
themselves against root and branch (either to be reimbursed their holy purchases,
or for some other sordid respect) were tempted not only to fell and cut down, but
utterly to extirpate, demolish and raze, as it were, all those many goodly woods and
forests, which our more prudent ancestors left standing for the ornament and service
of their country. And this devastation is now become so epidemical, that unless some
favourable expedient offer itself, and a way be seriously and speedily resolved upon,
for a future store, one of the most glorious and considerable bulwarks of this nation
will, within a short time, be totally wanting to it.*

How could such condemnation and command be ignored? Evelyn later published
his views in his seminal work *Sylva*, in which he entreated the landowners of the
nation to plant trees. It would seem that *Sylva* spawned much tree planting, and
an abundance of treatises and forestry manuals on the subject were soon published
to guide prospective planters and woodland managers. *Sylva* (later *Silva*) went
to eleven editions by 1825. Great pressures were put on oak stocks, principally
the coppice wood for tan bark and charcoal, but also the increased demand for
ship-building timber in the eighteenth and early nineteenth centuries, as world
trade expanded along with the men of war required for the Royal Navy to
defend the realm.

A wealth of literature provided advice to planters of oak, although everyone
seems to have had their own particular idiosyncrasies and preferences for how

to achieve the best results. In their *Trees of Great Britain and Ireland* (1906–13), Henry John Elwes and Augustine Henry offer up much of this fascinating debate, tempered by various experiences and correspondence from around Britain. From the eighteenth century onwards, some authorities believed young saplings transplanted into woodland would always fare better than sown acorns (the traditional method up to this period). This is a reasonable assumption, since mice, squirrels, pigeons, rooks, and jays are all keen devourers of acorns, and mice will often ring bark or chew right through young seedlings. Some planters believed that cutting out the leaders of young oaks stimulated better growth, while others, such as naturalist Robert Marsham, even advocated cutting young saplings that were not thriving down to six inches or a foot high – a sort of premature coppicing – which in his experience led to renewed vigour. Different mixtures of understorey trees were recommended as nurse trees to protect the developing young oaks (usually hazel, hawthorn, blackthorn, or holly).

Obviously, what worked well for some planters didn't necessarily breed success for others. In the *Gardeners' Chronicle* of 1900, Professor Fisher confirms that the English oak is essentially the tree of wet soils (lowlands) while sessile oak thrives on dry ground (uplands). He further states:

> *Nurserymen rarely distinguish them and are, as a rule, careless of the source from which their seed comes, provided it will produce good nursery plants. I should strongly advise all oak planters to select and grow their own oaks from the trees which thrive best on similar soil in their own district, or in places with similar soil and climate.*

Sensible advice that still holds good today.

THE OAK TREE AND OAK WOODS TODAY

So, where is the oak today? What are the different types of environment in which the tree occurs? Oak features in some measure in virtually all types of woodland, and often its situation will reflect its historical place and purpose. Oak has been selectively nurtured, favoured, or planted for thousands of years because it was such a multi-purpose tree. With the increased use of woodland for amenity purposes today, it's easy to simply admire and value oaks for their aesthetic qualities, quietly forgetting how important a utilitarian function they had previously performed.

These days, oak can be found as naturally occurring maiden trees in mixed woodland with a variety of understorey species, depending on soil types, situation, and climate, and as intentional timber trees planted in established woods. Sometimes pollards can be found along woodland boundaries either on the outer edges of woods or on the traces of long-forgotten internal boundaries. Coppice stools can also be found in some of the woods where a historical regime of coppice with standards might once have prevailed. With other woods, the oak coppice is the dominant feature. This is particularly true of difficult terrain, where growing and harvesting large timber trees would have been impractical, as well as areas close to the locations of old industries where bark and charcoal

were paramount. Some of the nation's most ancient and impressive oaks survive as pollards in wood-pasture settings. This is usually the case in old deer parks, some of which date to medieval antiquity and a few of which still survive intact. Others have reverted to the woodland from which they were once carved many centuries ago, or been remodelled by the great eighteenth-century landscapers. Fortunately the likes of Brown and Repton saw the visual merits of great old oaks, and retained them as part of their grand designs. Oaks are also found in natural recent woodland – leave a field untended for a few years and a wood will take over. Oaks have been planted as part of numerous amenity woodland projects around Britain. There are many commercial oak plantations and for many years English oak took precedence here, but since 1970 much more sessile oak is being planted.

Sometimes described as linear woods, hedgerows contain a great many fine oaks, although some of these trees have been put under great stress in recent times. A heavy level of salt distribution on roads and too much deep ploughing on arable land creates problems for root systems that are difficult to overcome. The roots of a large old oak can stretch well beyond the drip line of the canopy. Leaving headlands of fallow ground alongside hedges certainly helps the tree roots. A culture of removing hedgerows from the arable prairies of eastern England also saw losses. However, it's interesting to study some of the individual field oaks. Careful observation frequently reveals linear patterns where the oaks of long defunct hedges still plot their old hedge lines across open fields. These

trees occur as maidens and pollards, but also where there has been a long culture of hedge laying, some have effectively been regularly coppiced. Fine oaks are also found as part of urban parkland schemes and occasionally as street trees, although faster growing or smaller trees are often preferred. Village green trees and memorial plantings are more often oaks than any other species; the tree's iconic image making it an almost automatic choice.

Taking an overview of oak woodland in evidence today, it is nearly impossible to find an acre of ground that has not been manipulated by man for his needs. These woods are in a variety of conditions depending on what the current management plan (or lack thereof) might be. A popular belief is that a non-intervention regime in woodland promotes a true natural environment, where every organism lives out its life in a totally undisturbed habitat. Yet historical human influence has already quite often altered such woods, which contain introduced species, and even alien oaks. Many such woods have lost their original native oak status. Often they become tangled, impenetrable wastelands with reduced biodiversity, whose high forest will eventually mature and die and then the woodland will revert back to scrub. Good woodland management creates a marked contrast to this sort of dilapidation. Coppicing regimes, selective felling and planting, creating rides and glades, and excluding damaging herbivores (principally deer) encourages multi-generational tree cover and a vibrant ground flora. This in turn attracts a greater diversity of invertebrates and birds. Surely this makes for a more pleasant woodland for all to enjoy?

OPPOSITE TOP: Scruffy, small English oaks grow among a cluster of moss-clad granite boulders at Wistman's Wood on Dartmoor.

OPPOSITE BOTTOM: Early morning sunlight bursts through the fine oaks in the parkland at Penshurst Place in Kent.

Jumping back fifty or a hundred years from the well-managed commercial oak woods and oak plantations of today, necessary, functional, and productive for modern foresters, and yet sometimes a little uninspiring to the visitor's eye, one encounters many semi-natural ancient oak woods with a wealth of individuality, historical features, and atmosphere. A complete contrast with a commercial plantation might be one of many of the Atlantic oak woods of western Britain. In the southwest, gnarled, windswept Cornish woods of pure sessile oak hug the steep sides of the river valleys, running right down to the brackish shores of the estuaries. Oak is the dominant species throughout Cornish woods and is usually accompanied by an understorey of holly or hazel. Here the demand was for coppice-wood charcoal for tin smelting. In Devon, sessile oak is still the dominant species, but there are three strange and different woods on Dartmoor: Wistman's Wood, Piles Copse, and Black Tor Copse, which are all English oak woods. Opinion about their origins is divided. Some believe these are relics of post-glacial migration, surviving from a time before the sessile oak arrived; another theory is that these were planted woods from an earlier age, which were introduced because of their ability to bear heavier crops of acorns and thus vital for free-roaming pigs (pannage). Given the mossy, granite, boulder-strewn terrain, they would certainly have been extremely agile beasts. These woods have a magical, mysterious quality, wreathed as they are in ferns, mosses, and lichens, flourishing in the damp, sheltered valleys. The relatively small size of the oaks, which have grown very slowly due to adverse conditions and high altitude, belies their great antiquity.

On the west coast of Wales are places like Pengelli Forest. Often cited as 'the most beautiful wood in Wales', this is a 160-acre (once 500 acres), oak-dominant wood with a well-documented history of use going back more than 600 years. From the sixteenth century it was managed as coppice with standards, and many of the surviving oak stools could easily be that old. Ancient wood banks are evident, and the line of an old leat (millstream) that channelled water to a mill in the valley. There are detailed records of livestock that was grazed in the wood, accounts of sparrowhawks captured to be trained for hawking, honey collected from wild bees, and cockshoots – nets stretched across rides to trap low-flying game birds. The importance of these places, and their multifarious uses by the local communities down the centuries, is writ large here.

The Gwynedd oak woods of North Wales still have a remote, rugged, untouched feel about them, and that's how they have been for a long time. Look around woods such as Coed Ganllwyd and Coed-y-Rhygen and ancient, mossy oak coppice stools are abundant, often singled to allow a standard tree to develop. Man has moulded all these woods, which is frequently reflected in their names. In his book *The Wild Woods*, Peter Marren pulls out a few examples: Coed y Moch, or wood of the pigs (once used for pannage); Coed Cwm-y-Gof, or wood of the valley of the smithy; Coed yr Odin, or wood of the kiln; and Coed Bryn-yr-Efail, or hill of the smithy wood (marking these out as coppice woods for charcoal making to smelt ore). These are principally oak woods with birch and often rowan (trees that are well-suited to acidic soils). When these woods ceased to be intensively managed at the turn of the nineteenth-century,

ABOVE: A typical Atlantic oak wood on the Taynish Peninsula on the west coast of Scotland, where most of the oaks have been coppiced for hundreds of years.

sheep and goats were able to enter the woods and graze off all the new growth and damage the bark, a trend that has only recently been reversed by once again fencing off. Such woods are noted for their prolific colonies of mosses and lichens, with many rare and site-specific species.

The north of England has a great deal of similarity running through its upland oak woods on acidic soils and gritstones. Most are found in steep-sided valleys and are a mixture of oak with birch, some rowan, along with that alien interloper sycamore. In Cumbria, yew is a frequent element. The woodland floor is often heathlike in character. Again, most of these northern woods have been coppice woods. The oaks of Keskadale and Birkrigg, above the Newlands Valley, manage to scramble up the rocky slopes to 1,600 feet, making them the highest oak woods in England. For centuries they were regularly coppiced by man, fire, fungal attack, and the occasional rolling boulder.

The bulk of Scottish oak woods were managed for coppice, most actively between 1680 and 1880 but, regrettably, after this period many woods went into a general decline due to lax management, random felling regimes, and livestock or deer being allowed into woods. North of Glasgow, the extensive oak woods around Loch Lomond have a rich industrial heritage, which is still in evidence today. The old coppice was managed for charcoal and tan bark, but a lot of timber was taken in the eighteenth and nineteenth centuries for the Clydeside sawmills and shipyards. Many authorities also mention the famous Balmaha pyroligneus acid factory (there were others dotted around Scotland and even as far south as the Forest of Dean, but this seems to be the most frequently cited example), which survived into the early twentieth century and used copious quantities of coppice wood to produce pyroligneus acid, or wood vinegar (acetic acid). The process involved burning the wood in airless chambers, producing charcoal, but also the condensate that was collected and then used as a mordant for dyes in the textile industry.

In the Scottish lowlands, one or two interesting sites that were once the parks of large estates, show a past history of wood-pasture. Lochwood Oaks in Dumfriesshire (now a wood) and Cadzow Oaks near Hamilton in Ayrshire (still somewhat parklike) contain some of Scotland's oldest oak pollards, trees so important that they were used for the first dendrochronology studies in the UK. Near Edinburgh, in Dalkeith Park, some of the oldest oaks display a previous history of having been coppiced, so were obviously once in woodland before the park was established about 400 years ago.

Returning to the Atlantic oak woods, the west coast of Scotland is the place to discover outstanding, romantic, seemingly primeval woods of epiphyte-clad, twisted, and contorted oaks, particulary in places such as Ariundle, above Loch Sunart, or the Taynish Peninsula. Here, the high annual rainfall, mild climate engendered by the Gulf Stream, and supremely clean air creates a lush woodland garden of mosses, lichens, liverworts and ferns, cloaking boulders and tree boles in a sort of living carpet. Like all oak woods, these places have undergone intensive periods of exploitation in the past, much of the coppice wood firing the furnaces of Bonawe or Furnace ironworks. Today they are nature reserves, treasured for their rich repositories of plants and wildlife.

Almost all of the previously mentioned sessile oak-dominant woods stretching along the west coast of Britain have a distinctive Atlantic commonality about their character. Move eastwards into the Midlands and East Anglia, as well as down into the southern counties of England (the lowlands), and oak takes on a very different woodland presence. English oak appears to be much less dominant in many of these woods, even a rare woodland type in East Anglia, with far more serious competitors to contend with. On calcareous soils, the ash is frequently dominant; in much of Kent, parts of Essex, and in the Forest of Dean, great tracts of sweet chestnut hold sway. In Lincolnshire it's limewoods, while in the Chilterns or the New Forest, beech rules. Certainly oak still does well in the New Forest, but the beech with the deep shade that it casts will always make young oaks struggle.

Oliver Rackham states that there was an 'Oak Change' around 1900, when naturally sown oaks stopped growing from seed within woods. He believes this was due to a combination of increased shade that was itself due to the downturn in woodland management such as coppicing, in combination with the 1908 introduction of oak mildew from America, which soon became extremely widespread. Even though young oaks rarely thrive in deep shade, Rackham suggests that the mildew appears to make them even less shade-tolerant. Obviously, the oak is not threatened, as it has been planted in many woods where shade is not an issue and natural regeneration in non-woodland sites continues unabated. The oak has risen down the millennia to become our National Tree and at this stage there should be few worries about its wholesale decline… although, elsewhere in this book, some of the agents marching against the oak will be examined.

MAJESTY AND THE
FREDVILLE OAKS

To the south of the village of Nonington in Kent lies tranquil parkland that was once the expansive demesne of Fredville – a substantial two-storey, Adam-style mansion, built in the 1740s to the order of its new owner Margaretta Bridges. Today you can stroll through the parkland and still see the mighty oaks and sweet chestnuts that have made it famous for hundreds of years. In 1750, John Plumptre of Nottingham married Margaretta, and in so doing began a long line of Plumptres (all called John – a tradition going back well into the seventeenth century) who have owned the estate to this very day.

Edward Hasted first published his definitive work, *The History and Topographical Survey of the County of Kent*, as four folio volumes between 1778 and 1799. The work appears to be the first to mention the huge oak in front of the house:

> *At a small distance from the front of Fredville-house, stands the remarkable large oak tree, usually known by the name of the Fredville oak. It measures twenty-seven feet round in the girth, and is about thirty feet in height; and though it must have existed for many centuries, yet it looks healthy and thriving, and has a most majestic and venerable appearance.*

A delightful aquatint by William Green shows a group (perhaps servants) with arms outstretched and linked around the huge bole of the oak, while a group on horseback (John Plumptre and guests?) look on. Is this an example of tree measuring? Or perhaps this is the earliest image of tree-huggers!

Several writers would come to visit Fredville over the years. A short while after Hasted's visit, correspondents writing for the *Annals of Agriculture and Other Useful Arts* visited Fredville on 6 July 1793, and reported the following:

> *Call on John Plumtree, Esq. of Fredville, who very politely shews us his famous oak, called Majesty – measure this tree; 4 feet from the ground the circumference is 31 feet; it is supposed to contain 36 to 42 tons of timber. Two branches separated from this tree about four years ago, in a calm day, which contained three tons of timber. Another oak, called Beauty, 14 tons of timber; girt 4 feet from the ground, 16 feet 4 inches, is 63 feet high, perfectly straight, and a beauty indeed!*

In 1818, the traveller and writer John Evans also recounted a visit to Fredville:

OPPOSITE: The imposing form of Majesty in Fredville Park which sadly lost a huge bough in 2012.

BELOW: The author beneath
Majesty showing the vast scale
of the tree.

Not far from Waldershare is Fredville, the seat of John Plumptree, Esq. – in the park belonging to which are oak-trees, the most extraordinary for height and size in the kingdom. They are distinguished, by appropriate names; but the most remarkable of them are those called 'Majesty', 'Stately', and 'Beauty'.

Evans then divulges the statistics of the latter pair:

But 'Majesty', the most wonderful of all these trees, has, eight feet from the ground, a circumference of twenty-eight feet four inches … The total contents of this huge bulk of timber are thirty-six tons, bark not included.

Jacob George Strutt drew these trees for his *Sylva Britannica* in 1824. In his second edition of 1830 he wrote:

Nearly in front of the family mansion of John Plumtre, Esq., in his park at Fredville, in the parish of Nonnington, Kent, is a group of oaks known by the names of Majesty, Stately and Beauty. Seldom are trees so different from each other in individual character, and so interesting altogether, to be found in such near proximity.

Strutt delivered his statistics, much in line with Evans, and somewhat prophetically speculated about their future:

The pleasure with which the spectator views their different characteristics, is heightened by a sense that they are likely to remain cherished and protected equally in their decay as in their prime. Protected from violence, they will probably stand many centuries; and it may be hoped that they will as long continue to delight the descendants of the family by whom they are at present so highly valued, and so carefully preserved.

It is astounding to think that almost two hundred years later, the Plumptre family still own the estate and still treasure their great trees, despite the effects of time, the elements, and even industry. In 1890, an offer of £100 was made for the timber of Stately, but the offer was rebuffed, and the tree was not cut down. Writing in the 1920s, Lillian Boys Behrans stated that two of the largest oaks near the house were recorded in 1554, and known as the Ancient Bear and King Fredville Oak, the latter being Majesty, while the

Oaks at Fredville.

former was either Beauty or Stately. If these trees were of significant enough size in 1554 to warrant names, then surely they would have been at least 400 years old by then. It therefore seems perfectly feasible that Majesty could be 1,000 years old.

The demise of the old house followed a similar narrative to those of many others across the country: Requisitioned for military use during the Second World War, it suffered a catastrophic fire and was finally demolished in 1945. Thankfully, the fire did not take the great oaks.

Walk around the corner from the surviving stable block today, brush through the undergrowth, and you are suddenly pulled up in your tracks, struggling to take in the enormity of Majesty, squatting resolutely within its own little glade. Hidden from passing stares, this oak is a gargantuan beast of a tree; a monolith, a survivor, a record holder – with a girth of 40 feet, the biggest maiden English oak in Britain. It may have shed an enormous bough last year and, of course, the tree has been completely hollow for many a year, but it still looks set to last another century or two.

WILBERFORCE OAK. KESTON.

THE WILBERFORCE OAK

I N THE GROUNDS OF HOLWOOD HOUSE, near Bromley in Kent, a stone bench sits forlornly beneath … well, nothing much at present, although until 1991 it would have been the perfect place to stop and view the ancient Wilberforce Oak – a tree with monumental connections.

In 1783 William Pitt the Younger became Britain's youngest Prime Minister, at the tender age of twenty-four. He bought Holwood House during a visit to the estate on 12 May 1787, when he and William Greville met the politician and philanthropist William Wilberforce. Pitt urged Wilberforce to bring up his anti-slavery motion in the Commons. A Wilberforce diary entry in 1787 reads:

> *At length, I well remember after a conversation with Mr Pitt in the open air at the root of an old tree at Holwood, just above the steep descent into the vale of Keston, I resolved to give notice on a fit occasion in the House of Commons of my intention to bring forward the abolition of the slave-trade.*

Wilberforce knew he would have an uphill battle on his hands, for many influential families and powerful companies had built their fortunes using slave labour. He first brought his anti-slavery Bill before Parliament in 1791. It was defeated, largely due to a conservative backlash in the wake of the French Revolution and a reaction to radicalism. Another attempt to push his anti-slave-trade Bill in 1792 led to a diluted compromise solution of 'gradual abolition' over a number of years – a ploy to delay the process indefinitely. It was twenty years before Wilberforce was able to see 'An Act for the Abolition of the Slave Trade' finally passed in the Commons; the Bill receiving Royal Assent on 25 March 1807.

The Act might have abolished the slave trade in the British Empire, but it did not stop slavery itself. The ensuing mass protests against this iniquitous extension to the bonds of slavery resulted in an absolute end to all slavery in 1838; only 50 years after Wilberforce first set forth on his crusade under the tree that bears his name.

During the nineteenth and early twentieth centuries, the Wilberforce or Abolition Oak became the focus of many a pilgrimage, attested by the numerous different Edwardian postcards of the tree and its attendant seat, which was installed in 1862. Sadly, the great old pollard declined through the twentieth century, and by 1969 was considered to be dead. The old shell lingered on until 1991 when gales laid it low. The stone bench bearing its prophetic quote from Wilberforce's diary stands still – a modest memorial to a great and good man.

OPPOSITE TOP LEFT: One of many pilgrims who visited the Wilberforce Oak. Already the tree is beginning to deteriorate and zinc sheeting has been pinned over the broken boughs to provide some protection to the interior of the tree.

OPPOSITE TOP RIGHT: William Wilberforce, steel engraving by E. Scriven, after George Ricmond, *c.*1850.

OPPOSITE BOTTOM: London historian Jeffrey Green has researched this group portrait of seven pilgrims at the old oak, and tells us that it was taken in 1873 and consists of seven members of the Church Missionary Society, including Bishop Samuel Ajayi Crowther (at the back, against the tree), who was the first African Anglican bishop in Nigeria. The image was later published during the Edwardian era on postcards by Medhurst of Bromley.

THE BONNINGTON LAW DAY OAK

Opposite top: The Bonnington Law Day Oak before the storm in 2011.

Opposite bottom: The gathering of the parish council in 2013.

O N 14 MAY 2011, I MET A VILLAGER who was particularly knowledgeable about this famous oak. Apparently, a regular gathering of parish officials still convenes beneath the old oak every third Tuesday in May, according to an ancient tradition described in Edward Hasted's *The History and Topographical Survey of Kent* (1799):

> *There used to be a court leet holden here for the boroughs of Bonnington and Hamme, at which the borsholders of those boroughs were elected, but it had been discontinued ever since about the middle of queen Elizabeth's reign, only the memory of it remained, by a great old oak standing in the high way where it used to be held, and from thence called the law-day oak.*

I was disappointed to miss this traditional council meeting, but promised myself a return in 2012, but in October 2011, I learnt that severe gales had wrenched a large part of the tree to the ground, changing its wonderful spreading profile for ever. Fortunately the roots and part of the lower bole were still intact, which meant that there was half a chance that the tree might eventually regenerate.

The Law Day Oak is mentioned in several county accounts. Perhaps one of the most lyrical descriptions comes from the pen of a Mrs White, writing in 1889:

> *In the out-of-the-way villages on the borders of Romney marsh, the former home of shepherds and smugglers, the light of civilisation has not long shone, and many rites and superstitions connected with the worship of the oak are still persisted in by the inhabitants. A special sacredness appertains to the vows of lovers exchanged beneath the Bonnington oak, and its leaves, gathered with a certain formula at a certain time of night, are still sought by childless women and made into a medicinal draught, with the same intention as in Druidical days.*

A visit to the 2013 council meeting revealed that the oak has managed to stay in the land of the living. Two boughs were still intact, pushing forth a very healthy flush of new leaves. Members of the council convened at 7.30 p.m., and a variety of village issues and concerns were debated, in much the same manner as they have been for hundreds of years. Bonnington's Law Day is the last vestige of similar traditions that must once have taken place in scores of villages up and down the land. Thankfully, the venue for this long-held annual gathering endures, as does the villagers' desire to hold it.

Sir Philip Sydney's Oak.—Penshurst.

SIR PHILIP SIDNEY'S OAK

THROUGHOUT THE EXPANSIVE PARKLAND THAT SPRAWLS beyond the splendid fourteenth-century manor house of Penshurst Place, near Tonbridge, in Kent, stately and magnificent oaks dominate the scene. Perhaps the most celebrated of all the oaks is now little more than a shadow of its former grandeur. A single, prop-supported bough remains its last grasp on life. The oak derives its appellation from the fact that it was supposedly planted at the birth of the poet Sir Philip Sidney on 30 November 1554 (d. 1586), a tradition that was reaffirmed by one Mr Rawley, corresponding with *The Gentleman's Magazine* in 1794:

> *The tree I speak of is an oak in Penshurst park, in Kent; of which I send you a very accurate drawing by a young lady… It goes by the name of Bear Oak, or perhaps Bare Oak, from a supposed resemblance to that which, Camden says, gave name to the county of Barkshire. The tradition here is, that it is the very tree planted on the day that the celebrated Sir Philip Sidney was born.*

Rawley goes on to say the following:

> *Some late writers, however, have questioned this, and think it to have been a different tree, which was cut down some years ago, and was indeed much larger than this. I remember being once in the hollow of the present oak with the late Sir John Cullum; and his opinion then was, that its antiquity was greater than the period assigned. But, I assure you, the tradition of this place is constant for this tree; and, in confirmation of it, an old lady of 94 years of age (now living), has told me, that all the tenants used to furnish themselves with boughs from this tree, to stick in their hats, whenever they went to meet the Earls of Leicester, as was always the custom to do at the end of the park, when they came to reside at their seat here. This fine old oak stands upon a plain about 500 yards from their venerable mansion, near a large piece of water called Lancup-well.*
>
> *Within the hollow of it there is a seat, and it is capable of containing five or six persons with ease. The bark round the entrance was so much grown up, that it has lately been cut away to facilitate the access.*

Sir Philip Sidney.

At this time the tree was measured comprehensively, revealing a height of 73 feet and a girth of 24 feet at 5 feet, which would seem to bear out the suspicion that it was much older than 240 years. Some recent estimates have suggested the tree is 1,000 years old, but this is possibly the whim of a wishful imagination. So where does this place the tree in respect to Sidney? The best guess is that this was a tree that could have been one of his favourites, beneath which he might have composed verse, although much of his finest prose appears to have been written around 1580 while he was staying with his sister at Wilton, near Salisbury. Whether Sidney's association with this ancient oak is based on fact or hearsay is debateable, but a good story is sometimes worth the belief.

A couple of entries in William Hone's *Every-Day Book* (1830) also appear to cast doubt upon the veracity of the tree's Sidney association:

An oak was planted at Penshurst on the day of Sir Philip Sidney's birth, of which [Thomas] Martyn speaks as standing in his time, and measuring twenty-two feet round. This tree has since been felled, it is said by mistake; would it be impossible to make a similar mistake with regard to the mistaker?

The poet Robert Southey also seemed to assume that the original Sidney oak had shuffled off, but from old age rather than malpractice, as the following verse suggests:

Upon his natal day the acorn here
Was planted; it grew up a stately oak,
And in the beauty of its strength it stood
And flourished, when its perishable part
Had mouldered dust to dust. That stately oak
Itself hath mouldered now, but Sidney's name
Endureth in his own immortal works.

Sir Philip was an accomplished poet, brave soldier, ardent Protestant, and esteemed courtier of Elizabeth I. He was well travelled and well connected in literary circles. By 1585, Sidney had been appointed Governor of Flushing in the Netherlands, where a British presence was thought expedient in the face of increasing Spanish incursions. Sidney acquitted himself well at the storming of Axel. However, he did not fare so well the following year, when he participated in a skirmish against the Spanish at Zutphen. He was wounded by a musket shot to the thigh and died of gangrene three weeks later, at the age of thirty-two. Sidney was deeply mourned and legend has it that along the route of his grand funeral procession, Londoners cried, 'Farewell, the worthiest knight that lived.'

The world and its weather has been tough on Sir Philip Sidney's Oak in recent times. It has been struck by lightning, broken in half and, to add insult to injury, was set on fire by children during the 1990s. On a more cheering note, acorns from the old oak have been planted all over the world by Sidney family members and, most recently, cloned saplings are being planted around the estate to ensure the continuity of the genetic line.

QUEEN ELIZABETH'S OAK, COWDRAY PARK

OPPOSITE TOP: A 1920s postcard of the tree. The pond in the background has now completely disappeared.

OPPOSITE BOTTOM: Queen Elizabeth's Oak, Cowdray Park, Midhurst.

THE DEER OF THE COWDRAY ESTATE PARKLAND may have given way to cattle today, but many of the great old oaks and sweet chestnuts still dot the landscape, as they must have done for many centuries. Greatest of all has to be the rugged, squat, ancient pollard known as Queen Elizabeth's Oak; a monumental sessile oak, a little over 41 feet in girth, making it the third largest of its species in Britain, and generally thought to be about 1,000 years old.

Royal connections are often based on hearsay, but at Cowdray Park, in Sussex, a rare, early pamphlet documents evidence of Elizabeth's visit between 15 August and 21 August 1591. The queen had been personally invited by Sir Anthony Browne, a prominent Catholic keen to display unstinting loyalty to his monarch.

The week was spent in lavish entertainments (a rather obsequious sequence of events designed to flatter the monarch, by all accounts), much feasting and, of course, the queen found time to 'hunt' in the park. On Monday, 17 August, 'Elizabeth rode to her bower in the park, took a crossbow from a nymph who sang a sweet song, and with it shot three or four deer, carefully brought within range'. A painting by Francis Philip Stephanoff depicts the 'weak, feeble woman' taking aim. It is said that the queen rested her bow against this mighty oak, a casual action that would be remembered and celebrated for centuries. Other accounts say that she sheltered here from a rainstorm. Whichever it was, the tree was immortalized.

In his *Cowdray: Its Early History* (1922), Torrens Trotter recounts that:

Tradition has it that Lady Kildare (the sister of Lord Montague) incurred the displeasure of the Queen by daring to shoot with her, and although she only killed one deer, we read Elizabeth was so annoyed that she (Lady Kildare) did not afterwards dine at the royal table.

In recent years, the tree has been fenced off to protect it from bark nibbling by livestock and compaction from both trampling animals and devoted visitors. Visually this may have stolen a little of the tree's appeal, and it has allowed a dense growth of nettles to spring up, along with the most unusual clump of butcher's broom. This oak has changed significantly since images of it were published on postcards between 1910 and 1920, when the bole appeared almost sound. A huge split has since opened up, revealing the hollow interior; this process quite probably allowed a little splaying, and helped to exaggerate its girth from under 38 feet in the 1940s to the present 41-plus feet. Some of the upper boughs have also been lost, but those remaining appear to be keeping the tree in fine fettle.

QUEEN ELIZABETH'S OAK, NORTHIAM

Q UEEN ELIZABETH SEEMS TO HAVE BEEN PARTICULARLY FOND of spending time beneath the shade of great oak trees. Queen Elizabeth's Oak in the Sussex village of Northiam is still hanging on to the last remaining stump of evidence of her visit on 11 August 1573, which she made while travelling with her entourage from Hempstead to Rye.

Tradition relates how George Bishop and his family, who lived at Hayes Farm on the edge of the village green, served up a fine meal (described variously from a picnic to a banquet) for the queen. One wonders whether they knew she was coming, and quickly rustled up a feast fit for a queen. No matter, the monarch was clearly pleased with her meal, but perhaps not so taken by her footwear. She changed her shoes and, as a token of appreciation, left her cast-offs 'of green damask silk with heels two and a half inches high and pointed toes' with the maid servant of the Frewen family. R. Thurston Hopkins mentions them – 'Ah! Those awfully tiny things! So reminiscent of the vanity and capriciousness of good Queen Bess!' – in his *Kipling's Sussex* (1921). For many years the shoes resided at Brickwall House, the home of the Frewen family since 1566. They still belong to the family, but latterly they have been tucked away in a bank vault.

In Loudon's *Arboretum et Fruticetum Britannicum*, the only significant Sussex oak he mentions is, 'the venerable oak at Northiam':

Famed for its size, and for having given shelter to Queen Elizabeth, who once breakfasted under its extensive branches, on her way through the village to London, was partially blown down in a storm in 1816.

This passage would seem to indicate another sojourn during her return from Rye.

The tree and its story clearly aroused much interest during the nineteenth and early twentieth centuries. Plenty of photographs, lantern slides, and postcards show the tree while it was still in pretty good shape, although in its declining years it was held together with great cables and braces.

The tree finally died in the late twentieth century, but a replacement oak had already been planted right next to it. In 1991, this tree also died, and yet another young oak was planted to replace the replacement. Hayes Farm is now The Hayes Inn, and the remains of the old oak are sadly little more than a stump, overrun with ivy.

OPPOSITE TOP: An Edwardian postcard of the tree.

OPPOSITE BOTTOM: Queen Elizabeth's Oak, Northiam, drawn by Miss Samworth, of the Anastatic Drawing Society, 1870.

BELOW: The green damask silk shoes that Queen Elizabeth left behind.

THE CROUCH OAK

OPPOSITE: Early morning at
the Crouch Oak with a prop
beneath the bough which
once stretched horizontally
for 48 feet.

BELOW: Charles Haddon
Spurgeon was a renowned
Particular Baptist preacher
who was known as the 'Prince
of Preachers' and is reputed
to have preached to over ten
million people during his
lifetime.

AN ANCIENT OAK TREE GROWING IN THE LEAFY LONDON commuter
belt town of Addlestone, Surrey, may seem a little incongruous in an
essentially twentieth-century setting. But this is no ordinary oak – it marks
the south-east boundary of the old Windsor Forest, long since fragmented
and lost beneath urban sprawl. This tree is a true survivor.

The best guesses to its age put the Crouch Oak at about 800 years old,
which, with its girth of almost 24 feet, might seem a rather liberal estimate.
Local legend credits its vintage at 1,000 years (a popular figure for ancient oaks
throughout the country, but usually an over-exaggerated estimation). The name
is variously attributed to either its low, crouching form, or to a corruption of the
crutch that has long supported the main branch, or even to a cross that was once
placed upon it to distinguish it as a boundary marker.

The Crouch Oak bears a host of alternative names: Addlestone Oak, Queen's
Oak, Gospel Oak, Wycliffe's Oak, Whitefield or Spurgeon Tree. A succession of
influential preachers appear to have capitalised on the commanding presence of
the Crouch Oak as a platform for their rousing sermons. John Wycliffe (1330–84)
was reputed to have preached here, although one suspects this oak was not all that
impressive in the fourteenth century (perhaps there might previously have been
another large oak close by). John Knox (1505–72) is supposed to have visited, as
did George Whitefield (1714–70). Charles Haddon Spurgeon (1834–92), perhaps
the nineteenth century's most prominent preacher, held forth here in 1872.

Tradition relates that Queen Elizabeth once partook of a picnic in the shade
of the tree. A less glamorous, but mischievous story suggests that the queen was
caught short near the tree after feasting nearby – hence 'Crouch'! Yet another story

recalls how the queen narrowly escaped a
fatal charge from a rampant stag near this
tree. She was saved by the selfless act of
one of her huntsmen, who threw himself
in front of the beast and sadly perished.

Naturally enough, the tree is hollow
but still in good health, despite an arson
attack in 2007. Fortunately, the local fire
brigade's rapid response saved the tree
from burning to the ground and it seems
to have rallied. It is rare to find an ancient
tree in an urban context, and is clearly
held in deep affection by the local
community so its loss would have
been a tragedy.

THE OAKS OF DEER PARKS

The whole idea of parkland has had several different connotations over the last 1,000 years – from the first enclosed spaces set aside for deer, to the recreational spaces of the twenty-first century set aside for peoples' relaxation and enjoyment.

THE POPULAR PERCEPTION OF A DEER PARK is of an enclosed area that is usually part of a large private estate, in which deer are contained. This has been the state of affairs for well over a 1,000 years; the assumption being that deer parks entered the landscape after the Norman Conquest. However, Rackham has unearthed evidence in an Anglo-Saxon will of 1045 that shows that Ongar Great Park in Essex was probably a pre-Conquest deer park. If there was one Anglo-Saxon deer park then undoubtedly there must have been others. Indeed, the Anglo-Saxon word *pearroc* means 'a piece of land with a fence around it'.

The native red deer has been around for thousands of years, migrating north into Britain as the ice retreated. It formed a staple part of the diet as well as providing hides for clothing and shelter, and bones and antlers for tools for Mesolithic people. After recent archaeological discoveries at Fishbourne Roman Palace, it is now thought that the Romans first attempted to introduce the fallow deer. Whether or not this was a long-term success remains to be verified from other archaeological findings. Soon after the Normans arrived, in the late eleventh century, they imported their favoured fallow deer from France, a slightly smaller species than the red. This set in motion a whole new culture and infrastructure of parks and deer management, which would lead to an explosion in the number of deer parks. The Domesday Book lists about 35 deer parks, and yet by the end of the thirteenth century, this number had jumped to about 3,000.

Landscapes associated with traditional deer parks follow the same management regimes as those of wood-pasture; essentially large individual trees, often pollards,

OPPOSITE: Ancient oaks in Richmond Park.

ABOVE: Powis Castle deer park, steel engraving by J. C. Varall, 1831.

or small clumps of trees with extensive glades and launds of grassland in between. Many historians have viewed this as the most likely status of the British landscape, in contrast to the popular myth that Britain was comprised of dense continuous wild wood for thousands of years before the Neolithic people began making serious inroads into the natural vegetation to farm. The theory that large, wild herbivores originally maintained this landscape is conceivable, yet still hotly debated among experts.

When the Normans enclosed their deer parks, they also laid claim to the hunting rights in the royal forests. The parks were usually simply for holding and farming deer for the table, and, by association, conferred high status on those privileged enough to maintain them. Deer are voracious nibblers of trees, so wherever they were kept, due provision had to be made for the management of woodland and trees.

The perimeter fencing of parks was constructed to keep deer inside. This required a park pale, traditionally of alternate long and short staves, or sometimes a high stone wall, with a ditch around the inside to prevent the deer from leaping. Sometimes there was also a ditch on the outside. The logistics of harbouring a large beast like a red deer would be challenging. Considering that they can leap 7–8 feet, and that the sheer bulk of a 500 lb stag could flatten all but the strongest fence (long before the days of steel mesh), any construction would have had to be well considered.

Small compartments of woodland within the park had to be defended from the deer if they were required for coppice produce. Where the deer could freely

roam within the park, any harvesting of timber was done by regular rotations of pollarding; cutting branches about 8–10 feet from the ground where deer could not reach to browse off new growth. Pollarding has held the lives of many of our veteran trees in a kind of stasis, sometimes for many centuries longer than their normal lifespan. The legacy of this regime today has been a wonderful collection of veteran broadleaf trees – not just oaks, but also sweet chestnuts, beeches, ashes, and limes – in many parkland landscapes, whether still actively managed, transformed through later management regimes, or simply allowed to go wild.

Forests and chases were designed for the pursuit of the hunt. Here the deer were naturally gathered in the wild, but keepers would still watch over them, answerable to the local lords or even the king, and particularly adept at deterring poachers. If fencing was needed in the forest, then it was to keep deer out rather than in. Where coppicing was practised, compartments of woodland required periods of regeneration to take hold from the stools without being nibbled off by deer. As new growth matured, compartments would often be opened up again. These cycles of management are still observed in places like the New Forest. In and around many woods, the historical remnants of old defensive hedges, banks, and ditches can still be observed today, although some have been replaced by modern fences to keep the wood-pasture management regime intact. Deer in the wild may be shy, secretive beasts, but the impact that they have on the ground flora and young growth of trees is often dramatic, and potentially changes the whole ecology of a wood.

Private parks have seen several different phases of use through the centuries. By the beginning of the fourteenth century, deer parks were in a state of gradual decline because the expense of their upkeep was fast becoming something of a luxury and the land could often be put to better economic purpose. That being said, something of a park renaissance took place under Henry VIII, a fanatical huntsman as well as a voracious acquirer of wealth, land, property, and deer parks. Suddenly the high social status of owning a park was all the rage. Queen Elizabeth I, who also had a passion for hunting, would later prolong the fashion for parks. Although hunting in the sense of a day-long chase through wild forest was not undertaken within the parks, a kind of controlled chase in the form of deer coursing with dogs (usually greyhounds) became popular with the Tudors and lasted well into the seventeenth century. Sometimes the quarry was brought down, sometimes it survived to be chased another day, but the focus of these events was of wagers won and lost on the dogs; and so, undoubtedly, the roots of modern greyhound racing sprang from these events. Old maps sometimes delineate these deer courses, such as the one in Windsor Little Park in 1607. The National Trust's Lodge Park in Gloucestershire still contains its deer course, complete with viewing grandstand.

The late sixteenth and early seventeenth centuries saw something of a surge in the building of large country houses. These were usually surrounded by substantial parks, which reflected the high social status of the owner and effectively maintained a safe distance from the lower orders, who were beyond the park pale (source of the expression that someone or something is 'beyond the pale' which we still use). By the mid-seventeenth century, deer parks once again entered a phase of disuse and decline. Many were converted into arable farmland or became woodland, either by neglect or design. Where grazing continued, it was no longer the preserve of the deer; sheep, cattle, and horses frequently shared the pastures. In addition, the over-exploitation of timber trees inside the parks makes one wonder how many splendid old trees were swept away that had otherwise survived since the Conquest. Shipbuilders would have sought the crooked limbs of healthy old pollards, but if the trees had already begun to rot and hollow, they were probably deemed to be of little economic value.

In the eighteenth century, a whole new era began for deer parks; their main function was not as deer larders, but as extensive adornments to the large houses of the nobility. Deer were present, but, like the artistically arranged trees, avenues, and clumps, waterways, cascades, and lakes, they became just one element of the manufactured Arcadian idyll. Those familiar names such as Bridgeman, Kent, 'Capability' Brown, and later, Humphry Repton, all made their own distinctive contributions to the art and artifice of the new romanticized parkland landscapes. Fortunately, they saw fit to include many of the old trees that had once functioned in the medieval wood-pastures or hedgerows. William Gilpin, instigator of the 'Picturesque' movement, offered his opinions on parks in his *Remarks on Forest Scenery* (1791). While admiring 'the many improvements of the ingenious Mr. Brown', he suggests that 'As a park is an appendage of the house, it follows, that it should participate of it's neatness, and elegance.' He further notes:

ABOVE: Traditional park paling around Moccas deer park in Herefordshire.

As the park is a scene either planted by art, or, if naturally woody, artificially improved, we expect a beauty, and contrast in its clumps, which we do not look for in the wild scenes of nature. We expect to see its lawns, and their appendages, contrasted with each other, in shape, size, and disposition; from which a variety of artificial, yet natural scenes will arise. We expect that when trees are left standing as individuals, they should be the most beautiful of their kind, elegant and well-balanced. We expect, that all offensive trumpery, and all the rough luxuriance of undergrowth, should be removed; unless where it is necessary to thicken, or connect a scene; or hide some staring boundary. In the wild scenes of nature we have grander exhibitions, but greater deformities, than are generally met with in polished works of art. As we seldom meet with these sublime passages in improved landscape; it would be unpardonable if any thing disgusting should appear.

Protective belts of trees were expected to be used with great effect to mask the boundaries of the park (once, the old pale) and make a natural-looking barrier between the privileged classes and the masses. Seemingly pandering to the delicate sensitivities of his upper class audience, Gilpin insists that:

From every part of the approach, and from the ridings, and favourite walks about the park, let all the boundaries be secreted. A view of paling, tho in some cases it may be picturesque, is in general disgusting.

Gilpin also voices his opinions about the most appropriate livestock for a picturesque park. He acknowledges the usual inhabitants of parks as fallow deer, 'and very beautiful they are', but suggests that sheep and cattle are 'more useful, and, in my opinion, more beautiful'. He notes furthermore that:

Sheep particularly are very ornamental in a park. Their colour is just the dingy hue, which contrasts with the verdure of the ground; and the flakiness of their wool is rich, and picturesque. [Although he cautions,] *I should wish them however to wear their natural livery; not patched with letters, nor daubed with red-ochre.*

Lastly, it is worth mentioning that Gilpin was an unreserved and ardent fan of the oak, as he eulogizes: 'It is a happiness to the lovers of the picturesque, that

this noble plant is as useful, as it is beautiful.' The oaks that captivated Gilpin were big, spreading oaks with contorted, twisting limbs: 'Indeed, where it is fond of its situation, and has room to spread, it extends itself beyond any other tree; and like a monarch takes possession of the soil.'

After so many phases of rise and decline and remodelling, it is a miracle that any of the ancient oaks that populated the parks had survived. During the nineteenth century, prolific numbers of exotic trees were imported from all over the world. Big trees such as monkey puzzles, cedars, and redwoods needed plenty of space, and the landowners who bought them were keen to show off their latest prize specimens. These became the new parkland trees, often planted at the expense of the old 'dodders'. Remarkably, by the 1960s there were only 112 parks that still contained deer. From the late nineteenth century, the emphasis on ironclad ships removed the demand for the type of timber once used by the shipbuilders. If anything, the ancient pollard oaks were viewed as commercially useless, and even visual eyesores. Thank goodness that a few landowners, like their eighteenth-century forebears, still appreciated their aesthetic qualities in their parklands and took pains to retain them. Today the best surviving deer parks are those that are believed to most closely resemble their medieval roots. A combination of historical documents and maps, along with evidence found in the field, have helped to build a picture of their chequered past.

Very few parks truly resemble their medieval roots, but one of the most impressive examples is Staverton Park in Suffolk. Considered by many to be the finest assemblage of ancient oaks in Europe, the 220 acres of parkland contain around 4,500 oak pollards, many of which are 400–500 years old. The park also contains some truly remarkable, extremely old hollies, some of which have overtopped and shaded out the oaks. These 70-feet-high hollies could quite easily be 300 years old. Staverton has had relatively low levels of intervention over the last 150 years, so much of the open space between the oak pollards has filled in with birch and rowan, as well as the hollies. Where the rest of that open space would once have been grass, the lapsed grazing by domestic livestock has now allowed it to become infiltrated by bracken, as well as impressive swathes of bluebells in the spring. There are still deer, but not enough to have a high impact on the vegetation. The neglected oak pollards, some thriving, some dying, some completely dead, are a wonderful habitat for invertebrates. Many of the oaks support impressive 'cuckoo' hollies and rowans, long ago sewn in hollows by visiting birds.

The fact that most historic deer parks have been in private hands for many centuries has probably been a blessing. Certainly since the eighteenth century, the raison d'être for maintaining a park as a larder, or even for the occasional stage-managed chase or hunt, has all but disappeared. Parks became appendages of status, exhibiting an aesthetic exuberance and symbolizing competitive affluence. The addition of serpentine drives, sweeping avenues, ornamental lakes, follies, grottoes, and feature trees and clumps, not forgetting the occasional herd of deer, all created a specific image and message: a suggestion that the estate owner was master and manipulator of his demesne. Nature was almost at his mercy. Money, being no object, rather helped as well.

Whether or not these principles have changed today is debatable. What has changed is that many of the landed gentry now actively invite the British public to enter their parks, gardens, and houses. This is probably driven more by necessity than a spirit of munificence. However, there are conflicts in the process of opening up a landscape of ancient trees. Ancient oaks are not always the most stable of structures, and are known to shed large boughs unpredictably (that is, not always under the stresses and strains of adverse weather conditions). These trees are often in a gradual state of decline. While this phase of life brings with it many habitat benefits, their fragile and unpredictable structures are a continuing source of concern to their owners. In a world where litigation seems to run unchecked, nobody wants the worry of a possible personal injury claim as a result of the falling chunks of an ancient tree. Because of these concerns, many areas of incredibly interesting and beautiful park remain off-limits to the public.

Staverton is a private estate, although a single public footpath runs along the eastern edge. It is well worth a visit, if only to get a sniff of this magical place. Moccas Park, in Herefordshire, is another superb park, which most unusually still retains its park pale of oak staves. Again, fear of falling timber stalks the land, and access can only be gained through special permission from Natural

ABOVE: A skeletal oak in Holme Lacy deer park has been left as standing dead wood, providing important habitat for many invertebrates.

England, who steward the park for the estate. There are several extremely rare invertebrate species here too – including a beetle that is specific to a single tree! A strange management regime of stacking fallen timber and dead wood around the bases of the oaks seems to be in vogue here. One hopes there is a good reason for this. Perhaps it stops animals from compacting the ground close to the trees, or from chewing the bark (although oak bark is not usually a favourite). Heaven forbid that it's to make the park look tidy. All told, it looks most unnatural. Moreover, abnormally large piles of dead wood may concentrate equally abnormal quantities of fungi and invertebrate colonies very close to the healthy, living tissue. One assumes that the various species that have thrived in this park over many centuries have done so exactly because the natural cycles of life and death among the treescape suited them, including the random dispersal of dead wood. One might counter that, until the twentieth century, most dead wood was probably carried away for firewood, relieving the park of part of its biodiversity. Still, one can't help feeling that this wood-stacking regime tips the balance too far in the opposite direction.

Several fine parks are associated with some of our favourite great houses. The National Trust have some great parkland landscapes in their care. Calke Abbey in

Derbyshire, once owned by the Harpur Crewe family, has a park that was enclosed in the early seventeenth century, although some of the oldest oak pollards clearly predate this period; typically the Old Man of Calke, which has a girth of 33 feet. Was this a remnant of an earlier park or a hedgerow? Croft Castle, in Herefordshire, has some splendid oak pollards, as well as its numerous noted Spanish chestnuts – reputedly the two species mark the battle formations of the English and Spanish galleons of the Armada. Some of the oldest oaks are lost in a sea of conifers, but are slowly emerging again as the Forestry Commission sets the right course.

Dinefwr Estate in Carmarthenshire is another splendid park, noted for some fine old oak groves and prominent clumps that hint at the eighteenth-century influence of Capability Brown. The site is also famed for its abundant mosses and lichens, again, many of these associated with the oaks. The park rangers have done well to leave plenty of lying dead wood where it falls. Also in Wales, the rolling parkland of the Powis Estate has contained some of the very best oaks in the whole principality for well over a century. After a visit in 1904, H. J. Elwes commented on the park's outstanding oaks:

In April 1904 the Earl of Powis showed me some trees growing in his ancient park at Powis Castle [...] which I believe to be actually the champion oaks of Great Britain at the present time.

Assisted by a Mr Addie, the agent for the estate, Elwes spent a lot of time meticulously recording the vital statistics of the oaks. 'The Champion Oak' was an impressive maiden hybrid oak with a girth of 23.5 feet and a towering height of 105 feet . It would have been ideal, one would have thought, for the forester's axe, but maybe sentiment ruled the day, and a stay of execution saw the tree survive until 1939 when gales laid it low. By then it was 24 feet in girth and 110 feet high – reputedly the largest oak standing in Britain. Probably the greatest girthed oak that ever grew in the park, however, was a tree known appropriately as 'The Giant'; almost 34 feet around, it finally fell in 1961. Fine oaks may have come and gone here, but the Powis Castle Estate parkland has maintained its distinctive character, and remains intact, with mighty oaks and a herd of deer.

Numerous old houses throughout Britain are still able to boast either flourishing parkland landscapes or at least remnants of former parks. Chatsworth in Derbyshire, Duncomb Park and Ripley Castle in Yorkshire, and Bradgate in Leicestershire all still contain many ancient trees and are a delight to visit. In Herefordshire, Moccas Park is certainly highly regarded by naturalists, not only for its oaks, but also for its remarkable array of invertebrates; however, a much lower profile, but somehow more evocative atmosphere, attends Kentchurch Court (see p.182) deer park, which almost straddles the Welsh border, at the southwest corner of the county.

Within striking distance of London are two of the largest and perhaps finest examples in the land: Richmond Park and Windsor Great Park (see p.112). For some people they might appear to be too overrun with visitors, particularly on a hot summer weekend. Even I was astonished at the 'racetrack' of lycra-clad cyclists hurtling round the Richmond Park 'circuit' one Sunday morning. However, both these parks have many quiet corners where you can get away from everyone. Richmond Park covers 2,500 acres, is London's largest royal park, and contains at least 1,000 veteran oaks, some as old as 700 years. Although it certainly functioned as a hunting ground from the Tudor period, it was first enclosed as a park by Charles I in 1637. The red and fallow deer still roam freely, but nature conservation (the park has both SSSI and NNR status) and public amenity have displaced the hunt. Over 500 species of butterflies and moths have been recorded here, reed buntings, skylarks, and meadow pipits nest here, and more than a thousand beetle species are in evidence. Along with wild flowers, mosses, lichens, and rare fungi, it is obvious why this is such a special place. Certainly the more widespread importance of the habitat in all our deer parks is typically in evidence here.

Every single park has its own unique history and its own specific assemblage of trees and wildlife. I will undoubtedly have omitted to mention someone's favourite here, but all I can do is highlight a small selection and encourage everyone to get out there and explore these very special landscapes. Many are open to the public, but watch out for those special or occasional opening times for some of the country's most 'secret' parks.

BELOW: Ancient oaks in the eighteenth-century parkland at Ickworth in Suffolk. These trees create the false impression of a medieval deer park. They are probably the remnants of old hedgerows, grubbed out when the park was created.

OLD KNOBBLEY

OPPOSITE: Old Knobbley
spreads its welcoming arms.

A CERTAIN OAK IN ESSEX HAS WHILED away the centuries with few, the villagers of nearby Mistley excluded, knowing of its existence. Then, in 2000, everything changed. One of those villagers, Morag Embleton, decided it was high time to dedicate a website to 'Old Knobbley'. At the ripe old age of about 800, the tree found itself online at www.oldknobbley.com, a timely entry to the new millennium, and one of the first oak individuals endowed with a persona and its own dedicated website.

Mistley lies on the Stour estuary, just east of Manningtree. On the edge of the village lies a beautiful woodland called Furze Hills. Furze Hills contains some mighty oak pollards, harking back to a time when this was wood-pasture, and most probably a deer park. At the beginning of the eighteenth century, the land was part of the Earl of Oxford's Estate, although Old Knobbley and the three other impressive oak pollards in the wood clearly predate this era. There is evidence of a long history of coppicing here. The Rigby family, who owned the estate from 1703 until the mid-nineteenth century, planted many oaks, which were regularly pollarded. Mistley Hall, the Rigby family home, which lay less than half a mile to the east of Furze Hills, is described in William White's *Directory of Essex* (1848) as having 'a beautiful and well-wooded park of 700 acres'. This wooded park must surely have included Furze Hills, which was by then probably woodland rather than open parkland.

During the Second World War, Furze Hills was acquired by the army, and numerous huts and a secret bunker were constructed in the wood, but fortunately no damage was caused to the old trees – in fact, they probably provided perfect cover from the Luftwaffe. After the war, Mistley Parish Council bought Furze Hills to look after the wood and provide a wonderful public amenity.

In a small clearing in the middle of the wood sits Old Knobbley. Its massive frame, with a girth of 31 feet, looks like some huge torso bursting from the mould, its huge expansive 'arms' thrown wide in exuberant greeting, or perhaps just simple astonishment, thrilled still to be around after all these centuries. One senses the old tree-being watching you, trusting that you mean it no harm; for in the distant past it has had to survive a fire within its hollow bole and gales have ripped away several boughs. Its crusty old bark is highly polished by generations of clambering children, and once, it even played host to a nest of hornets.

A nationwide network of ancient and heritage trees with their own dedicated websites would be a very positive step forward. Such a project would be particularly relevant and engaging for children and schools as it would create a deeper understanding of trees and woodland, and engender a sense of caring and pride. After all, we are the custodians of trees such as Old Knobbley, tending them for the benefit and pleasure of future generations.

THE FAIRLOP OAK

OPPOSITE TOP: View of
Fairlop Oak, a copper
engraving by Owen from a
drawing by Edward Dayes,
1796. A picnic in progress
beneath the tree, while the
carriage awaits and other
visitors drive past. Clearly a
popular spot for an outing.

OPPOSITE BOTTOM: This
engraving of the Fairlop Oak,
published in *The Gentleman's
Magazine* in July 1806, is
effectively a news picture of the
day (except it was about a year
after the event). On June 25
1805, the fire described in the
text (also mentioned in TGM
in 1805 under 'Country News
– Domestic Occurrences')
caused this serious damage to
the old oak, which would
contribute to its final demise
only 15 years later.

BELOW: Watercolour entitled
*Fairlop Oak Tree drawn by
Dr J. Webster, Anno Œtat 80,
Of Chigwell Row, AD 1800.*

OF ALL THE FAMOUS OAKS DOWN THE CENTURIES, there are a select few that have attracted a notoriety that has reserved them an indelible place in the nation's history long after they have departed. One such tree is the Fairlop Oak, a magnificent old tree that once stood in the Forest of Hainault. Not only has the great tree now disappeared, but much of the forest was ruthlessly cleared for agricultural land in around 1851 – an act that today would be seen as nothing short of rank vandalism.

Several accounts of the tree exist from the late eighteenth and early nineteenth centuries, much of which is plagiarized from William Gilpin's *Remarks on Forest Scenery* (1794):

> *In a glade of Hainhault-forest in Essex, about a mile from Barkinside, stands an oak, which has been known through many centuries, by the name of Fairlop. The tradition of the country traces it half way up the Christian era [c900 years old]. It is still a noble tree, tho it has now suffered greatly from the depredations of time. About a yard from the ground, where its rough fluted stem is thirty-six feet in circumference, it divides into eleven vast arms; ... Beneath its shade, which overspreads an area of three hundred feet in circuit, an annual fair has long been held, on the 2d of July; and no booth is suffered to be erected beyond the extent of its boughs.*

Gilpin mourned the parlous state of the tree in its obviously declining vigour, which he felt was certainly due to neglect and ignorance:

> *In the feasting that attends a fair, fires are often necessary; and no places seemed so proper to make them in, as the hollow cavities formed by the heaving roots of the tree. This practice has brought a speedier decay on Fairlop, than it might otherwise have suffered.*

The annual fair can be traced back to about 1720, when one Daniel Day, a block and pump-maker from Wapping popularly known as 'Good Day', who had a small estate nearby, would repair to the shade of the great tree on the first Friday in July, inviting all his friends and colleagues to dine with him on beans and bacon. The food he would provide from a nearby hostelry called The Maypole. It didn't take long before many more people were attracted to this summer beanfeast festivity, and by 1725 a large fair was up

ABOVE: This remarkable image of the Fairlop Oak, from *Arbores Mirabiles* by Joseph Taylor, 1812, shows the old tree amid the general hubbub of the annual fair. Bizarrely, to one side a stall with a large sign offers pieces of the oak for sale as keepsakes. Clearly the opportunistic vendors considered the tree's fame and popularity an excellent way to turn a buck.

and running. By 1765, the gathering was a huge affair with as many as 100,000 people visiting each year. One contemporary observer bemoaned how 'a great number of people meet in a riotous and tumultuous manner, selling ale and spirituous liquors and keeping tippling booths and gaming tables to the great encouragement of vice and immorality'. Sadly, scenes such as those described above came at a great cost to the aged oak and, as J. C. Loudon remarks:

> The project of its patron [Daniel Day] tended greatly, however, to injure his favourite tree; and the orgies annually celebrated to the honour of the Fairlop Oak, yearly curtailed it of its fair proportions.

In 1767, a few years before Day died at the ripe old age of 84, a storm ripped a large bough from the tree. Taking this as an omen of his own imminent demise, he commissioned his own coffin to be made from the wood. The Revd C. A. Johns provides a slightly different account of this, as he had heard reports that several of Mr Day's friends had promised that he should be buried in timber of the tree and to this effect had actually 'lopped off one of the branches, for which trespass an action was brought against the party, fortunately for whom some flaw was found in the pleadings, and the plaintiff was non-suited. It was, however, proved that the fact committed was not injurious to the tree, but a *fair lop*.' Day lies buried in Barking churchyard, where his gravestone is still recognisable to this day.

In 1791, members of the Society of Archers (the Hainault Foresters) became concerned about the tree's rapid decline and paid the grand sum of 6d to William Forsyth, who was gardener to George III, to apply a supposedly curative 'composition' to the remaining healthy wood of the by now decrepit tree. Apparently this magical poultice was comprised of 'cow-dung, old ceiling lime, wood ash, river sand, and burnt bones'. A notice was then affixed to the tree: 'All good foresters are requested not to hurt this old tree, a plaster having lately been applied to his wounds.' Whether or not this was beneficial in any way is unrecorded.

Clearly the Fairlop Oak was a popular attraction at this time, as numerous artists painted and drew the tree, and several delightful engravings exist showing the ancient stag-headed tree in its final throws of life. No matter how much it was valued by many, there was still an inconsiderate minority who continued to abuse and neglect the tree, most notably in 1805:

> *From a party of about sixty cricketers, who had spent the day under its shade, and who carelessly left a fire burning too near its trunk. The tree was discovered to be on fire about eight in the evening, two hours after the cricketers had left the spot; and though a number of persons, with buckets and pails of water, endeavoured to extinguish the flames, the tree continued burning till morning.*

Unfortunately it was downhill from there for the tree; high winds in February 1820 finally dashing the old bole to the ground. Some of the timber was salvaged by a Mr Seabrooke, who was building the new St Pancras church, and converted into a fine, ornate pulpit, which survives to this day. Among many other items large and small that were made from it, a tea caddy belongs to the Essex Field Club and a fine pedestal table resides in a private collection. The Fairlop Oak lives on.

BELOW: The oak pulpit in St Pancras church made from the Fairlop Oak, 1820.

THE CHANDOS, OR MINCHENDEN OAK

OPPOSITE: The Minchenden Oak in its own little park in Southgate, north London. In the nineteenth century this was known as the Chandos Oak, a vast spreading tree. The scars of its many huge lateral boughs can still clearly be seen.

THE DEVELOPMENT AND EXPANSION OF LONDON over the last two hundred years has seen the disappearance of almost all of the open countryside and farmland, which has been overwhelmed by the ever-increasing and all-consuming urban sprawl. Here and there the occasional common, river or canal bank, or woodland marks a tiny retreat that has somehow survived the march of twentieth-century change. In Southgate, in north London, adjacent to Christ Church, a small public park called Minchenden Oak Garden, that was set aside in 1934 as a garden of remembrance, contains what is probably one of, if not the oldest oak tree in London.

Today the tree is known as the Minchenden Oak, but two hundred years ago it was celebrated as the Chandos Oak. Minchenden House and Gardens were built and laid out in around 1747 by John Nichol, a wealthy London merchant. Nichol did not live long to enjoy his fine new home and died leaving all to his daughter and sole heiress Margaret. In 1753 Margaret married James Brydges, Marquis of Carnarvon and subsequently the third Duke of Chandos. In 1813, upon the death of the Duchess Dowager of Chandos, the Duke's second wife (Margaret having died aged only 33 in 1768), the estate passed to the Marquis of Buckingham. From 1822 onwards it seems that the house was surplus to requirement, and several attempts were made to rent it out, but apparently the condition of the estate must have deterred potential tenants. By 1827 the beautiful villa was said to be in 'a most deplorable state'.

Relatively little seems to be known about the tree prior to 1800, although Dr James Beattie, friend of Dr Johnson, had visited in 1772 and reported upon the splendid Chandos Oak he had seen; so the tree had already gathered the appellation of the Chandos family then in residence. Enter Jacob George Strutt with his artistic passion for Britain's great trees, probably at some date between 1822 and 1826, when his first edition folio of *Sylva Britannica* was published. Strutt usually gives detailed measurements of his chosen trees, and again he doesn't disappoint:

Its girth at one foot from the ground is eighteen feet three inches; at three feet it is fifteen feet nine inches. The height of the stem to the branches is eight feet, and at that distance from the ground it is seventeen feet in girth. It is sixty feet in height, and the extremity of its boughs includes a line of one hundred and eighteen feet. It is in this last particular that its great attraction consists. When it is in full pride of its foliage, it strikes the spectator with sensations similar to those inspired by the magnificent Banyan trees of the east. Its boughs bending to the earth, with almost artificial regularity of form and equidistance from each other, give it the appearance of a gigantic tent; with verdant draperies, drawn up to admit the refreshing breezes that curl the myriads of leaves which form altogether a mass of vegetable beauty and grandeur, scarcely to be equalled by any other production of the same nature in the kingdom. It is a magnificent living canopy, impervious to the day.

From Strutt's beautiful sketch it is clear that this was an oak that had been open grown, with plenty of room to spread wide for several centuries. Judging by the relatively short bole, it may have also been pollarded. The dimensions of the tree might suggest an age of around 400–500 years. Prior to the building of Minchenden House there had been another estate and house in close proximity. Dating back to 1551, it was called Arnold(e)'s Grove, subsequently Arnold's or Arnold's Court – from which today's Arnos Grove is derived (the apostrophe having been somehow lost many years ago). It is quite conceivable that the oak was part of the parkland of the original sixteenth-century house and, if it had been managed for deer, a wood-pasture regime incorporating pollarding would have held sway. The tree is marked on a map of 1582 and described as the meeting place of the Edmonton Hundred Court, so if it really is the same tree it must already have acquired a respectable size by that date to have fulfilled such a role. Could this history vindicate claims that the tree is currently 900 years old?

With its girth of 19 feet 6 inches, it is still of a relatively modest size to be of that vintage, but if it really is that old maybe we should be calling it the Arnold Oak or the Court Oak?

The old mansion at Minchenden was demolished in 1853, and the land absorbed into the Arnos Grove Estate, but fortunately the great oak must have been regarded as something special and thus survived the change in fortunes going on around it. Two large limbs were lost in gales in 1900, but when the tree was measured again it had obviously grown significantly since Strutt's visit. Now the girth was 21 feet 3 inches with a canopy spread of 136 feet. A postcard published around 1920 shows the Minchenden Oak (no longer known as the Chandos Oak) minus a couple of large boughs, but also presenting more of an upright form than its previous spreading shape. The land about it looks rough and unkempt, so perhaps at this stage the tree's future would have been uncertain. When the local council stepped up in 1934 to convert the land into a Garden of Remembrance, it was a lifeline for a tree that could easily have been felled to make way for a modern housing scheme or industrial development.

Today the tree is once again cherished in its own little park. It has changed little in appearance over the last century and once more sports the seating around the base that Strutt drew in 1822. The tree has also gained fame as part of the Borough of Southgate coat-of-arms; the accompanying motto '*Ex Glande Quiercus*', meaning 'from the acorn, the oak', reflects Southgate's rise from a small community to its present prosperous status. Those famous acorns are so prized that members of the Southgate Green Association grow seedlings from them, which they sell from their stall at local school fairs. This is a brilliant way to keep the biological lineage of the tree alive, while raising awareness through the younger members of the community – the future stewards of the famous old oak.

ABOVE: This 1920s postcard appears to show a transitional phase of the Minchenden Oak's form. The impressive spreading lower branches so celebrated in early descriptions of the Chandos Oak are laid beneath the tree, after some recent dramatic pollarding. The area still looks semi-wild and the image certainly pre-dates the establishment of the park in 1934.

TURPIN'S OAK

ICK TURPIN WAS BORN IN HEMPSTEAD, ESSEX, in 1706, the son of a butcher and innkeeper. As a young man he teamed up with the notorious Gregory Gang who went on brutal and sadistic robbing and poaching sorties around London. However, Turpin soon turned his hand to highway robbery. Legend tells of Turpin, lying in wait on Finchley Common, intending to relieve a mail coach of its valuables. The account is almost certainly fictitious, as there is no record of Turpin ever having committed any crimes there.

Dick Turpin met up with another infamous highwayman, Tom King, in 1735. For several years they carried out many dastardly deeds, yet somehow managed to evade arrest. However, in 1737 King was trapped at a Whitechapel tavern with a horse that Turpin had stolen. On realizing what was happening, Turpin drew his pistols, and shot and killed King, presumably because he knew his partner's arrest would undoubtedly blow his own cover. Sensing that London would soon be a difficult place to remain undetected, Turpin headed north and spent the next two years in Lincolnshire and Yorkshire, where he committed the odd felony in order to support a comfortable lifestyle.

Turpin's Oak, at the corner of Oak Lane and the High Road in East Finchley, does not appear by name until about 1830, more than twenty years after the last recorded highwaymen were accosted on Finchley Common, and almost a century after Turpin's exploits around London. In 1853 an account in *English Forests and Forest-Trees* made the following claim:

> *The notorious Dick Turpin was in his time accustomed to take up his station behind this tree when he was intent upon a freebooting errand in this part of the country; in other words, this tree was his ambush.*

Again, this claim is completely unfounded. The tree actually died in 1952 and was finally cut down in 1956. Upon examination, the old bole was found to contain numerous old pistol balls, which certainly bolstered the assertion that many passing coachmen were wont to fire at the tree as a matter of course to deter any potential villains who might be lying in wait.

The law finally caught up with Turpin in 1739. He was arrested at York, tried (bizarrely, considering his much darker deeds) for horse stealing in Lincolnshire and, upon conviction, committed to the gallows. A huge crowd of onlookers came to witness his flamboyant farewell.

OPPOSITE: Turpin's Oak, wood engraving from *English Forests and Forest-Trees*, 1853.

BELOW: An Edwardian postcard of Dick Turpin's Oak in East Finchley with two prospective trainee highwaymen.

TURPIN'S OAK, AT FINCHLEY.

THE ELFIN OAK

OPPOSITE: The Elfin Oak in 1996 before it's all-encompassing steel cage was placed around it.

WHEN FIRST I FOUND THE ELFIN OAK in 1996 it was by a happy accident. Walking to a meeting through Kensington Gardens, I chanced upon a huge old stump set within its iron railings in the middle of the park. I marvelled at this bizarre fantastical sculpture, took a few photographs, one of which would later confuse and confound explanation, and moved on.

There appear to be two varying accounts of how the old stump evolved into its enchanting form. The plaque beneath the actual stump, where it now stands near the Princess Diana Memorial Playground in Kensington Gardens, asserts that the carvings were executed in 1911 by Ivor Innes when the old tree still stood in Richmond Park. It was later uprooted and moved to the gardens.

Another version of accounts avers that it was actually Lady Fortescue who, in 1928, commissioned the children's book illustrator Ivor Innes to create a carving from an old oak stump that had been salvaged from Richmond Park. Depicting a vast array of 'little people' and a variety of birds and beasts, Innes carved a tiny wonderland of magic that appeared to exude from the very heart of the ancient oak. Perhaps the truth lies in a mixture of both accounts, and Innes simply embellished and added to the work he had already begun in Richmond Park. It seems possible that some of the carvings were actually made from the carcass of the tree, while others were carved or even moulded in plaster and later attached. Either way, the age of the stump is set variously at between 600 and 900 years old.

The politician George Lansbury became the First Commissioner of Works in the 1929 Labour government. Seeing that life in the inner cities in the midst of the Great Depression was pretty grim for many people, Lansbury instigated a 'Brighter Britain' campaign in the hopes that creating parks, lidos, and playgrounds might lift everyone's spirits a little. The Elfin Oak, completed and opened to view in 1930, was just one small aspect of this effort to improve conditions and cheer the populace.

Ivor's wife, Elsie, wrote a children's book called *The Elfin Oak of Kensington Gardens*, which was published in 1930. The book describes the story of the old oak:

For centuries now [the oak] *has been the home of fairies, gnomes, elves, imps and pixies. In the nooks and crannies they lurk, or peer out of holes and crevices, their natural windows and doorways. It is their hiding-place by day, their revelry place by night, and when the great moon tops the bare branchless tree the Elfin Clans come out to play and frolic in the moonlight.*

From this book we know the names of many of the 'little people' carved into the oak stump: Wookey the Witch, Huckleberry the Gnome, Grumples and

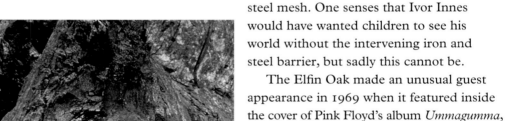

OPPOSITE: Various details of the Elfin Oak with the benefit of Spike Milligan's restoration.

BELOW: Two of the little elfin characters just before the last round of restoration in 1996.

Groodles the Elves, and many more. Ivor, of course, provided the illustrations. He would tend his creation until he died in the 1950s, at which point Elsie continued with the duty of care.

The late, great Spike Milligan (1918–2002), writer, comedian, eccentric and all-round good egg, who for many years lived close to the park in Bayswater, had been enthralled by the book as a child. When, in 1964, Milligan took his daughter Laura to see the tree, they discovered it to be in a very sorry state. Laura's disappointment galvanized Spike into a mission to restore the tree. He used his influence to convince Rentokil to preserve the timber (and to kill the woodworm, the bore holes of which are still evident today) and persuaded British Paints to supply special waterproof paint. With a team of friends he lovingly brought the Elfin Oak back to its former glory. Their work lasted well, but by 1996 the ravages of time, the elements, and a few less than respectful visitors meant that the oak required another round of conservation. Once again Spike was there to tend to his beloved tree. By now the concerns about vandalism, something that depressed Spike intensely, meant that the Elfin Oak was obliged to be protected, not only within iron railings, but now with added steel mesh. One senses that Ivor Innes would have wanted children to see his world without the intervening iron and steel barrier, but sadly this cannot be.

The Elfin Oak made an unusual guest appearance in 1969 when it featured inside the cover of Pink Floyd's album *Ummagumma*, behind a photograph of band member David Gilmour.

In 1997, with encouragement from English Heritage, the tree was accorded Grade II status under the Listed Buildings of Special Architectural or Historic Interest. If a dead tree can achieve this recognition, then how long must we wait before some of our greatest living trees – our Green Monuments – receive the same level of protection?

FOLKLORE, MYTH <u>AND</u> LEGEND

Exactly how far back through history the oak has been held sacred
is uncertain, but about fifteen years ago the discovery of a woodhenge
that was more than 4,000 years old on the coast of Norfolk brought
the subject to life. Seahenge, as the media dubbed it, had already been
known to the local populace for several decades, as it was occasionally
uncovered on the beach at very low tides. The ancient ceremonial
structure was composed of 55 oak staves standing upright in an oval
alignment around a central, large upturned oak stump. Exactly what
the structure was used for is still the subject of much speculation,
and whether the specific use of oak was portentous is also unknown.
It might simply have been the durable nature of oak compared to other
available timber. Other woodhenges have been recorded in other parts
of Britain. Most notable among these is one not very far from Stonehenge,
which turned out to have a child's burial at its centre.

T HE EARLIEST RECORDINGS OF SPIRITUAL ASSOCIATIONS with oak
in Britain date back to the Druids of the Celtic people, as reported by the
Romans when they arrived 2,000 years ago. The very name 'Druid', in Welsh
'*derwydd*', derives from *derw* – an oak tree. The Roman author Pliny the Elder
observed that 'the Druids, for so they call their divines, esteem nothing more
venerable than mistletoe, and the oak upon which it grows'. The oak had long
held an almost universal significance, revered by Greeks, Romans, Britons,
and Celts alike, as had the strange semi-parasitic mistletoe plant.

OPPOSITE: Druids cut the
mistletoe from the sacred oak.
Wood engraving from *English
Forests and Forest-Trees*, 1853.

THE MISTLETOE OAK
The Druids were usually described as performing their rites within sacred
oak groves or beneath great oaks, and if mistletoe grew on these, then so much
the better. It is probable that mistletoe oaks have always been very rare, thus
ordaining them with mystic significance – trees chosen by the gods. There are
several accounts of Druids venturing in search of mistletoe oaks on the sixth day
of the lunar cycle. White-clad Druids would climb the tree and cut the mistletoe
with a gold sickle or knife, which would be caught below in a white sheet so that
it did not touch the ground, thus dispelling its mystic, celestial powers. A pair

of white bulls were also sacrificed as part of the ceremony. The mistletoe symbolized eternal life to the Druids, as it stayed green in winter, and was known to them for its remarkable healing abilities. Mistletoe from oak was particularly valued in treating 'falling sickness', known today as epilepsy.

The Victorians were clearly entranced by these mystic connotations and the rarity of mistletoe oaks, and seemed to have spent much time seeking them out. Cautionary tales attend the removal of mistletoe from oaks. In a paper Dr Bull wrote for the Woolhope Club in 1870, he mentions a couple of fateful instances: the St Dial's mistletoe oak, near Monmouth, was cut down by the bailiff in about 1853, and the owner of the estate immediately dismissed him for doing so; and a woodman who climbed an Eastnor tree to get some mistletoe for a Malvern visitor, fell down and broke his leg. Whatever the penance, it seems that human interference has had severe consequences for these trees, as mistletoe on native oak no longer appears to exist anywhere.

THE YULE LOG

The significance of fire for warmth, cooking, or forging metal may be rather taken for granted today, but historically it has been of paramount importance to all cultures. Thousands of years ago it was believed that the Druids held the mystery of the creation of fire. Loudon tells us that:

> The druids professed to maintain perpetual fire; and once every year all the fires belonging to the people were extinguished, and relighted from the sacred fire of the druids. This was the origin of the Yule log, with which, the Christmas fire, in some parts of the country, was always kindled; a fresh log being thrown on and lighted, but taken off before it was consumed, and reserved to kindle the Christmas fire of the following year. The Yule Log was always of oak.

It is believed that 'yule' is derived from the Celtic god of fire – Baal, Bel, or Yiaoul – who was worshipped under the form of an oak. 'Baal was considered the same as the Roman Saturn, and his festival (that of Yule) was kept at Christmas (Yuletide), which was the time of the Saturnalia.' A fragment of the previous year's log was often used to kindle the new yule log; sometimes it had to burn for twelve hours, while in other districts it was fortuitous to let it burn throughout the twelve days of Christmas, but it was always quenched before burning away completely. An abundance of variations on this custom existed up and down the country. In her *British Folk Customs* (1976), Christina Hole avers that:

> The Yule Log was the domestic counterpart of the great communal fires of the midwinter and midsummer festivals, and like them, it was associated with fertility and continuing life, and with preservation from evil.

Hole also discusses the various rituals surrounding the acquisition of the log (very unlucky to buy one's log), as well as its ceremonial homecoming and anointing. Writing about Cornish customs in 1890, M. A. Courtney describes the chalking of a man's image on the log, which then slowly blackened and faded over the Christmas period, and suggested that this might be redolent of sacrifice. The ancient Britons' belief that the sacred yule fires renewed good fortune and combated evil has carried down the centuries, and the yule log ceremony is still observed in some households to this day.

THE GOSPEL OAK

Even though Christianity had been the chosen faith of a few as far back as the late second century, when Augustine and his band of missionaries set foot in Britain in 597, they must still have encountered pagan veneration of trees among the Anglo-Saxons. Word from Rome was one of caution: Do not alienate the people you want to convert, but absorb their icons and symbols into the new faith. A striking 1758 engraving from Francis Hayman's original work depicts this process of conversion, with a defiant Druid brandishing mistletoe in an oak tree, while a Christian throng with cross aloft draws near.

The balance of power is about to shift from the Druids to the bishops. Oaks, for so long the temples and totems, now ordained meeting places, scenes of courts, and boundary markers, as they probably already had been for centuries, but now the Christian preachers also used these trees as Gospel Oaks to spread their message. Jacob George Strutt leaves a fine account and sketch of the Gospel Oak at Stoneleigh, Warwickshire, in his *Sylva Britannica* (1830). He relates that:

The custom of making the boundaries of parishes, by the neighbouring inhabitants going round them once a-year, and stopping at certain spots to perform different ceremonies, in order that the localities might be impressed on the memories of the young, as they were attested by the recollections of the old, is still common in various

ABOVE: A Fownhope Heart of
Oak Society group photograph
c.1890. Note the oak bough
held aloft at the back with club
banners blowing in the breeze.

parts of the kingdom. The custom itself is of great antiquity, and is supposed by some to have been derived from the feast called Terminalia, which was dedicated to the God Terminus, who was considered as the guardian of fields and land-marks and the promoter of friendship and peace among men.

The custom of beating the bounds accompanied by readings from the scriptures was introduced among Christians about 800 by Avitus, Bishop of Vienna, and usually performed at Rogationtide. One of the most famous Gospel Oaks was a tree at Polstead in Suffolk, which stood until 1953, and was believed to be at least 1,000 years old. All that remains of the grand old tree today is a pile of dead wood, but close by a young oak grown from one of its acorns thrives. Every year the local community still gathers nearby for a service.

In north London there is a place called Gospel Oak. This was named after an oak tree that stood on the boundary between the parishes of St Pancras and Hampstead, when this was a relatively rural area. The tree featured in the annual beating of the bounds, when a priest would lead the community on a walk around the parish boundaries. It is known that the tree was still marked on maps of 1840, and Victorian prints show the eighteenth-century preacher George Whitfield addressing a crowd beneath a tree in Gospel Oak Fields. Was this the Gospel Oak? Apparently, Gospel Oak Fair was held here until 1857, but the fate of the oak itself is uncertain after this time.

Scores of Gospel Oaks have come and gone throughout Britain. One of two national-champion girthed English oaks (measuring a staggering 42 feet around) continues to survive on a remote Herefordshire farm (see p.180).

ABOVE: A wonderful snapshot of
village life at Great Wishford –
the Oak Apple Day procession
of 1911 about to move off.
The four nitch girls may be
seen (even a nitch baby in the
pram at the front of the picture).
The addition of 'Long Live The
King' to the banner and the
abundance of Union Jack flags
celebrates the impending
coronation of George V on
22 June.

ROYAL OAK DAY

The most famous oak association has to be Royal Oak Day. Sometimes known
as Oak Apple Day, it is celebrated on 29 May every year in remembrance of
Charles II's triumphal return to the throne in 1660. This was not only the day
he marched back into London, but also his birthday. The oak was adopted as the
symbol of allegiance to the monarchy in the wake of the famous story of Charles
having hidden in the Boscobel Oak to avoid capture by the Parliamentarians,
after the Battle of Worcester (see p.169).

The date of the Restoration was made an official day of thanksgiving,
a public holiday for celebration, and recreation (something that had probably
been available in very short measure during the Interregnum), by order of
Parliament in 1664. Everyone was expected to wear sprigs of oak to show their
loyalty to the crown or suffer a punishment (which typically involved being
splashed with water, pelted with rotten eggs, or stung with nettles). The most
sought after sprigs were those bearing oak apples, little round galls, known in
some parts as 'shick-shacks'. Oak boughs were hung in cottage porches and
from church towers. In many communities the day was often substituted for
the old May Day, with many of the customs, including maypole dancing,
May Queens, Jack-in-the-Green, and celebratory parades with oaken boughs,
featuring prominently. Almost 1,000 years on from Augustine, an adherence to
a fusion of Christian beliefs entwined with the old pagan rites and symbolism
of fertility and renewal proliferated – much to the dismay of some observers.

Several Friendly Societies sprung up around the country and chose 29 May
as their annual day of celebration. Most were established during the nineteenth

century and were formed principally to provide mutual assistance for members of the community in times of financial, labour, or health hardships. Members paid a small subscription and the Club Day, a time for merriment, marching, and reaffirmation of the community bond, would also be a source of fund-raising. One of the last surviving Societies is the Heart of Oak Friendly Society in Fownhope, Herefordshire, officially established in 1876, although recent evidence has come to light suggesting that it dates back to the 1790s. At first light on the nearest Saturday to 29 May, the club chairman repairs to the nearby woods to cut a large oak branch, which is then decorated with red, white, and blue ribbons, before being carried aloft in front of the club walk around the village. The Society banner is proudly unfurled; many marchers carry floral displays on long staves (prizes are awarded for the best display); a brass band drives the procession onwards and, after the church service of thanksgiving, a good lunch, and plenty of alcohol-fuelled toasts and speeches at a variety of hospitality stops around the village, the day is rounded off with an evening of song and dance. The oak bough, the flowers, and the carousing clearly hark back to the pagan rites of spring.

At Great Wishford, in Wiltshire, an ancient ceremony once linked to Whitsuntide, has, since the Restoration, been relocated to the 29 May, bringing the date further significance. The roots of the ceremony can be traced back to 1603, when a manorial court was held in nearby Grovely Wood to settle a dispute between the villagers and the new lord of the manor, Sir Richard Grobham, over wood-gathering rights. These were rights of fundamental importance to all rural communities for hundreds of years. A charter was established, enabling the villagers to 'lawfully gather and bring away all kinde of deade snappinge woode, boughs and stickes', for fuel throughout the year. Once a year they were also allowed to take green boughs of oak from the wood, but none thicker than a man's arm, and only those that could be pulled without mechanical aid. In 1292, 1318, and 1332 unsuccessful attempts were made to quash the rights of the villagers. The charter of 1603 affirmed their rights in perpetuity, and all seemed well until 1807, when the Earl of Pembroke bought the Manor of Wishford and promptly attempted to introduce an Act of Enclosure in 1809. In 1825 yet another attempt was made to exclude the villagers, but this time Grace Reed, a young woman of eighteen, and three of her friends, resolutely went into Grovely Wood to gather firewood. They were instantly arrested, taken to Salisbury, and thrown into gaol, as they were too poor to pay their fines. Public outrage and intervention by a lawyer thankfully secured their release, but the acrimony between landowner and commoners would rage on throughout the nineteenth century.

By 1892 matters had come to a head, and seventy-four Wishford villagers established the Oak Apple Club with the motto 'Unity is Strength'. The upsurge of socialist thinking and trade unions was clearly the underlying spirit of this founding group. Despite further rumblings during the mid-twentieth century, the villagers still assert their rights each year.

The day begins early, very early, when the villagers are awoken at daybreak, around 4 a.m., by a cacophonous 'band' of rattles, bells, pots and pans traipsed

ABOVE LEFT: The Nitch Girls
outside the church at Great
Wishford on Oak Apple Day.

ABOVE RIGHT: The club
march of the Fownhope Heart
of Oak Society.

around from door to door. Before breakfast, everyone repairs to Grovely Wood
to gather oak boughs. One will be the 'marriage bough', later hauled up the
church tower, and supposed to bring good luck to all who marry in the church
over the coming year. Others will decorate houses or be carried in procession.
Prizes are awarded for the most handsome boughs (preferably those bearing
oak apples). In his *Wildwood: A Journey Through Trees*, Roger Deakin encapsulates
the spirit of this tradition perfectly:

> *Ceremonies such as the Grovely rite were originally performed with the most serious
> possible intent: to promote the general fertility of every living thing in the parish
> for the whole of the coming season. People really believed there was a sanctity in
> the living bough: that it contained the invisible god of growth. It was a kind of
> sacrament that might bless the house and all who went in and out, and, by being
> carried in procession around the village farmyards and into the fields at the high
> point of spring, might impart its power of regeneration and growth to everything it
> encountered.*

After everyone has breakfasted, they travel to Salisbury Cathedral, where four
women, the nitch girls, dressed very much as Grace Reed and her friends might
have been, dance in the close before the club banner. Bearing their bundles of
oak and hazel faggots, or nitches, they enter the cathedral, march to the altar,
and loudly proclaim their rights: 'Grovely! Grovely! Grovely! And all Grovely!'
The task completed for another year, the villagers' rights preserved, all return to
Great Wishford for a fine lunch, a beating of the bounds, and various revelries.

'DANCING TREES'

The Revd Sabine Baring-Gould, a prodigious collector of folk traditions, song, and dance at the turn of the nineteenth century, records several colourful examples of West Country 'dancing trees' in his *A Book of the West* (1900). Usually these trees were oaks, although the famous Moreton Hampstead Cross Tree, of which excellent detailed records survive, was an elm. Baring-Gould tells the following tale about a 'dancing' oak at Dunsford, between Okehampton and Exeter:

OPPOSITE: A Green Man at the springing of the arches of the fourteenth-century sedilia in All Saints Church, Weston Longville, Norfolk.

[It was] *woven and extended and fashioned into a flat surface. The story in the neighbourhood used to be that the Fulfords, of Great Fulford, held their lands on the singular tenure that they should dine once a year on the top of the tree, and give a dance there to their tenants. But this usage has long been discontinued.*

Again another dancing tree is at Trebursaye, near Launceston. This also is an oak, but is now in a neglected condition and has lost most of its original form, looking merely as a peculiarly crabbed and tortured old tree. Here anciently a ghost was wont to be seen, that of a woman who had fallen from it during a dance and broken her neck, and many stories were afloat relative to horses taking fright at night and running away with the riders, or of passers-by on foot who were so scared as to be unable to pursue their journey, through seeing the dead woman dancing on the tree.

In the end Parson Ruddle of Launceston, a famous ghost-layer, was called to exorcise the unquiet spirit of the tree:

The ghost had so effectively frightened people that the dances on the top of the tree had been discontinued. They were never resumed.

One wonders what Health and Safety would have had to say about these remarkable arboreal shindigs.

GREEN MEN

If the Jack-in-the-Green character has personified the vibrancy and unquenchable energy of the life force first recorded in May Day rites during the late eighteenth century, then his image has been around much longer. In her excellent book *The Green Man* (1978), Kathleen Basford does not see an immediate connection with Jack-in-the-Green, but reveals that foliate heads have been known throughout Europe since the second century. However, their widespread occurrence in Britain does not appear to take hold until the twelfth century. Why are they there, and what might they signify? Basford has no categorical answer, but observes:

While it is possible that some of these leafy faces might allude to the May King or to the idea of the revival of nature in springtime, the Green man more often evokes the horrors of the 'silva daemonium'. A Green man who, at first glance, may seem the very personification of springtime, and 'summer is i-comen in' may, on closer inspection, reveal himself as a nightmarish spectre. The imagery can be ambivalent. The Green man can be at once both beautiful and sinister...

... The despair and anguish expressed in some of the faces is even more disquieting

because it is so human. The evil is so much more frightening because it is human as well as diabolical. It is when the fantasy is expressed most naturalistically that it seems most eerie and touches us most powerfully.

To place such images, redolent of pagan tree worship, within the confines of the Christian Church seems something of an anachronism. However, perhaps the absorption of old ways into the new typified the power that the Church desired to signal to its flock, and signified a cautionary message. The Green Man peers out of the wild wood, where physical and metaphysical dangers lurk, beyond the safe haven of the Church and the straight and narrow path of the Christian doctrine.

The Green Man seems to have held a popular place inside the Church between the twelfth and fifteenth centuries, a culture that undoubtedly came over from Europe with the Norman invaders. One finds areas, typically parts of rural Devon, where a very distinctive style of crude yet startling imagery recurs, probably passed down through several generations in a family of carvers. The tradition seems to have been instinctive, unquestionable, perhaps incomprehensible, for there are no contemporary accounts that reveal the purpose of the Green Man carvings. Oak wood is almost inevitably used for these carvings and, again, oak imagery of leaves and acorns recurs with some regularity, as it does in the work of the stonemasons.

Green Men images of the last few years are mostly joyous, kindly souls beckoning us back to reconnect to our green roots, to rekindle the harmony human beings once held with their natural surroundings. The reconnection doesn't necessarily indicate pagan veneration, for surely being at one with the infinite wonder of the natural world transcends any religious dogma or affiliation.

OAK SAYINGS AND BELIEFS

Many sayings attend the oak. Perhaps most familiar is that of the first flushing of foliage of oak and ash, and the type of summer they predict. The most common variations include:

> *If it's oak before ash,*
> *We're in for a splash.*
> *If it's ash before oak,*
> *We're in for a soak.*

For the last fifty years or so, ash has only come into leaf first on four occasions. This could be an indication of climate change, since the rhymes first surfaced several hundred years ago. Perhaps the ash once regularly leafed first. It is said by some that rising temperatures trigger oak leafing, while ash is triggered by sunshine. Of course genetic variation within both species also leads to quite a wide range of leafing times. It is not uncommon to see groups of oak or ash with trees well into leaf side-by-side with others that have barely broken bud. There are a few inconsistencies in evidence for this saying, as Charles Mosley, writing in 1910, quotes:

Oak before ash
Have a splash;
Ash before oak
There'll be smoke.

and:

When the oak comes out before the ash,
There'll be a summer of wet and splash;
When the ash comes out before the oak,
There'll be a summer of dust and smoke.

These verses may simply be regional variations, as there could easily have been dramatic differences from one end of Britain to the other, or even between upland and lowland trees.

John Dryden's (1631–1700) famous observation on the lifespan of oaks is indisputably well-founded and, again, extremely familiar:

The monarch oak, the patriarch of trees,
Shoots rising up, and spreads by slow degrees.
Three centuries he grows, and three he stays
Supreme in state; and in three more decays.

The timespan Dryden indicates would be exceptional for a maiden oak, although there are a few in existence that may approach this vintage, notably the famous Majesty at Fredville (see p.34). Certainly 900 years and a little more is quite easily within reach for a pollarded tree.

The acorn has long been revered as an emblem of fecundity. First held sacred by the Druids, the acorn and its cup are the earliest phallic symbols – the acorn being the male member, while the cup represents the female. In fact, the name of the head of the penis is *glans*, from the Latin for acorn. In line with these beliefs, acorns were frequently carried in pockets or little bags to ward off illness and ensure fertility, potency, and longevity.

Several popular nineteenth-century beliefs about acorns were recorded by various folklorists: if a young couple dropping two acorns in a bowl of water should see them float together, then they were bound to marry; couples unable to have children improve their prospects by embracing an oak; standing beneath an oak would confer protection from evil spirits and witchcraft. Good fortune and happiness were also believed to attend those who were married in the shade of an oak.

KETT'S OAKS

OPPOSITE: Kett's Oak amid the undergrowth at Ryston.

THE STORY OF ROBERT KETT AND THE UPRISING that he orchestrated in Norfolk in 1549 has gone down in the annals of history, initially as the work of a traitor, but latterly as a folk hero. Kett's Rebellion was born out of a period in history that has been often repeated, when the wealthy landowners were intent on grabbing land for themselves at the expense of poor commoners.

The 1540s was a time of inflation, unemployment, rising rents and declining wages, a situation that resonates to this very day, and the common people seeing their land being snatched away became increasingly incensed to the point where something had to give. In July 1549, a group of agitators made their way to a farm at Hethersett, a few miles south-west of Norwich, to tear down the hedges and fences of Sir John Flowerdew, reviled for his role in the demolition of Wymondham Abbey during the Dissolution. Flowerdew confronted the mob and bribed them to target their anger on an old adversary, Robert Kett, who had an estate at Wymondham. When they came to tear down Kett's enclosures he called the rioters to halt, listened to their grievances and, deciding they were fully justified in their cause, joined them, tore down his own enclosures, and then returned to Flowerdew's estate to remove his enclosures.

With Robert Kett taking the mantle as leader and hordes of disaffected common folk rallying to the cause, the protest movement grew. Kett and his followers marched to Norwich and set up camp on Mousehold Heath. Thousands joined him outside what was then the second city of England, with a population of about 12,000, until the camp became larger than the city. An oak at the centre of the camp, called the Oak of Reformation, was adopted by Kett as a place to administer the cause. There he held council with representatives of the Hundreds of Norfolk, issued warrants for obtaining supplies, and arrested those who contested their cause.

The rebels drew up a list of their grievances and submitted it to the Protector Somerset. His response was to dispatch a herald from London to order the illegal gathering to be dispersed and to grant a pardon. The rebels would have none of it, and on 21 July 1549 they stormed the city and took control. Despite one failed attempt to dislodge them by forces commanded by the Marquis of Northampton, the rebels' rule in the city only endured until 27 August, when the Earl of Warwick arrived with 14,000 well-equipped and trained men. The fighting was fierce and bloody before the final battle at Dussindale, just outside the city. It is said that about 3,000 rebels lost their lives here and that the rest fled the battlefield.

Robert Kett was captured at Swannington the following day and, with his older brother William, was taken to the Tower of London to be tried for treason. Duly convicted, both men were then returned to Norwich in December.

Robert was hanged from the walls of Norwich Castle, while William was hanged from the west tower of Wymondham Abbey. After barely six months, the whole rebellion was completely quashed and for many years Robert Kett was remembered as a 'reviled symbol of rustic violence.' In fact, for over a century the city of Norwich celebrated 27 August as a day of deliverance from the rebellion.

It was only in the mid-nineteenth century that some writers and historians began to view Kett's uprising with a more benevolent attitude. Conceding that his methods might not have been the most expedient, the moral conviction of the man, and a landowning man by birth at that, surely gave him the right to be remembered as a champion of the common people. Today, Kett might seem an even more relevant historical figure in the light of current social and economic strife. The Mousehold Heath oak was lost many years ago, a sad version of events suggesting that Norwich City Council cut it down in the 1960s in order to make a car park.

The best known of the Kett's Oak trees is the one that sits on the verge of the old Wymondham to Norwich road near Hethersett, where Kett is supposed to have made his intitial rousing speech to the masses before they marched to Norwich. If this was a substantial tree in the mid-sixteenth century, one might expect it to be a little larger. Norfolk County Council offered three possibilities: that it has been incredibly slow growing, and is the original tree; that it was planted soon after the rebellion from acorns of the original tree (still, it seems a bit small to be 450 years old); that it is a tree that was planted a while later. The latter seems the most plausible.

An oil painting by Samuel Wale from the 1740s is titled 'Robert Kett, under the Oak of Reformation at his Great Camp on Mousehold Heath, Norwich, receives the Earl of Warwick's Herald, August 22nd 1549.' The distinctive shape of the oak has led some to believe that this was in fact the Hethersett tree, which bears more than a passing resemblance. Obviously this is not so. Several different artists subsequently produced engravings based on this painting, reflecting the increasing popularity of Kett as the nineteenth century progressed.

Concern about the welfare of the Hethersett tree has clearly been an issue in the past and at some point the hollow bole was filled with concrete (well meant no doubt, but not usually recommended). In 1967 the local council also carried out remedial work that included the great triangular prop.

Less well known is a tree dubbed Kett's Oak that stands on the edge of Kett's Oak Wood on the Ryston Hall estate, near Downham Market, some forty miles west of Norwich. Some doubts have been aired as to whether Kett was ever here, but accounts tell of several rebel camps that were established around the county. The earliest reference to this tree is on a seventeenth-century map, where it is a noted landmark. Francis White's *History, Gazetteer and Directory of Norfolk* (1854) mentions the oak, and Kelly's Directory for 1883 states that, '300 yards south of Ryston Hall, stands Kett's Oak, or the Oak of Reformation, where Coniers, the

chaplain of the rebels, read prayers and preached, and their court sat to administer justice and regulate disorders'. In 1528 Richard Pratt married into the Guylour family, who then owned Ryston. By 1549 he was evidently lord and master and, one assumes, happy to tolerate the presence of the Kett sympathisers on his estate. However, we are less sure about his response to a bit of sheep stealing. Even rebels must eat, and a small stone slab near the oak tree (carved in 1896) bears a strange bit of doggerel rather cheekily recounting the illicit acquisition of a few sheep. It is believed to have originally been left pinned to the tree after the rebels departed. Titled 'THE OAK OF REFORMATION KET'S REBELLION, 1549', it states the following:

Mr. Prat, your Shepe are Very fat
and we thank you for that
we have left you the skynns
to buy your Ladye pinnes
and you must thank us for that.

This Kett's Oak is a true contender as a substantial tree in the sixteenth century. In 1906 Elwes and Henry received details of the tree from Mr E. R. Pratt of Ryston Hall, his account including the above verse, and the oak was stated to be, 'fairly sound and vigorous', and measuring 26 feet 6 inches at 3 feet. Today it measures 27.5 feet and, although bearing a healthy crown, is well hollowed within.

ABOVE: *Robert Kett, under the Oak of Reformation at his Grand Camp on Mousehold Heath, Norwich, receives the Earl of Warwick's Herald, August 22nd 1549.* Oil on canvas by Samuel Wale (1721–1786)*. A splendid historical scene with an oak at the very centre of events. Public affection for Kett and his uprising was reflected by several nineteenth-century copy engravings made from the original.

THE WINFARTHING OAK

ALMOST CERTAINLY THE LARGEST OAK that has ever been recorded in Norfolk was the Winfarthing Oak, which once stood on the Earl of Albemarle's estate at Quiddenham Hall, Winfarthing, near Diss. With its girth of 40 feet at shoulder height recorded in 1820, and accounts of it having been called the 'Old Oak' at the time of the Norman Conquest, popular opinion held that it must have been around 1,500 years old – a truly exceptional age, if it were true.

There is a strong probability that the oak is one of the last ancient pollards of Winfarthing Great Park, once belonging to Sir William Munchensy in the thirteenth century.

Early nineteenth-century accounts mention that the oak's hollow interior was reputed to have once held 30 people. Tables and chairs were allegedly also placed inside, perhaps for parish or evangelical meetings. There was once a brass plate nailed above the hollow entrance to the tree's hollow bole, bearing a short verse that solicited donations to the Bible Society:

Ye who this venerable oak survey
Which still survives through many a stormy day,
Deposit here your mite with willing hands,
To spread in foreign climes, through foreign lands,
The Sacred Volume, so divinely given,
Whose pages teach the narrow way to heaven
DANIEL DOGGETT [apparently the tenant of the Lodge Farm,
where the tree stood. A collection box was provided.]

Corresponding with the *Gardener's Magazine* in 1836, Samuel Taylor, Esq., paints the following picture of the tree:

It is now a mere shell – a mighty ruin, bleached to a snowy white; but it is magnificent in its decay; and I do wonder much that Mr. Strutt should have omitted it in his otherwise satisfactory list of tree worthies. The only mark of vitality it exhibits is on the south side, where a narrow strip of bark sends forth the few branches shown in the drawing, which even now occasionally produce acorns.

Taylor, who had known the tree for forty years, denied reports that it had seriously declined in recent times. The tree had endured for 'an important portion of my life, but a mere span of its own'.

OPPOSITE: The Winfarthing Oak, wood engraving from J. C. Loudon's *Arboretum et Fruticetum Britannicum*, 1838.

OPPOSITE BOTTOM: An Edwardian postcard of the tree which is still clearly alive, although wreathed in ivy. By 1953 the old frame had finally crumbled and fallen.

THE TEA PARTY OAK

OPPOSITE: The massive Tea Party Oak within its own little enclosure in Ickworth Park, Suffolk.

THE ICKWORTH ESTATE, THREE MILES SOUTHWEST of Bury St Edmonds in Suffolk, has been in the hands of the National Trust since 1956. After almost 500 years, on the death of the 4th Marquis of Bristol, the Hervey family had handed over the great house and a large endowment in lieu of death duties (a familiar scenario with so many of the nation's large estates). An area to the west of the fine neoclassical house, with its giant rotunda, is still known as the Old Deer Park. This was supposedly the original thirteenth-century deer park. A licence for about 50 acres of imparking was granted between 1259 and 1264.

In 1655 the whole estate amounted to 1,188 acres, the majority of which comprised small fields with hedgerows, blocks of woodland, farmsteads, and cottages. By the beginning of the eighteenth century, the Herveys had swept away these farms and villages, rehousing the ousted tenants in nearby Horringer, expanding their park and reintroducing the deer.

A visit today reveals a landscape that has all the appearances of a genuine medieval deer park, with a wealth of old pollards in evidence, but on closer examination there is a lost landscape here. Gone are the cottages and farms, gone are the woods and hedges, and yet there are signs of old wood banks, huge coppice stools that must once have been contained and fenced within woods, and linear alignments of old oaks that most certainly signify lost hedgerows. Nobody ever set out to deceive the landscape historians of the future here; what is on view are simply the vestiges of changes of use of the land ordained by whim or purpose of a succession of landowners. Oliver Rackham coined this a 'pseudo-medieval park'.

Many impressive old oaks appear throughout the park. Two particularly picturesque examples near the car park look like they are about to lock in an arboreal embrace. At the centre of the park stands one of the largest and oldest oaks in the whole of East Anglia – the Tea Party Oak – estimated to be about 700–800 years old. With a girth of almost 38 feet, this shattered giant beckons you forward with a massive bleached, claw-like lateral bough. The Tea Party Oak derived its name from the fact that the local children from the nearby village of Horringer used to gather for tea parties beneath its vast spreading canopy on high days and holidays from about 1860 onwards; a custom that lasted for about fifty years. For an oak of such great size to go unmentioned in any of the books on trees in the nineteenth and early twentieth centuries seems a strange and unexplainable omission. Usually the owners of great trees were only too eager to broadcast their presence in a world where garden and park one-upmanship was keenly contested. However, nothing more exciting ever came its way beyond a tea party – how frightfully British.

ICONOGRAPHY, SYMBOLISM <u>AND</u> ETYMOLOGY

What's in a name? Every place name, every person's name, has a meaning or derivation. A glance at the map of Britain quickly reveals a host of place names derived from or associated with the oak. Gathering the necessary lexicon for a search through the oak etymology of British place names is the first port of call. Old English gives oak as 'ac' (sometimes 'ak', 'aak', or 'ack'). The Scots had 'aik', the Old Irish was 'daur', and the Celts of Wales had 'derwen' and 'derw', derivative 'deri', as well as 'derlwyn' – an oak grove.

T HE MOST OBVIOUS OAK-INFLUENCED PLACE NAMES include 'oak' as part of their designation. A broad sampling include: Oakenclough (Lancashire) – oaks in a steep valley or ravine; Oakenholt (Flint) – oak wood or copse; Oakthorpe (Leicestershire) and Oakerthorpe (Derbyshire) – the village or hamlet by the oak; a lot of Oakleys – a settlement in a field or clearing near the oaks; as well as all manner of plainly obvious associations in Oakford, Oakfield, Oakgrove, Oakhill, Oakridge, Oakhanger, Oaklands, Fairoak, several Broad Oaks and, of course, Sevenoaks … whose name endures even though the gales of 1987 reduced what was once seven oaks to one! Less well known, there are also Five Oaks (Kent, West Sussex and Jersey), Four Oaks (East Sussex and West Midlands), and Three Oaks (East Sussex). Copt Oak (Leicestershire) refers to pollarded oaks – 'cop' meaning head in Old English, and pollarding referring to oaks with their heads cut. Some names that appear to have obvious associations have no relation to oak whatsoever. Take, for example, Oakham in Rutland, whose name is actually derived from the Anglo-Saxon 'Oca's Hamm' – the meadow or riverside pasture belonging to Oca.

Surviving Anglo-Saxon charters (some counties well represented, but others barely so) show oak mentioned second most frequently, after thorn trees, in the perambulations made to identify boundaries. Many places with names beginning with 'Ac' hark back to their Anglo-Saxon beginnings, many of which were recorded in the Domesday Book: Most obvious might be the several Actons, denoting oak farm, 'Ac tun', or farm by the oaks. Acomb (Yorkshire and Northumberland), derives from 'Acum', at the oak trees; Oakworth (Yorkshire), from 'Acurde', an

OPPOSITE: The Whiteleaved Oak on the Malvern Hills.

oak enclosure; Occold (Suffolk) is recorded as 'Acholt' in Domesday – so, once again, oak wood or copse. Matlock takes the 'ock' variant, the name signifying a meeting place, 'maethel', near the oak.

The Lancashire town of Accrington is a little more complex. The town was known as Akarinton in 1194, Akerunton, Akerinton, and Akerynton in 1258, Acrinton in 1292, Ackryngton in 1311, and Acryngton in 1324. It is thought that an Anglo-Saxon conjunction of acorn, 'aecern', and farmstead or village, 'tun', might have led to the name. It is also said that the Lancashire dialect for acorn was 'akran'. There is a place called Acre in Lancashire. Acre or aker is derived from 'aecer', which translates loosely as a field, land, cultivated land, and later a defined area that a yoke of oxen could plough in a day. This obviously relates to 'aecern', so possibly an area cleared out of oak wood (where acorns might have been harvested), a field with oaks, or one planted with oaks. Most etymological descriptions involving references to 'oak' cite these connections, but remain quite broad in their translation. Finding the meaning of an oak place name usually involves a choice between Old English derivations from oak or acorn, and discovering whether some local lord or landowner might have imposed his name as right of ownership to the settlement.

In Wales there is Derwen (Denbigh); Deri (Caerphilly); Derwenlas (Powys), which means green oak; Cwmderwen (Powys), the oak in the valley; while in Cumbria the Old Norse 'aik' or 'eik' would seem to make Aikton the oak farm or farm near the oak. Up in Orkney, one finds Aikers and Aikerness, which certainly denotes the Norse influence up there, but there were no oaks in Iceland, so it is thought that in this instance 'aik' would simply signify the presence of trees. However, Eakring (Nottinghamshire) also claims the Old Norse roots of 'eik' plus 'hringr', indicating a ring of oaks (or trees?); it also appears in the Domesday Book as 'Ecringhe'.

Surnames, sometimes the same or similar to some of the place names mentioned here, reflect oak associations. For example Ackroyd (also Acroyd, Akeroyd, Akroyd, Aykroyd, Ackred, Akred, Ecroyd), which is most commonly from Yorkshire, is a name conjoining oak with the Old English 'royd', meaning a clearing or farm, so the name means a dweller in the clearing or farm near or among the oaks. Akkerman (and variants) suggests a ploughman or tiller of the land – literally 'acre man' (see p.102). If 'bourn' is a stream, then Ayckbourn (and variants) translates as a dweller near the oak by the stream; and if worth comes from the Anglo-Saxon 'uurt', then Ackworth (and variants) is an enclosure or homestead.

Hundreds, if not thousands, of farmsteads, cottages, street names and, of course, public houses have oak associations. This, of course, conveys the omnipresence of oak in the landscape, as well as an enduring affection for our most recognisable and favourite tree, and the enduring historical symbolism of the Restoration of the monarchy in 1660, which is for ever associated with the epic account of King Charles II hiding in the oak tree. Many oak place names are worthy of note. A short arbitrary selection will reveal just a few of the many micro-histories of oak to be gleaned throughout Britain.

BELOW: The Broad Oak at Winwick, near Warrington, from a sketch made in 1836 by Dr Kendrick.

HATFIELD BROAD OAK

Hatfield Broad Oak in Essex, which is situated in close proximity to the Hatfield Forest, part of the ancient Forest of Essex, took its name from one of the huge, wide-spreading and ancient trees that once grew at the north end of the parish, where it ran into the forest. But which tree? The reference to 'broad' in the name immediately suggests one of the big old pollard trees, typically associated with the wood-pasture regimes that were maintained in the forest. An oak still figures on the Hatfield Broad Oak village sign, but there now appears to be some dispute or confusion about exactly which oak gave the village its name. The original broad oak has long since departed, but in a splendid engraving from 1802 this rickety old character of a tree is shown to resemble an old person crawling along with the aid of two sticks. This image makes it seem incredible that a timber merchant once offered Sir John Barrington (1615–1683) 100 guineas for the tree when it was in its prime. Was this the original tree? Another tree known as the Doodle Oak, which once grew in the north-west corner of Hatfield Forest, is favoured by others as the original tree. This tree was felled in 1859, but 850 annual rings were counted in the old stump in 1949, certainly adding credence to the association dating back to 1295, when this tree would have been almost 300 years old.

THE BROAD OAK

The Broad Oak at Winwick, near Warrington, Lancashire, was, in its day, also a much celebrated landmark tree. It seems to have given its name to a nearby Broad Oak Farm, but not an actual settlement name. The illustration that comes down to us from

BELOW: A 1904 postcard of the
Seven Oaks at Sevenoaks in
Kent. The company of
Valentines (of Dundee) vied
with Frith to publish all the
most famous and saleable views.

1836 shows it to have been a magnificent specimen, and justly deserving of the epithet 'broad'. The artist Dr Kendrick recorded the canopy spread as 99 feet north to south, and 87 feet east to west. Its girth was a relatively modest 11 feet 6 inches at 5 feet. One Sir Phipps Hornby was a naval captain during the Napoleonic Wars, in command of the frigate *Volage*. On 13 March 1811 he helped to secure a fine victory against the French and Italian fleets off the Island of Lissa, capturing the French battleship *Corona* in the process. He returned home to Winwick an acclaimed local hero. In his honour, the community put on a celebratory dinner beneath the Broad Oak where, 'on the 26 August 1811, a numerous party sat down to congratulate their friend and commemorate the occasion'. Loyal toasts were drunk and songs written specially for the occasion were sung:

> *Beneath their own oak, England's favourite tree,*
> *Hung with wreaths of true blue, shall the festival be,*
> *For them the bright circle, in hall and in bower,*
> *With the feast and the dance shall prolong the gay hour.*
> [from a song called 'Winwick' written by Mr Fitchett]

The oak stood for all that was most clearly defined as British: steadfast, strong, enduring. Where else could one hold such celebrations? A local bard also composed a triumphal poem for the special day. An extract from 'The Oak Speaks':

> *Renowned for generous shade,*
> *Behold in me a monarch oak of thrice a century;*
> *Ye kindred trees, let memory cease to dwell,*
> *On those sad days, when struck by fate ye fell,*
> *And turn to when, beneath my verdant shade,*
> *A social throng the votive banquet made.*

The Seven Oaks, Sevenoaks.   Valentine's Series

On 4 February 1850, while Captain Hornby was still alive, by now knighted and also an admiral, the Broad Oak, 'a beautiful and time-honoured ornament of Winwick, was blown down by the wind, to the great grief of the neighbourhood'.

Dr Kendrick believed that the tree's demise was largely down to 'a sadly premature decay occasioned by the unchecked trampling of cattle round its base'. It is interesting to note that more than 150 years ago, root compaction was considered detrimental to tree health.

SEVENOAKS

Sevenoaks in Kent, surely one of the best known 'oak towns', cannot be overlooked. The name reputedly derives from the Anglo-Saxon 'Seouenaca', which is believed to have been the name of a chapel near seven oak trees, located roughly where Knole Park lies today, at some point during the ninth or tenth century, although clear evidence of the group of oaks does not appear until 1122 in the *Textus Roffensis*. Clearly, these trees would have done well if they had all survived since the twelfth century, so the seven oaks must have had several manifestations down the centuries. In *Britannia Depicta* (1731) the trees are merely referred to as 'seven oaks of extraordinary size which grew in or near it [Sevenoaks] at its first building but have been long since cut down'. The next reference to seven oak trees appears only in 1871, when they are represented in a line near the White Hart pub on the Ordnance Survey map. Black's 1874 *Guide to Kent* also mentions these trees. The same trees also appear on many Edwardian postcards.

An exact planting date for these trees has long been debated. Some believe they might have been planted in the early eighteenth century. It is, however, more realistic to assume that the reference to a purchase in the Knole Estate accounts, dated 11 September 1807, and mentioning payment to 'Mr. Modsell for the Seven Oaks near White Hart inn £78' is a reference to the trees. The size of the trees in the postcards a hundred years later seems to vindicate the 1807 planting date. In 1902, seven oaks (turkey oaks, not native English or sessile) were planted along the northern edge of the Vine cricket ground to celebrate the coronation of Edward VII. The infamous storm of 1987, with its 100 mph winds, battered six of these trees to the ground. Amid much media publicity, seven new trees (sessile oaks this time) were planted, making a total of eight oaks (an extra safety-margin tree was planted to allow for any future disasters). Sadly, only a year after planting, five of the trees had been vandalised. Determined, the local community replanted all seven, but this time with larger trees and protective railings.

Many years previously, the seven oaks near the White Hart had succumbed to the misguided actions of the local council who, in 1955, had been erroneously informed that the trees were unsound. They promptly felled the lot. Seven replacement English oaks were soon planted by Vita Sackville-West and Councillor E. Viner, and these trees still survive to this day. Subsequently, an American oak has been planted at the end of these seven, so it would appear that both current groves of seven oaks are in fact eight oaks. Time to change Sevenoaks to Eightoaks? Certainly not, given the increasing regularity of climate-change-induced violent storms that occur in Britain.

SELLY OAK

Selly Oak, a southwest suburb of Birmingham, has been deprived of its landmark oak tree for over a hundred years, but much local history elaborates on its place in the community. The Domesday Book records the area as 'Escelie' or 'Eschelli', which means that Selly might reasonably be derived from 'scelf-lei' or shelf-meadow, a pasture located on a shelf or terrace of land. Another meaning has been ascribed to 'sel' (salt) and 'ley' (meadow), the saltway through the meadow (from nearby Droitwich). During the sixteenth century, the area was known as Selly Cross, and the first mention of the name Selly Oak only appears in manorial court rolls for 1746. The name Sally Oak is marked on a 1789 canal map by John Snape, which gave rise to a fictitious association between the oak and a local witch called Sarah or Sally.

The Old Oak, often depicted on Edwardian postcards, and most beautifully rendered in an oil painting of 1897 by W. Stone, stood on the roadside, at the crossroads of Bristol Road and Oak Tree Lane. At the turn of the nineteenth century, large branches were chopped off and the roots of the tree were badly damaged during nearby house-building work. By 1909, the tree was thought to be unsafe and was felled. The stump ended up in Selly Oak Park, with a little brass plaque that read: 'Butt of the Old Oak Tree from which the name of Selly Oak was derived. Removed from Oak Tree Lane, Selly Oak, 1909.' A recent dendrochronological sample taken from the stump reveals that the tree had been planted between 1710 and 1720, which lead some to theorize that the oak became a landmark when the Bromsgrove to Birmingham road was turnpiked in 1727. Even at seventeen years, this would still have been quite a diminutive tree, but perhaps by 1746 it was large enough to be the eponymous oak. Since 1985 three 'new' Selly Oaks have been planted in the vicinity.

WHITELEAVED OAK

A small hamlet at the southern end of the Malvern Hills called Whiteleaved Oak has a long-standing association with an oak tree that reputedly bore white, or variegated, leaves. The tree has long departed, but an account by one Henry Dingley, a verderer of Malvern Chase in 1584, notes that 'a great Oake caulled the white leved Oake bereth white leaves', near the southernmost boundary of the Chase. The Worcestershire botanist Edwin Lees also wrote in 1877 of the tree 'that existed within living memory, whose leaves being variegated with white blotches, caused it to be considered a curiosity and prodigy'. Even though the original tree no longer exists, a splendid ancient oak (bearing no white leaves), with a girth of 25 feet and probably aged at about 800 years old, grows atop

ABOVE: A variety of votive offerings on the Whiteleaved Oak.

a strange rocky plinth above a small pit or old quarry, and has taken on the mantle of the legendary arboreal anomaly.

In recent years many followers of alternative faiths, including pagans and ley-hunters, have defined the Whiteleaved Oak's location as sacred, citing its geometric alignment with sites such as Glastonbury and Stonehenge. As a boundary tree, it also sits at the junction of the three counties of Herefordshire, Worcestershire, and Gloucestershire. The tree's celebrity status is evidenced today by the numerous gifts and offerings of ribbons, messages, jewels, and crystals that it has attracted. These votive offerings effectively make the Whiteleaved Oak what the Scots would call a 'clootie tree' ('clootie' meaning a strip of cloth or rag). Venerating the spirit of the tree (often associated with a sacred well or spring) or signifying a prayer for well-being or healing, the custom of leaving such offerings is one that is believed to have Celtic roots. Indeed, a natural spring with an attendant dew-pond lies close by the oak. Does the white sports sock that was left indicate the hope of a remedy for an ankle or foot injury? Does the bra indicate the hope for a cure of breast cancer? Many of the messages left at the tree are very specific and personal. We will never know their backstories, or the success of their pleas, and can only wish for the best possible outcomes for these oak supplicants.

BUTTON OAK

In the Wyre Forest, in Worcestershire, is the village of Button Oak. Some people believe the name derives from the oak galls, sometimes called oak buttons,

which might have been prevalent on the local oaks or on one particularly large,
landmark oak. A more likely explanation derives from the 'booth' (boothen, *plural*),
or shelter, that was used by the many charcoal burners in the forest while they
kept watch over their charcoal mounds.

ROYAL OAK

In 1651, after King Charles II was defeated at the battle of Worcester, he fled the
field with a small band of supporters, and famously holed up overnight at Boscobel
House, then in Staffordshire, where he was obliged to hide among the boughs of
an old oak tree to avoid detection by the pursuing Parliamentarian forces. Charles
eventually escaped to France, only returning to Britain in 1660, when he was
restored to the throne. The exact date of the king's triumphal procession back
into London was 29 May, also his birthday, and in honour of the oak that saved
the monarch, the day was duly dubbed Royal Oak Day. In celebration of the
Restoration, hundreds of pubs nationwide soon took the name of the Royal Oak.
Such has been the continuing affection for the monarchy that today there are
still something in the region of 600 Royal Oak pubs across the country. A vast
array of pictorial pub signs can be found, most of them bearing similar themes,
including a large oak, an oak with a crown above or amid the foliage, an oak with
a little portrait of Charles amid the foliage, various clusters of acorns, leaves, and
assorted crowns. However, there are a few very individual and imaginative signs
also to be found, often painted to order by local artists. There has also been a
long tradition of royal naval ships bearing the name *Royal Oak*, and sometimes
it's the ships rather than the oak tree that appears on some pub signs.

Royal Oak Day is celebrated each year at the Royal Hospital, Chelsea, in memory of the founder, Charles II. The statue of Charles, modelled after a Roman general by Grinling Gibbons in 1682, is adorned with oak boughs. Chelsea Pensioners must also wear a sprig of oak in their buttonhole for the day. The building of the hospital was commissioned by Charles in 1681, but the first pensioners did not move in until 1692, seven years after the king's death. Still, every year, on or around 29 May, King Charles is fondly remembered with a parade and inspection, often taken by a royal visitor.

'THE OAKS'

Every year, in early June, the Oaks, or more properly the Oaks Stakes, one of the five classic flat races of the season, is run at Epsom. The race for three-year-old thoroughbred fillies was first run in 1779, and is named after the nearby estate, to the east of Epsom. It is said that the 12th Earl of Derby, then the tenant of the estate, devised the race with a group of chums in 1778. His horse Bridget apparently won the inaugural race, which was no doubt very satisfying for Lord Derby.

SYMBOLISM: THE OAK LEAF

The oak leaf has been just one of many symbols frequently associated with the Jacobite cause of 1745, when Prince Charles Edward Stuart (Bonnie Prince Charlie) led an insurrection to restore his family to the throne of Great Britain. He failed, and his defeat at the Battle of Culloden in 1746 put an end to the Jacobite uprising. His long flight through Scotland and eventual escape to France is well documented, and it is a mark of the Scot's affection for the Young Pretender that nobody betrayed him to the English. Even in exile his supporters were able to show their allegiance through the secret symbols they employed within their society. Today, the highly collectable drinking glasses of the eighteenth century reveal the pictorial symbolism associated with the Old Pretender (Prince James Stuart and the 1715 rising) as well as the hope of a second Restoration for Prince Charles Edward. The oak leaf, a regular inclusion, particularly after 1745, quite obviously harks back to the original Restoration of 1660 and to Charles II's close ties to the oak and the famous Boscobel story.

Inspect many of the brightly coloured medal ribbons that are proudly worn on many scarlet coats and a small bronze insignia of an oak leaf may well be seen – a mark that a soldier has been 'mentioned in despatches', usually commended for some act of gallantry or selflessness. Oak leaves and acorns feature on various pieces of officer's uniform in the British Army, as well as in the regimental devices of several regiments, some of which are now disbanded or amalgamated. The image of the dependable, durable oak has featured as a symbol of courage, achievement, and victory since Roman times, when victorious leaders in battle or leading statesmen were customarily crowned with wreaths of oak leaves.

Various British coins have featured the oak, its leaves, and acorns. Both the silver threepence and sixpence, minted between 1927 and 1936, bore wreaths of acorns and oak leaves on the reverse side. Much more recently, pound coins of the 1980s bore an image of an oak tree with the trunk encircled by a coronet.

What better emblem to uphold the solidity and strength of the national currency!

Various organizations have chosen the oak or oak leaves as their logo. Two of the most familiar are the National Trust, which has had its sprig of oak leaves with acorns since 1936, and the Woodland Trust, which features dark green and light green oak leaves. Companies such as Hearts of Oak Assurance used the idea of mighty oaken warships that once defended our nation to suggest a solid, dependable company that one could rely on to protect and provide in times of need. With the number of members they attracted, it seems to have been a solid commercial decision.

The acorn is often found as a decorative feature of fixtures and fittings in the home, typically in Victorian houses, as newel post finials, light pulls, window cords, and clothes hook ends, and also some designs of door knockers. It was a popular belief that these devices would protect the house from lightning strikes.

Oak is one of the trees most often struck by lightning, probably due to its great size (the lightning hits it before lesser trees) and led to the old saying, 'Beware the oak, it draws the stroke.' Shards of lightning-singed oak were treasured as amulets and branches of stricken trees were placed in houses, on the principle that lightning doesn't strike twice in the same place.

In the language of flowers, the oak is the emblem of hospitality, and the oak leaf of bravery and humanity. In the words of Anne McIntyre, in her contribution to my *Silva* (1999), 'The acorn is a symbol of hard work and achievement – "great oaks from little acorns grow" – and of the cosmic egg, the source of all life and of immortality.'

WINDSOR GREAT
PARK OAKS

O N A HOT SUMMER'S DAY, WINDSOR GREAT PARK, only a few miles from
the western fringes of London, provides a marvellous retreat; a vast open
green space for thousands of city dwellers to unwind. In fact, around 2.5 million
people visit the park every year, whether to walk, cycle, ride, or simply picnic.

However, history reveals many different cycles of events in Windsor Great Park.

The old Windsor Forest once stretched over 28,000 acres of Surrey,
Berkshire and into Buckinghamshire, with a circumference of 120 miles – a vast
area indeed. By the early seventeenth century, however, this had shrunk to a
circumference of 77 miles, and by the end of the eighteenth century, only 56
miles. At originally about 4,000 acres, the size of Windsor Great Park has always
been a mere fraction of this area. First empaled as a deer park in 1277, the park
has had a long and varied history, principally as a royal preserve for hunting, but
also as a recreational area, which included tournaments, jousting, archery, deer
coursing, and even bear-baiting.

Until the eighteenth century, most monarchs enjoyed the chase, and none
more so than Elizabeth I, who rode out to hunt with some frequency. In 1602,
aged sixty-nine (and only a year before she died), she is said to have shot 'a
great and fat stagge with her owen Hand'. The image of the queen charging
along in hot pursuit of her quarry is almost certainly a fanciful one; more likely,
she would be strategically positioned to await a deer that would have been
driven within range of her bow. However, the park was not restricted to the
sport of the hunt. Elizabeth was acutely aware that her navy was constantly in
need of good-quality oak timber, and assented to Lord Burghley's 1580 order
to empale 13 acres of Cranbourne Walk, sow it with acorns, and thus create
the first recorded plantation.

With the accession of George I in 1714, much changed in the park, as the
Hanoverian monarchs were not as taken with hunting as their predecessors.
Instead they chose to construct gardens and lakes, as well as erect statues
and monuments. George III even imported Roman ruins from Libya.

A critical period for Windsor Forest and the park came at the beginning
of the nineteenth century. Enclosure was sweeping across England and dividing
the nation, as was succinctly observed many years later by the writer and poet
Thomas Love Peacock (1785–1866) in his essay 'The Last Day of Windsor
Forest' (*c.*1862). Peacock grew up on the borders of the old forest and often
rambled there, 'under antique trees, through groves and glades, through bushes
and underwood, among fern, and foxglove, and bounding deer'. In 1814, the

park was enclosed for the Crown, thus placing much of it off limits to the public. Of the 5,000 acres enclosed, some 2,000 acres are still private estate to this day. Peacock ruefully relates the following about the enclosures:

> They [enclosures] are, like most events in this world, 'Good to some, bad to others, and indifferent to the majority.' They are good to the landowner, who gets an addition to his land: they are bad to the poor parishioner who loses his rights of common: they are bad to the lover of rural walks, for whom footpaths are annihilated: they are bad to those, from whom the scenes of their youth are blotted from the face of the world.

If enclosure had secured the park for the Crown, it had not secured what were viewed as the king's deer from the forest, so it was not long before extensive deer poaching ran unchecked throughout the old forest. Furious at such disregard, the Crown was soon determined to drive what it viewed as its property into the safe harbour of the park. Peacock describes in great detail witnessing the amazing scene of two regiments of cavalry driving hundreds of deer from the forest and into the park pale. For him, this was 'the last day of Windsor Forest'.

The relaxation of forest laws and, subsequently, two hundred years of agricultural improvement and urban development led to the disappearance of virtually all of the old forest. The Crouch Oak (see p.50) at Addlestone is one of the last boundary trees of the Windsor forest. With 'progress' went the wonderful mosaic of wood-pasture that had evolved over many centuries – apart, that is, from the ancient landscape still to be found within Windsor Great Park. Although the demand for food production during the Second World War saw large areas ploughed up and many of the ancient trees felled, the park has since been returned to its former pastoral glory. As Graham Harvey notes in *Parkland* (2002):

> *The park contains the largest and most important assemblage of ancient trees in the whole of western Europe, and is one of the few places in Britain to have supported a continuous succession of old trees dating back as far as the original wildwood.*

A few of the ancient oak pollards for which the park has become so famous stand in single sentinel splendour, some dead, some in ragged decrepitude still hanging on, others, remarkably, in full vigour. Close examination of these individuals sometimes reveals linear alignments (the assumption being that these are very likely the remnants of long defunct hedgerows) – a feature that has been observed in several other deer parks. To find many of these ancient 'dodders' (such an appropriate name for these old stagers), one has to delve deep into some of the 800 acres of woodland. Some of these oaks are most definitely in the region of 800–1,000 years old. Almost all are hollow, most are stag-headed, but still they continue to bear lush foliage each year. Of course there are dead trees, but these are just as important in the ecology of the park, providing habitat for vast colonies of invertebrates, larders for birds, and roosts for bats. As long as they don't pose a hazard by falling on anyone, they also have a special sculptural presence.

It is generally assumed that most of the oaks are self-sown trees from the original forest. These were once regularly pollarded in a wood-pasture regime, but in recent times, the glades and lawns associated with this have become overgrown, closeting many of the trees in a dense tangle of bramble, bracken, and hawthorn. In 2003, the old regime was reintroduced into a wooded compartment of Cranbourne Park. By grazing the ancient breed of longhorn cattle first introduced into Britain by the Romans, the Crown Estates in conjunction with Natural England are emulating traditional management. The cattle graze back the secondary woodland and the undergrowth so that the character of the old wood-pasture returns, as well as improving the biodiversity. The big question now is whether they should readopt pollarding of the oaks – a difficult process to reintroduce to ancient trees that haven't felt the woodman's saw for a century or two.

There have been many famous oaks in the park – most notably Herne's Oak (see p.118) and its long tradition of unworldly associations. The largest oak in the park in the nineteenth century would have been William the Conqueror's Oak, near Cranbourne Lodge (demolished in 1865), described in *English*

BELOW: Queen Victoria's Oak, the inspiration for John Smeaton's Eddystone Lighthouse, built in 1759. Hand-coloured wood engraving *c*.1880.

QUEEN VICTORIA'S TREE.

Forests and Forest-Trees (1853) as measuring 38 feet round at 6 feet from the ground:

> *The venerable appearance of this fine old tree, 'his high top bald with dry antiquity' – the size and expanse of its branches – the gnarled and rugged appearance of its portly trunk – and the large projecting roots which emanate from it, fill the mind with admiration and astonishment.*

Marked on a map of 1904, today a mere rotting shard is the only evidence left of this once revered tree.

On the road leading to Cranbourne Lodge stands the tree that has taken over the mantle of the largest oak in the park; in 1853 its girth was 36 feet. Today it is known as Offa's Oak, a name devised for it by ancient tree expert Ted Green, who believes the tree might have been a sapling during King Offa's time (757– 796). It must now be 36 feet, or even a little more, but an exact measurement is difficult since a quarter of the tree has collapsed outwards, while an array of props hold the rest in place. An age in excess of 1,200 years for this tree might be a little generous, but naming the tree helps to give it a profile and a story, which is no bad thing when it comes to awareness and conservation.

A tree with a 31-foot girth near the Forest Gate, again in something of a ramshackle state, has often been misrepresented as William the Conqueror's Oak. One suspects that this is the same tree that Loudon notes as the King Oak (26-foot girth in 1838). The true William the Conqueror's Oak is illustrated in William Henry Burgess's *Eidodendron*(1827) and, judging by its shape, is clearly the same tree as the one mentioned in *English Forests and Forest-Trees* (above). The following delightful quote from Professor Burnet could only describe a tree with a girth of 38 feet:

> *We lunched in it, September 2, 1829: it would accommodate at least 20 persons with standing room; and 10 or 12 might sit down comfortably to dinner. I think at Willis's and in Guildhall, I have danced a quadrille in a smaller space.*

One of the most famous oaks in the nineteenth century was Queen Victoria's Oak or the Victoria Oak, which stood to the north of High Standing Hill. A tall maiden tree, it grew to perfection. The engineer John Smeaton claimed it was his inspiration for the lighthouse he designed for the Eddystone Rocks, twelve miles southwest of Plymouth. Two previous lighthouses on the rocks had succumbed – one to violent weather and the other burnt down. Smeaton admired the stability and elasticity of such an oak, and was convinced that it would serve well as a template. He used a hollow construction of interlocking granite blocks, dovetailed together using marble dowels and, on 16 October 1759, after little more than three years' work, it was finally commissioned. Smeaton's lighthouse would withstand the worst of the elements until 1877, when erosion beneath its foundations caused concern. It was dismantled and all except the base was rebuilt on Plymouth Hoe as a memorial to its inspired designer. A new lighthouse was erected in 1882. Designed by James Douglass, it drew heavily on Smeaton's work and stands to this day.

Numerous artists and photographers have long been entranced by the ancient oaks, their work providing a wonderful catalogue of images of the park in a wide variety of moods and compositions. Several eighteenth- and nineteenth-century artists issued aquatints and engravings, most commonly of Herne's Oak.

One of the most interesting portfolios was the collection of photographs in William Menzies' *The History of Windsor Great Park and Windsor Forest*, published in 1864 (making it the earliest published work illustrated with photographs). This was an elephant folio work (23 inches tall) containing numerous superb, large albumen prints from photographs taken by James Sinclair, 14th Earl of Caithness, and William Bembridge, and featuring many of the famous ancient trees of the day.

William Menzies (1827–78) was Deputy Surveyor of Windsor Park and Forest for twenty-nine years until, sadly, he died at the relatively young age of fifty-one, but in 1875 he was able to edit a rather unusual work. *Forest Trees and Woodland Scenery as described by Ancient and Modern Poets* was a beautiful folio, featuring twenty superb chromolithographs of trees, including several from Windsor Great Park. Printed by M&N Manhart, these coloured prints were after watercolours by Elphinstone, Walton, and Nutt. The remarkable archival quality of these prints means that the colours are as vibrant today as the day they were published.

ABOVE: Offa's Oak, the largest oak in Windsor Great Park.

HERNE'S OAK

OPPOSITE: Herne's Oak, an original pencil drawing by M. Parker, 1834. This is a remarkably faithful copy of a lithograph by Rowney & Foster of an 1821 sketch attributed to F.N., depicting the tree as it was in 1788.

I**F EVER AN OAK DESERVED IMMORTALITY,** then surely this accolade should go to the legendary Herne's Oak that once grew within Windsor Great Park. The earliest accounts talk of a tree that was already an old-timer by the reign of Queen Elizabeth. It first arrived in the nation's affections through its dramatic appearance in William Shakespeare's *Merry Wives of Windsor,* first performed in 1597. The Bard must clearly have been well acquainted with the legend surrounding Herne's Oak, for in Act IV, as the wives plot a trap for Falstaff in Windsor Park, Mistress Page declares:

> *There is an old tale goes that Herne the hunter,*
> *Sometime a keeper here in Windsor forest,*
> *Doth all the winter-time, at still midnight,*
> *Walk round about an oak, with great ragg'd horns;*
> *And there he blasts the tree and takes the cattle*
> *And makes the milch-kine yield blood and shakes a chain*
> *In a most hideous and dreadful manner:*
> *You have heard of such a spirit, and well you know*
> *The superstitious idle-headed eld*
> *Received and did deliver to our age*
> *This tale of Herne the hunter for a truth.*

A colourful story has long held sway in local folklore, that Herne was once a keeper or huntsman to Richard II (1377–1399), and that during a hunt, when the king was in the path of a charging stag, Herne threw himself in front of the king, killing the stag, but taking the brunt of the charge. He seemed mortally wounded, but a mysterious dark character (sometimes cast as one Philip Urswick) suddenly surfaced from the assembled crowd and offered to bring Herne back to health, but with the proviso that they should have the antlers of the slain stag strapped to Herne's head. The grateful king promised that if Herne recovered, he would be promoted to head keeper. At this, some of Herne's fellow keepers who bore him much ill will, covertly cut a deal with the dark character (surely the Devil incarnate) that would mean the recovered and promoted Herne (complete with antlers, which by now appear to have become irreversibly conjoined to his skull) would lose his powers as a huntsman. In due course this did, indeed, come to pass and as a result, the king dismissed Herne from his post. Devastated, the hapless, antlered hunter took himself to a large oak tree in Windsor Forest and hanged himself.

All was not well following Herne's suicide, and a succession of chief huntsmen proved totally incompetent. The hunters met with the dark stranger, who now desired his reward for bringing about the demise of Herne. The toll that

BELOW: *Herne's Oak in Windsor Park*, aquatint published for Samuel Ireland, 1799.

he levied upon the hunters was that they were obliged to ride for evermore with the ghostly apparition of Herne in a ceaseless chase. They took a great toll on the king's deer, until King Richard, exasperated by this, met with the spirit of Herne beneath the old oak and commanded him to cease. Herne agreed, but only if the king should hang all the scheming hunters who had plotted his downfall on that very oak. The king complied willingly, and Herne was seen no more.

All of this may seem to be a rollicking good yarn. It's worth bearing in mind that this version of events derives from a fanciful piece of romantic fiction entitled *Windsor Castle*, written by W. Harrison Ainsworth in 1843, and that it's likely that Ainsworth was embellishing a long-standing folk tradition.

Fertile imaginations and tenuous esoteric connections have fuelled conjecture ever since W. Harrison Ainsworth set pen to paper. If Shakespeare knew of this story, was it based on local hearsay in the old Windsor Forest of the sixteenth century? Was he privy to some documentary evidence of an actual person and event, or was it simply a mythical tale dreamed up by him to suit his own dramatic purpose? Several writers have suggested that Herne is drawn from the Celtic god Cernunnos or the Anglo-Saxon hunting deity Woden, whose Norse equivalent Odin is often depicted as a horned being, riding through the night sky with his Wild Hunt. Odin also hanged himself upon Yggdrasil, the tree of knowledge, in his quest to know the secret of the runic alphabet.

Fact-based evidence corroborates some of the fictional stories laid out above. Victorian writer and scholar James Halliwell-Phillips apparently discovered a sixteenth-century document referring to one Richard Horne, described as a hunter, who was apprehended for poaching the king's deer in the reign of Henry VIII. One assumes he was hanged for his misdemeanours ... perhaps from a tree. It is worth noting that the very first edition of *The Merry Wives of Windsor* (1602) spells Herne as Horne.

In 1792 Samuel Ireland in his *Picturesque Views of the River Thames* cites Herne as a real keeper during the reign of Elizabeth:

That having committed some great offence, for which he feared to lose his situation, and fall into disgrace, he was induced to hang himself on this tree. The credulity of the times easily worked on the minds of the ignorant to suppose that his ghost would haunt the spot. This rendered it a fit scene of action for the purpose of our bard to terrify and expose the cowardice of the fat knight [Falstaff]...

By 1790 Herne's Oak was reputedly dead. Even as Ireland wrote, he notes the following:

Some idea has prevailed of an intention to cut down this celebrated tree, which it is much to be wished may not be true … As I do not know that any engraving has been made of this tree, the annexed view may possibly afford some pleasure to the curious reader.

Given all of these accounts, it is perhaps no surprise that the story of Herne's Oak is somewhat complex. Ireland depicts the original tree in 1792, well before the 1796 date when it is supposed to have been cut down (reputedly as a result of misconceived or misunderstood orders from George III). According to these depictions, its distinctive shape continues well into the nineteenth century, being sketched, painted and engraved by numerous artists, until it actually fell in a storm in 1863. An etching by Thomas Medland, taken from a drawing by Thomas Thornton from 1792, shows the same tree delineated by Ireland. Both of these plates also depict the groves of English elms in the Home Park, among which the old oak was described as standing and, even though the oak's foliage in both of these images is rather sparse, it is clear that the tree was still alive.

It was only in 1838 that Edward Jesse, in his *Gleanings in Natural History*, muddies the waters by proclaiming that another oak in the Little Park was the true Herne's Oak. Jesse's account also repudiates the assertion that the oak had been felled in 1796; a story he deemed to be completely unfounded. As a consequence of Jesse's account, Loudon published an image of the alternative – and decidedly dead – Herne's Oak in his *Arboretum et Fruticetum Britannicum* (1838). Having talked to many of the local inhabitants, Jesse asserted that this was the original tree:

I can almost fancy it the very picture of death. Not a leaf, not a particle of vitality appears about it. The hunter must have blasted it. It stretches out its bare and sapless branches, like the skeleton arms of some enormous giant, and is almost fearful in its decay.

Loudon, seemingly bludgeoned into acceptance by Jesse's effusive account, which he quotes in full, does however also include a tiny rendition of another tree. This tree, claimed by many to be Herne's Oak, resembles the representations by Ireland and Medland, but then Loudon believed (erroneously, as it turns out) that it 'no longer exists.'

A stereoscopic card from around 1860 delineates the old frame of the tree, by this time probably dead, before it collapsed in 1863. A replacement for Herne's Oak was planted in 1866, but that only survived until a storm laid it low in 1906. Yet again, this time at the command of Edward VII, another Herne's Oak was planted in the Home Park. It survives to this day, but is off limits to the public.

As for the tales of ghosts and strange phenomena, they have persisted until quite recent times, with the blast of Herne's hunting horn, the beating hooves of his fiery black charger, or the baying of his hounds supposedly heard by several terrified unfortunates in the wooded depths of the old park. There have even been reports of occasional sightings of Herne, often presaging some great disaster for the nation or the royal family.

GOFF'S OAK

ONE OF THE MOST FAMOUS OAKS IN HERTFORDSHIRE was arguably Goff's Oak. The tree has a well-documented, ancient history, and a macabre twist in its nineteenth-century associations.

First mentioned by J. C. Loudon in *Arboretum et Fruticetum Britannicum* (1838), Goff's Oak, a tree some 32 feet in girth, stood on the south side of the Common near Theobalds, and gave its name to the nearby inn. At the time, a print of the tree was to be found inside the inn, bearing the following inscription: 'This tree was planted AD 1066, by Sir Theodore Godfrey, or Goff 'by, who came over with William the Conqueror.'

An 1843 print of the tree shows it already well into decline, and by the time Edwardian postcards featuring the tree were published, it had gained protective iron railings. J. H. Wilks indicates that there was a 'twin' oak planted in the grounds of nearby Beaumont Manor. This cannot be substantiated.

A bizarre story attends the tree during the mid-nineteenth century. Major Grant, then the owner of the nearby manor, put all his money on one of his racehorses to win a key race. It failed to win and so Grant, now a ruined man, shot the horse and buried it next to the oak. Devastated, the groom took up the same gun and promptly committed suicide. Legend has it that both horse and groom still haunt the manor house.

Goff's Oak finally collapsed in 1950, but a replacement oak from one of its acorns had been planted. Tragically, the replacement, badly damaged by the dreadful storm of 1987, itself fell later in that year.

OPPOSITE: Goff's Oak from a glass-plate negative taken in around 1900. In the background to the right is a tea shop, and at the left the premises of Mr Burgess, Smith and Farrier (also at Cheshunt). Although starting to look a little decrepit, the tree still seems to have been putting on plenty of foliage at this time.

BELOW: A brightly coloured Edwardian postcard of Goff's Oak with decorous lady and casual bicycle.

PANSHANGER OAK

OPPOSITE: Still thriving in the middle of the woods on the old estate, the Panshanger Oak is one of the finest and oldest maiden oaks in Britain.

BARELY A MILE TO THE WEST OF HERTFORD lies the old estate of Panshanger, for 200 years the home of the Cowper family. Sadly, Panshanger Park was sold off in 1953 shortly after the demise of Lady Desborough, who had decreed in her will that nobody else should live in the house. The following year her wish was fulfilled and the house demolished.

The Cowper family had lived on the adjoining estate of Cole Green Park from 1719, but having acquired the Panshanger estate, Peter, 5th Earl Cowper, decided a move was in order. In preparation, he commissioned the construction of Panshanger Park, built in the Gothic style between 1806 and 1809, and sited on a rise above the River Mimram. In 1799 Earl Cowper also employed the great Humphry Repton to create a stunning landscape to complement his new house, altering the course of the Mimram into several ornamental lakes. Two of Repton's famous Red Books still survive, depicting the grand plan.

Trees were always a very significant element of a Repton landscape, and it is to his credit that he appears to have retained many of the large oaks on the estate, notably the Great Oak of Panshanger. By the turn of the eighteenth century, the tree had already attracted many admirers. Its celebrity status was only enhanced by the legend that it was planted by Queen Elizabeth I.

What has always made this tree particularly special is that it is one of the largest known maiden oaks in Britain; most oaks that achieve great longevity usually being pollarded specimens. The famed diarist and naturalist Revd Gilbert White refers to the tree in his *Natural History of Selborne* (1788) as 'probably the finest and most stately oak now growing in the south east of England'. The first recorded girth measurement appears in Arthur Young's *Survey of the County of Hertfordshire*, in 1804, where he notes the following:

> On the grounds of Panshanger is a most superb oak, which measures upwards of seventeen feet in circumference at five feet from the ground. It was called The Great Oak in 1709. It is very healthy, yet grows in a gravel surface, apparently as sterile as any soil whatsoever, but it undoubtedly extends its tap root into soil of a very different quality. It is one of the finest oaks which I have seen, though twelve feet to the first bough.

By 1831, Thomas Medland, who had made a splendid drawing of the tree in 1814 ('drawn from nature, when the tree was at its greatest state of beauty'), measured the girth at 19 feet, which concurred with Jacob George Strutt's finding for his *Sylva Britannica* in 1830. Alex McKenzie, visiting in 1893, quotes a girth of 21 feet, and today's measurement shows that the old tree has grown to 25 feet.

The Great Oak at Panshanger.

Writing in the *Hertfordshire Illustrated Review*, McKenzie leaves a wonderfully detailed description of his visit to Panshanger:

> *We found it standing on a lawn, in a hollow, with a sloping bank on all sides, excepting the south, where the ground falls towards the River Mimram, in the valley. Its position is very striking and most deceiving, its immense size not being apparent ... In shape it is a truly royal Oak, straight, upright, and taper from root to crown, upwards of fifty feet in height, and the stem is as round as a circle can be drawn.*

OPPOSITE: The Panshanger Oak, stone lithograph by J. G. Strutt, 1830.

ABOVE: *Panshanger House*, a steel engraving by J. P. Neale, c.1820.

It seems that Mr McKenzie was not aware of the reputed Queen Elizabeth connection, for he questioned whether records existed of its planting. His estimate, allowing for it being 200 years old in 1719, was 374 years old, and today, a 25-foot girth would indicate an age of about 500 years old, which does put it within the realms of a Tudor planting date.

Clearly the Victorians firmly believed this tradition, for Prince Albert planted a seedling at the Speech House in the Forest of Dean in 1861, 'from a tree in Pansanger [sic] Park planted by Queen Elizabeth', which still thrives today with its little memorial stone beneath.

As for the Panshanger Oak itself, despite looking a little sickly in a 1940s photograph, it seems to have retrenched successfully and, although recently losing a large bough, is doing very well indeed. The tree is managed as part of the 1,000-acre estate owned by Lafarge Aggregates, a company with excellent green credentials, who are keen to look after all aspects of the wildlife habitat and landscape heritage in their care.

OAK ART ^{AND} LITERATURE

Whenever the oak is employed in lines of verse or prose, it is always with a certain sense of reverence. This could be because of the phenomenal scale of the tree, with its massive physicality and its ability to survive for 1,000 years or more, which is truly awesome in comparison to the puny human span. The oak has long been the indispensable tree, stretching back across the millennia to a time when human existence – and indeed survival – revolved around the facility of trees in every aspect of life.

OAK HAS SPIRITUAL PEDIGREE TOO; it was believed that the veneration of trees, and the sacred oaks in particular, provided a direct line to the gods. In pre-Christian Britain, Celtic priests or Druids were the empowered leaders, performing their rites in sacred oak groves. Sometimes seen as magicians, they held their subjects in thrall. The Roman poet Virgil (70–19 BC) portrays the oak with powerful solemnity in his second Georgic, translated by Dryden:

> ... Jove's own tree,
> That holds the woods in awful sovereignty,
> Requires a depth of lodging in the ground,
> And, next the lower skies, a bed profound.
> High as his topmost boughs to heaven ascend,
> So low his roots to hell's dominion tend;
> Therefore nor winds, nor winter's rage, o'erthrows
> His bulky body, but unmoved he grows.
> For length of ages lasts his happy reign,
> And lives of mortal men contend in vain.
> Full in the midst of his own strength he stands,
> Stretching his brawny arms, and leafy hands;
> His shade protects the plains, his head the hills commands.

Oak appears to be immortal in comparison to human beings, and in this verse the oak has become anthropomorphic, bringing the tree into even closer quarters

OPPOSITE: *Old Oak at Prince Consort's Gate, Windsor Forest,* chromolithograph by W. L. Walton from *Forest Trees and Woodland Scenery* by William Menzies, 1876.

with human existence. Of course every oak will eventually die, but in antiquity there must have been an overriding vision of an entity so vastly superior, not just of exceptional size and age, but with a mystical capacity to seemingly die and then be reborn every year. Poets appear to have been fascinated by the place of the oak in the landscape, its role in community life and perhaps more than anything else, the romance of the tree in decline, as with Shakespeare's much loved quote:

Whose boughs were moss'd with age,
And high top bald with dry antiquity.

Edmund Spenser (1552–1599), considered by many to be one of our greatest poets, waxed lyrically about an old oak in the 'Februarie' eclogue of his 'Shepheardes Calender':

There grewe an aged Tree on the greene,
A goodly Oaek sometime had it bene,
With armes full strong, and largely display'd
But of their leaves they were disarray'd;
The bodie bigge, and mightely pight,
Thoroughly rooted, and of wonderous hight:
Whilome had bene the King of the field,
And mochell mast to the husband did yielde;
And with his nuts larded many swine,
But now the gray mosse marred his rine;
His bared boughes were beaten with stormes,
His toppe was bald and wasted with wormes;
His honor decay'd, his branches sere…

In his 'Yardley Chase' (1791), Cowper celebrates the oak's lifespan, marvelling at how one tiny acorn begets a mighty, mature tree. His epitaph for the craggy, bare form of the departing veteran suggests nostalgia:

Thou wert a bauble once, a cup and ball,
Which babes might play with; and the thievish jay
Seeking her food, with ease might have purloin'd
The auburn nut that held thee, swallowing down
Thy yet close-folded latitude of boughs,
And all thy embryo vastness, at a gulp.
…Time has made thee what thou wert – king of the woods!
And time hath made thee what thou art – a cave
For owls to roost in! Once thy spreading boughs
O'erhung the champaign, and the numerous flock
That grazed it stood beneath that ample cope
Uncrowded, yet safe-shelter'd from the storm.
No flock frequents thee now: thou hast outlived
Thy popularity, and art become

Quercus pedunculata

(Unless verse rescue thee awhile) a thing
Forgotten, as the foliage of thy youth!

The Revd William Gilpin (1724–1804) formulated the notion of the picturesque during his travels in the 1770s. This philosophy promotes an aesthetic ideal in all aspects of the landscape. We learn from his *Remarks on Forest Scenery* (1791) that he was particularly well disposed towards the oak:

It is a happiness to the lovers of the picturesque, that this noble plant is as useful, as it is beautiful.

And commenting on the longevity and visual delight of the oak in decline:

I mention the circumstance of it's [sic] longevity as it is of a nature singularly picturesque. It is through age, that the oak acquires its greatest beauty; which often continues increasing even into decay…What is more beautiful, for instance, on a rugged foreground, than an old tree with a hollow trunk? Or with a dead arm, a drooping bough or a dying branch?…When the dreary heath is spread before the eye, and ideas of wildness and desolation are required, what more suitable accompaniment can be imagined, than the blasted oak, ragged, scathed, and leafless; shooting its peeled, white branches athwart the gathering blackness of some rising storm.

The theme of ancient, sometimes dead oaks evoked admiration, and this was not the preserve of the poets, for Gilpin was also determined to guide the untutored eye to appreciate the beauty of the oak tree. Contemporaries such as Edmund Burke believed that understanding the beautiful and the sublime was not an acquired art, but something instinctive.

Noel Thomas Carrington's (1777–1830) epic poem 'Dartmoor', explores a more sinister aspect to the oak. More accurately, it focuses on a very particular kind of wild and rugged oak wood on the top of Dartmoor; an alien, fearsome landscape where nature's struggle for survival is at the mercy of the raw elements. Though the poem was written in 1826, a visit to Wistman's Wood today on a wild, blustery type of day might easily transport you back to Carrington's 'lonely wood', for its character has changed little in 200 years.

> …*Thy guardian oaks,*
> *My country, are thy boast – a giant race,*
> *And undegenerate still; but of this grove,*
> *This pygmy grove, not one has climb'd the air*
> *So emulously that its loftiest branch*
> *May brush the traveller's brow. The twisted roots*
> *Have clasp'd in search of nourishment the rocks,*
> *And straggled wide, and pierced the stony soil*
> *In vain: denied maternal succour, here*
> *A dwarfish race has risen. Round the boughs*
> *Hoary and feeble, and around the trunks,*
> *With grasp destructive, feeding on the life*
> *That lingers yet, the ivy winds, and moss*
> *Of growth enormous. E'en the dull vile weed*
> *Has fix'd itself upon the very crown*
> *Of many an ancient oak; and thus, refused*

By nature kindly aid – dishonoured – old –
Dreary in aspect – silently decays
The lonely wood of Wistman.

A complete contrast with Carrington's brooding, forbidding oak wood is Mary Howitt's (1799–1888) joyous celebration of the oak in its kingly splendour in 'When We are Lowly Laid'. Despite the poem's jubilant tone, we are still reminded that the force of nature is irrepressible, and that oaks will outlast any mere mortal.

Sing for the oak-tree,
The monarch of the wood,
Sing for the oak-tree,
That groweth green and good;
That groweth broad and branching
Within the forest shade,
That groweth now, and yet shall grow,
When we are lowly laid!

Poet and naturalist W. H. Hudson (1846–1922), famed for his insightful observations of the natural world around him, revels in a New Forest vista in the Exe Valley in this extract from *Hampshire Days*:

…when the oak is in its 'glad light grene,' for that is the most vivid and beautiful of all vegetable greens, and the prospect is the greenest and most soul-refreshing to be found in England. The valley is all wooded and the wood is all oak – a continuous oak-wood stretching away on the right, mile on mile, to the sea. The sensation experienced at the sight of this prospect is like that of a traveller in a dry desert when he comes to a clear running stream and drinks his fill of water and is refreshed.

The late nineteenth and early twentieth centuries witnessed a burgeoning of observational, passionate writing on rural affairs, often focusing on wildlife and landscape. William Cobbett, who had published his highly detailed *Rural Rides* in 1830, was motivated to explore the sociological and political circumstance of his rural context. He observed common country folk in their daily struggle and frequently rebuked the politicians, taxmen, and bankers, who he held responsible for the plight of these honest toilers. As a document of rural life during a period when much of Britain was engulfed by the Industrial Revolution (*c.*1760–1820), his detailed records are invaluable, but it was writers such as Hudson, Richard Jefferies, and Edward Thomas who dug deep into the rich earth of country life, observing, but also provoking emotive responses.

In his dairy entry for 22 April 1876, after a ramble through Moccas Park with friends, Revd Francis Kilvert voiced the same awe-struck thoughts that so many before him have expressed in the presence of ancient oaks. In one breath, Kilvert is overcome with trepidation at the ancient tree 'beings' taking on a life of their own, 'waiting and watching'. Maybe his 'oak men' are not that far removed from

the Green Man, or the Wild Man, the primeval spirit of the wild wood and epitome of nature untamed. He writes:

I fear those grey old men of Moccas, those grey, gnarled, knock-kneed, bowed, bent, huge, strange, long-armed, deformed, hunchbacked, misshapen oak men that stand waiting and watching century after century biding God's time with both feet in the grave and yet tiring down and seeing out generation after generation, with such tales to tell, as when they whisper them to each other in the midsummer nights, make the silver birches weep and the poplars and aspens shiver and the long ears of the hares and rabbits stand on end. No human hand set those oaks. They are 'the trees that the Lord hath planted'. They look as if they had been at the beginning and making of the world, and they will probably see its end.

I spent much of my early childhood roaming the moors and woods above my Yorkshire home. I might not have been able to encapsulate my feelings for a wind-buffeted oak wood as a ten-year-old, but the emotion flooded back when I read this snatch of Francis Brett Young's (1884–1954) epic poem *The Island*. In the following extract, Adam Woodward and the Shipwright, Adam avers:

…Yet I confess
I love my woodland best when all its voices
Are raised in riot…
Then my brave oaks
Unbent proclaim their majesty, defying
The demons of the air. Oft have I leaned
With my ear pressed against them, striving to share
That fierce aerial tumult – yet not a tremor
Shaketh their steadfast boles! No progeny
Of earth is nobler or mightier than these –
No, nor yet wiser.

The image of the oak tree, the oak leaf, and acorns are recurring themes in all manner of pictorial representations and applied art forms. Often this was purely decorative, but sometimes it had a symbolic function. The use of the oak leaf device was often employed on Jacobite silverware and, even more so, on glassware during the eighteenth century. Such objects were seen to confirm the owner's leanings towards the Stuart dynasty and their desire for the Restoration, firstly, in 1715 of the Old Pretender – Prince James Stuart – and then, in 1745, the Young Pretender – Bonnie Prince Charlie.

The oak wreath and sprays of acorns have proved such potent patriotic symbols that they have often been employed in memorabilia associated with royal events – coronations, weddings, birth, and death, as well as celebrations of military victories, particularly in respect to naval engagements – the hearts of oak, our wooden walls. They have also been used on medals and certificates to honour artistic or sporting prowess.

In the nineteenth century, the creative industries began to embrace the use of birds, animals, flowers, and trees in design, particularly during the naturalism movement that gathered momentum during the 1870s, and is perhaps most synonymous with William Morris. Everything from architectural adornment, furniture, glass, ceramics, and textiles derived inspiration from the natural world, and the oak instantly became part of the designers' repertoire.

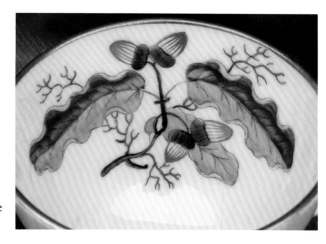

ABOVE: Hand-painted oak design on a late Georgian bone-china teacup from the 1820s. In the aftermath of the Napoleonic Wars and the great victory at Trafalgar, the oak was very likely viewed as a most patriotic motif to decorate one's tea service.

Oak imagery appears among the botanical illustrations from some of the earliest published books, notably the Herballs of the sixteenth and seventeenth centuries. A great diversity of style exists; in some of the crude representations, accuracy is initially encumbered by the technical limitations of early block making and printing. However, there is a certain rustic charm to these illustrations and, no doubt, they satisfied the role that was required of them – common identification – a basic necessity in the interests of correct prescription for ailments. By the eighteenth and nineteenth centuries, highly talented botanical artists were producing exquisitely drawn, hand-coloured representations, not just of native British trees and plants, but by now an ever-increasing herbarium of plant life from all over the world. Even with the benefit of photography, the skill of the botanical artist has endured into the twenty-first century.

In the latter half of the eighteenth century, many artists employed the oak as an allegorical device. George Stubbs (1724–1806) is rightly famous for his paintings of horses, but he should be equally revered for his depiction of the oak trees that situated his mares and foals in such a quintessentially English setting. Oaks have come to signify a number of different things: They might represent the power of the natural world, standing resolute, perhaps even storm-blasted as they shelter animals or little groups of woodlanders from the fury of the elements; or they might suggest the patriarch, the enduring symbol of the monarch, watching over his subjects. On the other hand, the oak tree might hark back to antiquity as the pagan symbol of respect and veneration, promoting some kind of benevolent, protective force. Essentially though, the trees and woodland glades are usually depicted as safe resorts; replete with oak, the great provider.

Many paintings and drawings of oaks were executed by locally based artists who we might describe today as gifted amateurs – those who simply knew and loved their local landmark trees and felt the urge to record them. Although many of these images would have been consigned to very personal portfolios, a few have come down to public collections. A watercolour of the famed Cowthorpe Oak by R. O. Hodgson resides in Manchester City Galleries, while a splendid oil on canvas of the tree by John N. Rhodes (1840) can be found in Leeds Museums and Galleries. *Glendower's Oak* by Tooke belongs to St Helens Council; *Cobbett's Oak at Tilford Green* (artist unknown) is in the Museum of Farnham; Henry

Dawson, an accomplished provincial artist, painted *The Major Oak* in 1844, and it may still be seen in Nottingham; and *The Winfarthing Oak* was painted by James Sillett in 1812. Several renditions of the Fairlop Oak attest to its popularity – a watercolour by Samuel Hieronymous Grimm in 1774, and oils by Laurence J. Cosse (*c.*1800), and Henry Milbourne in 1816. There are more, including those that were oaks of national historic importance, and others that were simply noted local landmarks. Were these paintings simply affectionate personal records of familiar trees with no specific commercial intent, or commissioned pieces from patrons?

Many of the late eighteenth and early nineteenth century topographical and historical books were illustrated with engravings or etchings, which were usually of landscapes, views of castles, cathedrals, ruins, and ancestral homes, but occasionally also illustrations of great trees. As more people began to travel in Britain they wanted guidebooks to show them the key attractions, as well as collections of images to keep as mementoes of their excursions. Etchings as well as copper and, later, steel engravings were used for better-quality publications, and many of these images were derived from paintings. This was also something of a boom time for the publication of all manner of magazines, which promoted knowledge of an increasingly accessible world to a questing populace. *The Gentleman's Magazine*, which ran from 1731 until 1922, and *The Penny Magazine*, which ran for a much briefer period of time (1832–45), were just two of a multitude that frequently ran accounts, correspondence, and occasionally also accompanying wood engravings of famous oaks. Just before the advent of photography, the demand for the art of the engraver was perhaps at its zenith.

One of the finest and earliest collections of tree images comes from the hand of Major Hayman Rooke who published his *Remarkable Oaks in the Park at Welbeck* in 1790. Here he depicts nine unusual oaks on the estate of the Duke of Portland, drawn by Rooke and engraved by W. Ellis. One of these, 'An Ancient Oak in Birchland Wood' (part of Sherwood Forest), is today known as 'The Major Oak', arguably the most famous oak in Britain (see p.224), named in honour of Hayman Rooke. Would that there were many more such detailed portfolios of historic trees on the great estates.

Jacob George Strutt (1784–1867) was probably the closest any single nineteenth-century artist came to creating a comprehensive visual record of some of Britain's most important historic and ancient trees. Oaks feature most prominently in his wonderful collection. A landscape artist and etcher, Strutt embarked upon his tree odyssey in 1822 and by 1826 had accumulated fifty illustrations gathered principally from some of the great estates across Britain, although he seems to have rather ignored or avoided Wales. The magnificent folio edition (22 x 15 inch plates) of *Sylva Britannica: or Portraits of Forest Trees Distinguished for their Antiquity, Magnitude, or Beauty* was initially published in parts between 1822 and 1826. Such was the favourable response that Strutt was pressed to publish a smaller edition of the work that might be more affordable to a wider audience; this was accomplished in 1830.

The vast majority of Strutt's selected trees are no longer in existence, although a few, such as the Panshanger Oak in Hertfordshire, the Chandos (now Minchenden) Oak in Southgate, north London, and Majesty in Kent are still in pretty good shape. Sir Philip Sidney's Oak, at Penshurst, hangs in there by a thread. It is fascinating to see that what we might now consider heritage trees were equally as fascinating to the Georgians as they are to us today. Strutt produced another work *Deliciae Sylvarum or Grand and Romantic Forest Scenery in England and Scotland* in 1828.

In 1839, William Henry Fox Talbot announced his process for the calotype – a salted paper negative from which prints might be made – and thus photography was born. Talbot chose subjects around his home at Lacock for his early experiments from 1835. He created his sun pictures using plants and leaves laid on light-sensitive paper to make striking, simple contact prints in reverse (the first negatives), as well as photographing his family, estate, and some of the trees in the surrounding countryside. The well-known image of an oak tree in winter at Lacock Abbey typifies the misty, impressionistic pictures of real life for which Talbot became known. In their subtle array of warm tones, these images opened up a brand-new avenue to the artist. Talbot patented his process in 1841, setting in motion the negative-to-positive print process that would dominate photography for the next 160 years.

LEFT: The King Oak in Savernake Forest – a J. G. Strutt original folio plate 'acquired' by William H. Ablett for his *English Trees and Tree Planting* of 1880. No mention of Strutt was made! Did such piracy go unnoticed?

With the ready availability of the collodion wet-plate process, by the 1860s many photographers – both professionals and a growing number of amateurs – were creating wonderful photographs of everything under the sun. Portraiture became affordable to the masses, and the increasing appetite for travel meant that landscapes were commercial goldmines for big companies such as George Washington Wilson, James Valentine, and the ubiquitous Francis Frith. As part of their stock in trade, these companies photographed, among just about everything else, some of the famous oak trees around Britain. With the exception of the Major Oak, it is relatively difficult to find copies of these prints now – perhaps they just weren't as popular as the images of castles, ruins, and coastal resorts that were also available for tourists to buy.

The Francis Frith Company made the transition from producing albumen prints for albums to printing copious quantities of postcards from about 1900 onwards. Many of their earlier negatives of trees suddenly found a new lease of life. The Edwardian postcard era was a socio-cultural phenomenon. Everyone was sucked into the mania for writing and sending postcards, and often for the flimsiest of reasons – 'I'm coming for tea' (posted the same morning!), 'Hope your cold is better', 'Just look at this tree!' and the like. In many respects it was as casual yet incessant as blipping over a text message or a tweet today. For today's collectors discovering postcards of famous old oaks can be a treat, yet one is immediately aware of the over-abundance of images of the Major Oak. Photographing this famous tree appears to have become something of an obsession at the time, almost certainly due to a steady demand for postcards from the tourists. Photographs of villagers, whole families gathered proudly around their old oak, children clambering over the boughs or peeping out of the hollow trunks, or people lined up, ramrod straight, staring fixedly at the photographer fiddling with his huge plate camera under a dark cloth, depict oak trees in all manner of different contexts. 'A pennyworth of art' they may have been, but postcards have left us with one of the most comprehensive records of famous and ancient trees from a century ago.

By the turn of the nineteenth century, book illustration had well and truly favoured photography rather than engravings. Much book illustration of the first half of the twentieth century was inferior-quality offset lithography, which appeared grainy and flat. However, the seminal *Trees of Great Britain and Ireland* (1906–13) by Elwes and Henry, privately published in seven volumes, is lavishly illustrated with large monochrome photogravure plates – stunning quality images (even by today's standards) of scores of Britain's greatest trees of the day.

Throughout most of the twentieth century, artists and photographers seem to have almost ignored the nation's famous oaks. There is no shortage of tree books, but the oak celebrities were scarcely noticed. If anything, many writers and commentators adopted a slightly derisory tone with respect to ancient pollard trees in general, as John Rodgers wrote in 1941:

> It is difficult, however, to see any beauty in them; their hollow gaping trunks, their gnarled and mutilated branches, and all the other symptoms of decay, are depressing and even sordid… [conceding only] that they have an appeal, both to curiosity and sentiment.

It wasn't until the 1980s and 90s that there was a reawakening of interest for ancient trees, due in no small part to the learned texts of landscape historian and naturalist Dr Oliver Rackham and the keen eye of Thomas Pakenham in his *Meetings with Remarkable Trees* (1996). At last the historical, biological, and cultural significance of ancient trees, large oaks very much to the fore, had a raised profile. In fact, Pakenham's book lead to a series of ten-minute films about some of the individual trees. Big trees were on television. Millions tuned in, and that in itself boosted awareness of how special these trees are. It also no doubt boosted book sales. Many people remember those shorts to this day – I can't think how many times I've been out photographing trees and been asked, 'Are you Thomas Pakenham?'

Present-day artists are still absorbed by the oak tree, its place in the landscape, and its distinctive form, but it's always interesting to see what happens and how the public responds when a radically different approach is adopted in an artistic rendering of our national tree. Artist Philippa Lawrence has recently been binding dead trees in the landscape with fabric, often highly coloured, creating an extremely bold visual statement in the midst of many rural landscapes. Philippa's project statement declares:

ABOVE: *Bound, Croft*, a cotton-wrapped deceased oak at Croft Castle, by Philippa Lawrence, 2009.

'Bound,' the use of cloth as a form of communication and connection. Temporary site responsive interventions utilising cloth in the landscape as a vehicle to draw attention to issues of boundaries and ownership.

Responses vary from an 'eyesore' to 'vision'. No matter where we stand, such art pushes boundaries and provokes reactions – these bound trees are certainly impossible to ignore, and that can't be a bad thing.

OAKS OF SAVERNAKE

OPPOSITE: The Big Belly Oak has survived despite its close proximity to a main road.

FOR MOST PEOPLE VISITING THE SAVERNAKE FOREST TODAY, the overriding impression is of a predominantly beech wood interspersed with conifer plantations, but there is also oak wood and many fine old oak individuals to be found here, too. The name Savernake is believed to be derived from Safernoc, a name that appears in a deed showing land granted to the Abbey of Wilton by King Athelstan in 934. The 'oc' at the end of Safernoc would seem to signify oak. Rather mysteriously, this name does not appear in the Domesday Book of 1086.

In the mid-eighteenth century Savernake covered 40,000 acres, but today it comprises a much more modest 4,500 acres. The dominance of beech is a legacy of a fashion for planting this tree in the eighteenth century, most notably evident in the Grand Avenue, which, at almost four miles in length, is the longest avenue in Britain. It was devised by Lancelot 'Capability' Brown in the 1740s for the 3rd Earl of Ailesbury as a grand approach to Tottenham House. Beeches have come and gone from this splendid feature, but replanting and natural regeneration has maintained the essence of the original scheme.

Since 1939 the Forestry Commission has leased much of the forest, and the main thrust of their planting was beech and stands of conifers. Taken in context, the main aim of forestry during the war and the immediate post-war period was to make sure that Britain would have enough timber in the event of any future conflicts. Amenity and conservation were simply not part of the agenda. This resulted in the neglect of many of the ancient oaks in the forest, not by design, but simply because they were not viewed as commercially useful trees. Until very recently, the evidence was plain enough to see in the decrepit hulks of ancient oak pollards. These had once clearly been part of a wood-pasture regime several hundred years ago, but had since crumbled in the shadows or were hemmed in by plantations. Recent times have seen some of these trees 'liberated' and given a bit more space and light, which might hopefully prolong their time.

If most of Savernake's ancient oaks are tucked away in the darker recesses of the forest, there is one tree that has become familiar to thousands of motorists whizzing along the A346 between Marlborough and Salisbury. Sitting right by the side of this busy highway is the Big Belly Oak, or Big Bellied Oak, a formidable beast of a tree. At over 36 feet in girth, it is the biggest oak in the forest, and thought by many to be about 1,100 years old. Its shape has also caused it to acquire the alternative name the Decanter Oak. A weird tradition asserts that the Devil himself will appear to anyone prepared (or foolish enough) to dance naked, anticlockwise, a dozen times around the tree at midnight. One can only imagine the effect that this would have on passing motorists in the middle of the night. In recent times, concerns were expressed about the safety

DUKE'S VAUNT.

aspects of such an old oak so close to a main road. A huge steel band was bound around the old bole and the crown was selectively cut back, with the aim of stopping top-heavy boughs falling and tearing the old pollard apart. On balance this should help, but there could be an issue with the steelwork pinching into the vascular tissue, perhaps constricting the flow of sap up the tree.

One would have thought that the massive dimensions of the Big Belly Oak, coupled with its very prominent position on an old road, would have given it some sort of celebrity status during the nineteenth century. Only in the Edwardian era did the tree start to figure on postcards. Loudon fails to mention it, and Strutt diverts his artistic attention to the King Oak which, he states:

Forms a conspicuous feature in Savernake Forest, one of the most interesting spots in the kingdom, to the lovers of wildwood scenery … The King Oak, its most venerable ornament, spreads its branches over a diameter of sixty yards, and is twenty-four feet in girt. The trunk is quite hollow, and altogether its age appears to warrant the idea that it may have witnessed in its infancy those rites and sacrifices of our Saxon ancestors which were held in these shadowy recesses, at once to increase their solemnity, and to shield them from the profane eyes of vulgar observers.

The King Oak barely outlasted the nineteenth century, and a 1901 photograph by Frith shows it merely as a revered stump behind its own little picket fence. There is now a replacement King Oak, signed by the Forestry Commission, but it has a long way to go.

Strutt also figured the Creeping Oak in his work. This tree was mainly interesting because a large limb had dropped away or split from the main tree, rested on the ground (probably layering itself in the process), and created the impression that the tree was creeping across the forest. Again, this oak is no more, but similar forms of semi-recumbent oaks can be found in the forest if you look hard enough.

I wrote in one of my previous books that an oak known as the Duke's Vaunt Oak was no longer in existence, but it seems I was mistaken. Hidden away in a small clearing among conifers, the last few shards of this old tree still wrestle with life. The old bole is now so fragmented that it's difficult to gauge a girth measurement, but it was measured at 30 feet when still complete in 1802. The name 'Vaunt' signifies that it was the boast or glory of the duke. The tree was supposed to have been much admired by Edward Seymour, brother of Jane Seymour, whom Henry VIII courted at Savernake (he eventually married her an unseemly three days after he had ordered the execution of Ann Boleyn in 1536). Jane bore Henry the son and heir he had craved for so long, but died in childbirth. Edward was made 1st Duke of Somerset and Lord Protector of the Realm, principally to act as guardian and mentor to the young Edward VI. The oak would certainly have already been a large tree in the mid-sixteenth century, so the connection to Edward Seymour is plausible.

Corresponding with *The Gentleman's Magazine* in 1802, Mr J. Stone describes the location of the tree in the forest, indicating that its purpose was as a boundary marker. He went on to say:

> *I remember, on a perambulation round the boundaries of that parish about 40 years ago, being one of twenty boys who were shut up together in the concavity; and also that a band of music, consisting of a violin, hautboy, and bassoon, played several tunes in it. There was then a door hung to it, which shut or locked occasionally … thereafter follows an appreciation of its great size and age … So that without any hyperbole we may assign him a date, perhaps little short of a thousand years!* [That magic number rears its head once again].

Today the Forestry Commission has grasped the fascination that old oaks have with the public, and given the old and revered trees their own name plaques, along with a host of new candidates such as Amity Oak, Cathedral Oak, King of Limbs, Spider Oak, Saddle Oak (1 and 2), and the delightful Old Paunchy – with his big, bulbous burry bole. There are more than twenty to discover.

ABOVE: The last remaining shard of the once massive Duke's Vaunt Oak in the depths of Savernake Forest.

THE NEWLAND OAK, FOREST OF DEAN.

J. W. Porter,   (Copyright)

THE "NEWLAND" OAK, 43 feet in girth.
(One of the largest in the Kingdom).

Coleford, C

THE NEWLAND OAK

OPPOSITE TOP: The Newland Oak in The Forest of Dean – wood engraving from *The Woolhope Naturalists' Field Club* journals, 1878.

OPPOSITE BOTTOM: The earliest known photograph of the tree dates to around 1900, by the Coleford photographer Mr J. W. Porter (an image much admired by Elwes and Henry). The photograph depicts a goodly array of local folk set around the grand old oak – one of the family. Clearly a popular image, it was made into postcards.

THE EARLIEST DEPICTION OF THE FAMOUS NEWLAND OAK is a 1772 watercolour by Major Hayman Rooke. Rooke depicts the craggy old pollard of perhaps 600–800 years old growing at Spout Farm, Newland, near Coleford. Measurement at this date records that the Newland Oak was a little over 34 feet at 3 feet above ground; the tree appearing quite sound and retaining some vestige of commercial value. It was, however, spared the axe and, as it settled into its dotage, hollowing out into 'the patriarch which, unfolding the history of many a winter's storm, remains the solitary survivor of the fittest in the original Forest of Dean' (as observed by the Woolhope Naturalists Field Club in 1889). It further reduced its crown by relieving itself of several boughs, and became celebrated both locally and from afar as one of the greatest girthed oaks in the land, by now some 43 feet around.

Arthur O. Cooke offers a detailed and affectionate portrait of the tree in his 1913 book *The Forest of Dean*:

> *The feeling at first sight, and more especially when standing close beside the massive trunk, may be of disappointment, for the great tree has long been little but a giant ruin. The girth is generally given as slightly over forty-four feet at a height of five feet from the ground; but it is difficult to see exactly how this is arrived at, so burr-incrusted, warped and twisted is the trunk, that it is impossible to pass a measuring tape around it with any degree of regularity. The gigantic bole stands ten or twelve feet high. Mount to the summit—not a task of difficulty, for the projecting burrs give ample and secure support—and it will be found entirely hollow within. But still the sap flows upwards yearly through the outer shell, and green leaves open on the boughs above.*
>
> *…Yet year by year the patriarch dons its scanty summer garb, and casts a thin and flickering shadow in which cattle rest at summer noon. Or when, on some midday of early spring, the wind blows down the high-lying valley from the north, its gnarled and bossy trunk has many crevices in which the lambs are wont to shelter from the blast. Even in this last stage of decay the veteran passes to its end in usefulness.*

By 1950 the tree had lost more of its boughs, but must have still been growing as girths of 45 feet are recorded, which would certainly make it a champion tree today. Heavy snow in the winter of 1955 caused all but one bough to crash to the ground, signalling that the end was nigh. Fortunately, in 1964 cuttings were taken from that last live branch, and three young oaks planted close by. Tragically, the remnants of the Newland Oak were set on fire by vandals in 1970. This was the final nail in the coffin, but the best of the three young oaks was retained and survives to this day, carrying on the genetic lineage of the great old tree.

GOG <u>AND</u> MAGOG
OAKS

OPPOSITE: Gog and Magog at Wick, near Glastonbury, Somerset. Gog is dead, Magog hangs on.

IN AN OLD GREEN LANE AT WICK, near Glastonbury in Somerset, stand two massive old oaks. One now dead, the other still struggling on, the trees are known simply as Gog and Magog. For how long they have held their strange appellations is difficult to divine, since there is no mention of them in pre-twentieth-century texts.

Discovering why they were so-named, and who or what Gog and Magog were, leads us back through a labyrinth of culture and counter-culture, and both biblical and Islamic texts. Their numerous references all suggest dark forces at work, whether that be harbingers of evil or, in the Christian context, the Antichrist. They take on ever-changing identities across numerous cultures, both geographically and chronologically, including warlike, barbarian tribes, and fierce giants stalking the land. The latter appears to have become a peculiarly British phenomenon, promoted by the folklore set down by writers such as Geoffrey of Monmouth in the twelfth century. In his *Historia Regum Britanniae* he mentions the giant Goemagot (sometimes, Goemagog), the last of a race of giants, who was slain by the Cornish hero Corin or Corineus, and then hurled from a high cliff into the sea; the cliff afterwards being called Langoemagog – Giant's Leap. The story of how one giant turns into two has a couple of possible roots. Some have proposed that Gog is derived from the Celtic deity Ogmios, and Magog is his consort, yet images of these two show them as both quite distinctly male. More likely, the two giants were originally named Corineus and Gogmagog, after the two combatants in the great struggle in what is now Cornwall.

Records from 1605 reveal that the Pageantmaster of the Lord Mayor of London's Procession refers to two effigies carried forth as Corineus and Gogmagog. They have long been an important part of the Lord Mayor's Show celebrations. The original effigies were lost in the Great Fire in 1666, and those subsequently carried in procession during the late seventeenth century were made of wicker. These didn't last long, as they were consumed by rats and mice, so two new wooden statues were carved in 1708. Sadly, these perished in the Blitz of 1940, and two more replacements were carved in 1953 by David Evans. A pair of new wicker effigies once more became a part of the Lord Mayor's Procession in 2006.

Given such widespread folklore it is perhaps no surprise to find the names of two infamous giants settled on two giant oaks. At Glastonbury it is known that these two decrepit oaks are the last remaining trees of a long avenue that once led up to the Tor. There are many claims that this ancient avenue was an oaken grove sacred to the Druids, however with girths of 23 feet and 11 inches and 24 feet and 7 inches, Gog and Magog don't come near the 1,000 years' vintage claimed for them.

THE KNIGHTWOOD OAK

OPPOSITE: The Knightwood Oak, a perennial favourite with visitors to the New Forest.

T HE NEW FOREST IS ARGUABLY THE MOST FAMOUS, most historically well-documented forest in Britain. Although the physical structure of a forest existed in Hampshire long before the Norman Conquest, it was William the Conqueror who annexed the area and designated it as a royal forest for his own pleasure in the chase, but more so for revenue. Here the deer were maintained for his table, and those to whom he chose to give them as gifts; venison was most probably sold (and undoubtedly poached), income was generated from the forest timber and rented land, and William instigated laws and installed officials to oversee his asset.

The story of William's appropriation of the forest in 1079 received a variable response from different quarters. The Anglo-Saxon Chronicle painted a very dark picture of murder and mayhem as whole communities were supposedly uprooted and dispossessed with churches, farms, and whole villages being laid waste on the orders of the king. Since the Saxon populace probably took a pretty dim view of these French imposters, it is understandable that their records contain anti-Norman antagonisms. Certainly William wanted to subjugate the Saxons, but the reality was probably a lot less spectacular and, although they would have been less than thrilled at having forest laws thrust upon them, life for most people probably continued much as it had done before; they simply had a new lord and master.

The ongoing history of the New Forest revolved around the management of the deer, the grazing and pannage of domestic livestock, and the production of timber. Numerous accounts reveal perennial concerns about the stocks of useful timber, particularly from the seventeenth century up to the end of the eighteenth century, mainly for shipbuilding. In 1632, *Necessarie Remembrances* reveals that there were barely '2,000 serviceable trees in the whole forest', and it was said that, 'there was nothing left but wind-shaken and decayed trees in the New Forest, quite unfit for building ships'. Under the Stuart kings the laws of the forest were increasingly disregarded or relaxed, much of the best timber was removed (or stolen) with little thought of replanting, so that by the time of the Restoration most forests were in a shameful condition.

Probably influenced by John Evelyn's *Sylva*, in 1669 Charles II ordered three hundred acres of the New Forest to be enclosed as a nursery for young oaks. The trees of the forest were still in decline, so William III passed an Act ordering the planting of 6,000 acres. However, the fates conspired and in 1703 a hurricane flattened about 4,000 of the best oaks in the forest. Once more, in 1789, a

Report of the Land Revenue Commissioners discovered the dreadful state of the forest: grazing went unchecked, deer were overstocked and died in the winter from starvation, timber was plundered, and 'the forest was, in fact, robbed under every pretext'. It was not until the middle of the nineteenth century that matters were stabilized within the forest, and some sense of order and regulated management installed once again. This has continued up to the present day, and has seen the New Forest returned to a more sustainable state.

Different pressures now attend the New Forest, principally from tourism, and the many millions who visit every year. With National Park status since 1999, the Forestry Commission, local councils, and forest officers drawn from local communities are managing the forest wisely and productively for a bright future.

Most of the finest broadleaf woods here are dominated by oak and beech, although clearly in the distant past native lime was a major component. This is reflected in the place name of the town of Lyndhurst, 'lynd' meaning lime and 'hurst' a wood producing fodder for cattle. Quite often what are now beech woods would once have been oak dominant, but the extreme shade and faster growth of beech has shaded out most regenerating oaks. Eyeworth and Pinnick are two woods particularly noted for their character, which has probably changed little over many centuries. Here, large trees, some outgrown pollards, remnants of old wood-pasture, grow with an understory of holly and hawthorn. There are indeed records from the seventeenth century of oaks being planted with holly and hawthorn berries scattered among them; the idea being that the thorny young plants would protect the emerging oaks from browsing animals. A few of these holly ringwoods can still be discovered around mature oaks today.

The prodigious number of postcards produced during the early twentieth century reflect the New Forest's popularity as a tourist destination. Several of its named trees, featured on these cards, had already become natural 'celebrities' by then; although perhaps not as many as one might expect from an area covering 67,000 acres. Certainly, the most famous today is the Knightwood Oak, a huge outgrown pollard with a fine fist of ascending boughs in the middle of Knightwood Inclosure, some two miles west of Lyndhurst. With a girth of a little over 24 feet, it is probably 300–400 years old, but its shape has changed very little since the numerous postcards of the Edwardian era. Mentioned by John R. Wise in *The New Forest – its History and Scenery* (1863), the Knyghtwood Oak was then only 17 feet 4 inches in girth, so a very respectable growth rate in 150 years. Wise paints a lyrical picture of the New Forest oaks:

The oaks here do not grow so high or so large as in many other parts of England, but they are finer in their outlines, hanging in the distance as if rather suspended in the air than growing in the earth, but nearer, as especially at Bramble Hill, twisting their long arms, and interlacing each other into a thick roof. Now and then they take to straggling ways, running out, as with the famous Knyghtwood Oak, into mere awkward forks. The most striking are not, perhaps, so much those in their prime, as the old ruined trees at Boldrewood, their bark furrowed with age, their timber quite decayed, now only braced together by the clamps of ivy to which they once gave support and strength.

ABOVE: The Knightwood
Oak, an engraving from *Our
Woodland* by F. G. Heath, 1878.

The Knightwood Oak is still surrounded by its picket fence and the woodland in which it stands has also performed well over the years as a shelterbelt from storms. Since it is marked on the Ordnance Survey maps, it is easy to find and still attracts many visitors.

A little further west, the King and Queen Oaks of Bolderwood were obviously equally as celebrated as the Knightwood Oak, but have since fallen.

A strange tale attends what is now little more than an ivy-clad, dead oak stump out on Wilverley Plain. Known as the Naked Man, the old stump probably acquired its name from the appearance of a bleached carcass that resembled a naked man with two arms, which, J. H. Wilks recounts, 'is popularly supposed to depict a man engaged in an act of nature'. Because of the ivy we'll never know! Tradition asserts that the name actually came from the gruesome fate of a highwayman, who was left hanging here until rooks picked his bones clean. The tree has also been known as the Tree of Good and Evil Knowledge, but the reason seems obscure. The first mention occurs at the end of the eighteenth century, as the tree upon which local highwayman Mark Way was hanged for his misdeeds, but is this a red herring? A highwayman of that name doesn't appear in the records. Maybe Mark Way is really a 'way mark' across the forest. A tank managed to knock the Naked Man down during the Second World War, but it was promptly re-erected and cemented in place.

Another oak of much renown took its place in history on 2 August 1100, when Sir Walter Tyrrell fired an arrow that glanced off the tree and struck King William Rufus in the breast, killing him instantly. The tree is long gone, but a stone still marks the spot. To this day nobody knows for sure if this was a genuine accident or a successful assassination.

THE SILTON OAK

ON THE EDGE OF THE TINY HAMLET OF SILTON, just within the northern bounds of Dorset, the shambolic remnant of the Silton Oak stands forlornly in the centre of a large pasture behind the church, marking the boundary limit of the all but forgotten Forest of Gillingham.

The Silton Oak has also long been known as Wyndham's Oak, the Great Oak, or, sometimes, the Judge's Tree, in memory of Sir Hugh Wyndham (1602–1684), appointed as a Judge of the Court of Common Pleas by Oliver Cromwell in 1654. Judge Wyndham was charged with deliberating upon the Royalist conspirators of the quashed Penruddock Uprising in 1655. Immediately after, Colonel John Penruddock was beheaded, with other ringleaders, while seventy other men were shipped to the West Indies and sold into slavery. Wyndham's actions during the interregnum would come back to haunt him at the Restoration, when he was briefly imprisoned in the Tower of London. He pleaded that he had hoped to save the accused from condemnation at his assizes, and was pardoned by the king.

Wyndham was a fortunate man and was able to return to the Manor of Silton, which he had purchased in 1641, and resume his practice. It is said that the old oak in the pasture behind the manor house and church was…

> … the favourite haunt of Judge Wyndham, under the shade of which he was wont to regale himself with his pipe, during his vacation from the labours of his profession, and at the same time enjoy the rich, cheerful, and extensive prospect it commands.

Wyndham died in Norwich in 1684 while on circuit. His body was brought back for burial at the church of St Nicholas in Silton. He is commemorated in what is regarded as Dorset's largest church memorial inside this modest little building.

The somewhat ominous aura about this tree might reflect the long-held local belief that two members of the Monmouth Rebellion of 1685, victims of Judge Jeffreys's 'Bloody Assizes', were hanged from it. An account of this avalanche of brutality and retribution by Jeffreys throughout the southwest comes down to us in a vivid depiction in John Tutchins's *The Western Martyrology* of 1705:

> Humanity could not offend so far to deserve such Punishment as he inflicted. A certain barbarous Joy and Pleasure grinned from his Brutal Soul through his Bloody Eyes, whenever he was sentencing any of the poor Souls to Death and Torment…

Did the old boughs just creak or groan … or was it perhaps the rasp of a rope above?

OPPOSITE TOP: *Silton Oak, Dorsetshire*, copper engraving by J. Greig from a drawing by J. Fenton Esq. Published in *The Antiquarian & Topographical Cabinet*, 1810. If the accuracy of this image is anything to go by, one might deduce that the tree is in better shape today than it was 200 years ago.

OPPOSITE BOTTOM: The massive bulk of the Silton Oak sits squarely in the middle of the pasture behind the church of St Nicholas in Silton.

THE MEAVY OAK

O N THE END OF THE VILLAGE GREEN AT MEAVY, on the southwest edge of Dartmoor, stands the Meavy Oak, with a stone-stepped preaching cross tucked in beneath its canopy. Whether the Christian cross was imposed upon the community, or was a subtle act of conversion is a story untold. The Revd Sabine Baring-Gould alludes to it in his *A Book of the West* (1900):

> The [Meavy] *Oak, however, is of vast age. It is referred to in deeds almost to the Conquest, and that it was a sacred tree to which a certain amount of reverence was given is probable enough. The cross was set up under its shadow to consecrate it, and probably to put an end to superstitious rites done there. Anyhow this tree till within this century* [nineteenth] *was. On the village festival, surrounded with poles, a platform was erected above the tree, the top of which was kept clipped flat like a table, and a set of stairs erected, by means of which the platform could be reached. On the top a table and chairs were set, and feasting took place. Whether dancing I cannot say, but in all probability in former generations there was dancing there as well as feeding and drinking. These trees where dancing took place are precisely the May-pole in a more primitive form.*

The old stone cross is thought to have been a preaching cross that probably pre-dates the building of the first church here in 1122. The oak is reputedly coeval with the church, making it also 900 years old, which seems a generous estimate for a tree that today only has a girth of 21 feet 6 inches. As to be expected, it is hollow, and has obviously lost a large part of its old bole. Records from 1833 reveal that it was then 27 feet in circumference.

The tree is sometimes called the Gospel Oak, and the fine steps of the cross plinth would have made an excellent pulpit. Alternatively it is the Royal Oak, as tradition asserts that King John knew the tree and, while hunting on Dartmoor, often used the building that pre-dates the nearby Royal Oak Inn as a hunting lodge. In 1826, in notes for Carrington's poem 'Dartmoor', there is an account 'that nine people once dined inside the trunk of the tree on the authority of the hostess of the Royal Oak Inn'.

Today the oak is still cherished, and protected by its little iron fence – a sign asks you not to tether your horse here. The inn sells Meavy Oak Ale and every year, on the third Saturday in June, there is still a Meavy Oak Fair with maypole dancing among the many attractions. A vestige of the old ways lives on.

OPPOSITE: The Meavy Oak on Dartmoor, Devon.

BELOW: Wood engraving of the Meavy Oak from J. C. Loudon's *Arboretum et Fruticetum Britannicum*, 1838.

OAK BUILDINGS

As soon as Neolithic people began to settle down in permanent communities where they could plant crops and graze livestock, a reliable and renewable woodland resource became fundamental. Timber was required to make fences to keep the animals from wandering and palisades to protect the community, and within these enclosures shelters were required. Archaeologists have revealed post holes dating back some 6,000 years, in formations that indicate the positions of walls with larger holes marking central aisle posts that would have supported the roof. Oak's strength and durability would have been best suited for this purpose. Roofs were woven with straw or reeds and walls would have been wattle and daub – probably hazel or willow caked with mud mixed with chopped straw.

WE KNOW THAT THE ROMANS BUILT TIMBER-FRAMED STRUCTURES, as the remains of several have been unearthed in London. They brought a new technical approach to building, using sawn and squared timber and rudimentary mortise and tenon joints; a little cruder than their medieval and later counterparts with tapered timbers set into holes hewn with axes, but still extremely effective and strong. Curiously, Roman builders favoured nails over the wooden pegs that medieval carpenters used to secure construction members.

Roman construction techniques were all but abandoned by the Anglo-Saxons, who reverted to methods more akin to those employed by prehistoric builders. Wood was worked in the round, timbers were cleaved, and lap and tongue and groove joints came back into use. This strange regression of technology perpetuated until the late twelfth century when, within a very short period, Roman technology was readopted and has effectively held sway ever since. Almost all of our evidence of standing timber-framed buildings dates from this period.

Heavy structural timber-framing applies to a building constructed in one of three ways: the box frame, cruck frame and aisle frame. All frames are pre-fabricated in two dimensions, before on-site erection into a three-dimensional building. The term box frame is sometimes only distinguished from cruck framing, but specifically this technique means that the exterior walls bear the roof's load. A cruck frame is formed from a series of pairs of curved or arced blades, usually cut from the same tree so they match. Sometimes these will run from ground to roof apex; sometimes they will shorter and in this case stabilised by tie beams. Aisled frames tend to be used in wider buildings, typically in great

OPPOSITE: Built in 1426 for Winchester College, Harmondsworth Great Barn is the largest timber-framed building in England.

ABOVE: The sixteenth-century Guildhall of Corpus Christi in Market Place, Lavenham, Suffolk, arguably England's best preserved medieval town with a wealth of timber-framed buildings built off the proceeds of the wool trade between the fifteenth and seventeenth centuries. Note the lime-washed timbers here, the way these building would have looked before the nineteenth-century fashion for blackening them.

barns, and employ rows of interior posts, which give the central aisle or nave, and side aisles, to increase the support for the roof. All of these structures provide a timber skeleton, a flexible framework around which a roof and walls may be added, along with internal walls, partitions and floors.

The framework is sometimes left exposed on the outside of the building, usually described as half-timbered, or is clad with weatherboard, stone or brickwork. Huge, well-seasoned pieces of oak timber were reserved for the most prestigious projects such as cathedrals and castles and often transported great distances. Small trees, roughly 9 or 10 inches in diameter, were suitable to build the average house and could be grown in about sixty years, but between 200 and 300 would be required for each building so that the timber would have been sourced from the nearest wood, cut and built in green wood on site. As I can attest from my own house, which has some elm tresses, this was not always restricted to oak – sweet chestnut, ash, and pine were also sometimes used, but only where the wood was not exposed to the weather. The means of joining these timbers from the medieval period to the twenty-first century has been exactly the same, with oak pegs in offset holes which, as they are driven, pull the frames snugly together. Since frames were often pre-cut and fitted, then dismantled and transported to the construction site, carpenters usually cut their assembly marks near the uniquely-fitting joints of frames and trusses to make sure that the correct components were matched together in the final erection. Even today these are carved in straight Roman numerals, although four is IIII and nine is

VIIII, probably in order to avoid confusion with XI and IX. Arabic numbers, possessing curves, are usually written rather than cut.

In many earlier and humbler buildings the timbers were left waney, even with sap wood and bark left on the corners, particularly in areas that would not be seen. Timbers would originally have been cut with felling axes and surface-finished with broadaxes – sometimes the little scallops made by these can be seen on rafters and beams. Later on, timbers were sawn, and close examination of the marks on the edges of the timber sometimes points to the use of pit or frame saws. It is worth dispelling a popular myth that old joints, holes, rebates and the like indicate the recycling of ships' timbers. Apart from a few buildings close to the coast, this is just not so; most recycled timbers came from other buildings.

R. W. Brunskill identified eighteen vernacular styles of architecture throughout Britain, five of which have a strong tradition of timber-framed buildings. Apart from East Anglia these occupy well-wooded regions, with Kent, Sussex, Surrey, and Hampshire all drawing on the richly wooded resources of the Weald; the Home Counties to the north and west of London; the West Midlands, particularly Herefordshire and Shropshire, but also the eastern borders of Wales; and Cheshire, with a few more localised areas of Lancashire and Yorkshire.

East Anglia, and Suffolk in particular, has a handful of villages and towns that can still boast a wealth of timber-framed buildings – Lavenham being one of the finest examples. When the timbers are exposed they are almost always

ABOVE: St Andrews Church, in Greensted in Essex, is the oldest wooden church in the world and the oldest 'stave-built' timber building in Europe. The fifty-one substantial oak planks that make up the walls, left in the round on the exterior, date from about 1060, although there is evidence of previous timber structures dating back to the late sixth century.

left bare of paint or pitch to silver gracefully with age but sometimes they are rendered over and the plaster decorated with patterns known as pargetting. Colour washes on the infill plaster are also common, and yet another distinctive feature of East Anglian buildings is close-spaced vertical studding.

The Wealden houses of the south-east are equally distinctive, with features such as curved braces across the studding, jettied upper storeys and frequent use of weatherboarding, sometimes completely covering the house (common on barns), sometimes upper storeys and/or gable ends. Many of these houses would originally have been built around a central hall reaching the full height of the building.

The houses of the West Midlands and the Welsh border counties are perhaps most readily distinguished by their striking black and white appearance, but this is a Victorian embellishment, for originally the timber would have been either left untreated or lime-washed. Usually of box-frame construction, panels tend to be strengthened and decorated by the addition of chevrons or diagonal braces. The local tourism in Herefordshire trades heavily on its monochrome village trail. These houses may look beautiful, but timber movement, shrinkage of plaster or brick infills (often only single brick thickness), lack of insulation, and the fact that many were built directly on to earthen floors four or five hundred years ago, can make them rather chilly and draughty. There are some magnificent individual buildings to be found, ranging from great and modest homes, handsome farmsteads such as Lower Brockhampton in Herefordshire, massive barns, inns and hotels (The Feathers in Ludlow is a fine example), dovecotes and then, most specifically, market houses or halls set at the centre of what have long been thriving market towns. Again, Herefordshire, Ledbury and Leominster still have handsome timbered buildings from the seventeenth century. The Grange, as Leominster's market house is now known, was built in 1633/4 by John Abel, a local man, known as the 'King's Carpenter' after he assisted King Charles I during the siege of Hereford, by constructing flour mills and gunpowder mills, to feed and arm the besieged army. It is regarded as one of the finest examples of his work.

One of the finest timber-framed market halls ever built in Britain used to stand in the centre of Hereford. Built in the late sixteenth century, and officially entitled the Town Hall, the building was 84 feet long and 34 feet wide, crowned by a lantern over 100 feet high and supported by twenty-seven oak columns. The first floor was used as magistrates' chambers and a court room, while the second floor was given over to fourteen craft guilds – bakers, barbers, barber surgeons, braziers, butchers, clothiers, coopers, cordwainers, glovers, joiners, mercers, tanners, tylers and weavers. The open space on the ground floor, among the pillars, was used for regular markets. Nikolaus Pevsner, in *The Buildings of England*, described it as 'a sight to thrill any visitor from England or abroad. It was the most fantastic black and white building imaginable, three-storeyed, with gables and the richest, most curious decoration.' Despite this the city fathers, concerned about the pressure that the structure was exerting on the timber pillars, decided to remove the upper storey in 1792 and, in line with the prevailing fashion, rendered over the timbering with plaster. By 1862 further

BELOW: Sarah Partridge at Orchard Barn in Suffolk cleaving oak shingles with a froe.

worries about the structure, combined with congestion in the city, led to the total demolition of a truly exceptional building – something today we could only consider as utter vandalism.

In Cheshire, Lancashire, and Yorkshire, the abundance of timber-framed buildings diminishes, but what is lacked in number is compensated by quality. Many fine houses still survive with visually arresting and intricate external ornamentation; none more so than Little Moreton Hall, near Congleton in Cheshire. Built between 1504 and 1610, this house has all the appearance of something out of a fairy tale – 'a gingerbread house' as the National Trust puts it. Chester, the county town, boasts one of the most phenomenal arrays of timbered buildings in Britain, perhaps only rivalled by the Shambles of York. Many of Chester's Rows have medieval roots, but a great deal of what may be seen on the face of the city today is the result of Victorian black and white revival. No matter; the overall effect is most impressive and imparts the feel of a bygone age. A few of the timbered buildings of Yorkshire and Lancashire also bear the same sort of elaborate exterior decoration as Little Moreton. Speke Hall, near Liverpool, completed in 1598 and little changed since, may be simpler in appearance yet equally as impressive.

To truly appreciate the design and construction skills required to erect a timber-framed building, there is no better way than visiting some of the great

barns that have survived from the fourteenth and fifteenth centuries. In many cases these were still in everyday use as utilitarian buildings, storing produce or sheltering livestock, until very recent times. Access for large, modern machinery or change of agricultural regimes led to many of them becoming redundant, but thankfully historians, archaeologists, enthusiastic communities with a keen sense of local heritage, and bodies such as English Heritage and National Trust have all pulled out the stops to save and renovate some outstanding barns.

One of the most awe-inspiring constructions is the massive aisled Great Barn in the village of Harmondsworth, wedged as it is between the M4, the M25, and Heathrow Airport. It was constructed by Winchester College in 1426 and measures 192 feet long, 37 feet wide and 39 feet high; the whole structure is supported by thirteen huge oak trusses, making it the largest timber-framed building in England. The late poet laureate Sir John Betjeman was so moved by this building that he named it, most appropriately, the 'Cathedral of Middlesex'. Indeed, the barn's template mimics the same structural design upon which many cathedrals of the period were based. Standing in the middle of this incredible structure, one feels nothing short of veneration – incredulity at the scale;

admiration and wonder for the skills of those medieval carpenters. Here one can get up close to massive oaks felled 600 years ago (accurately dated by dendrochronology), the main posts some 14 inches square; study in detail the shapes that lent themselves to the structure; pick out the assembly marks; and touch the traces of adze, axe and saw. Although this is a Grade 1 listed building, a period of great turmoil during the latter twentieth century saw it standing in a precarious situation with regard to its future and structural well-being. Fortunately, the local community and English Heritage stepped up in 2009 to begin a new phase of care and repair, and in 2012 it opened to the public (only Sundays, April to October, but well worth a visit).

An interesting cameo from John Evelyn mentions barn building on a more modest scale during the seventeenth century, but with an interesting twist:

> …*my worthy friend, Leonard Pinckney, Esq; lately First Clerk of his Majesty's Kitchen, did assure me, that one John Garland built a very handsome barn, containing five bays, with pan, posts, beams, spars, &c. of one sole tree, growing in Worksop Park.*

One can only guess how big such a tree must have been, and whether the barn might still exist today. A fascinating odyssey for the diligent researcher!

The cathedrals and great houses were able to flex their influential muscle and financial reserves to acquire the very best and largest oak timber for their grand projects, often transported over great distances at substantial cost and, much in

the mode of shipbuilding timber, requiring several years seasoning prior to use. The next tier of priority for oak timber usually resided with the church, and there are many thousands of these, the very oldest dating back to the ninth century. Although usually built of stone, oak was always needed for roof construction as well as for all the interior fixtures and fittings. Some of the most remarkable legacies of medieval craftsmanship and artistry have survived despite the efforts of the iconoclasts. Alongside the religious iconography reside carvings of Green Men, beasts and beings natural, fanciful and mythological, plants, flowers, leaves, scenes of biblical teaching, social and agricultural history, and, occasionally, pure unashamed ribaldry and humour. It seems that the wood carvers and stonemasons who toiled to build our churches were given the perquisite to leave their own very personal touches for posterity. If only we had written records from these men to know more of the background to their work.

The variety and number of timber-framed houses throughout Britain is a remarkable legacy and testament to the durability of the oak timber, even bearing in mind that much would have been used in the green state. When open fires for cooking and warmth and candles for lighting were the norm, fire must have claimed many of these structures. The destruction in London alone, among the overcrowded, narrow streets of almost exclusively timber buildings, after the Great Fire of 1666, and with the loss of over 13,000 houses and eighty-seven churches, makes it remarkable that anything prior to this date still exists today. After the fire, Charles II passed an edict stipulating that timber required for any rebuilding work in the city could only be oak.

Indeed, speaking from personal experience of a serious house fire, I have observed first-hand how old oak timbers can resist the intensity of an inferno. Examining the beams of a room that blazed for at least half an hour, the outer quarter of an inch was charred, but the inner timber was still perfectly sound and load bearing.

In the twentieth century, timber-framed construction was eclipsed by the increased use of steel and glass along with traditional, and seemingly more permanent, materials such as brick and stone. However, about thirty years ago something of a renaissance in the interest in timber-framing came to the fore, initially emerging from the business of restoration and conservation work, alongside projects to convert redundant barns into homes. Even so, the supply of derelict barns was not limitless and very soon a surge in demand arose for newbuild timber-framed dwellings.

Suddenly it became very fashionable to live in a timber-framed house – it was seen as ecologically sound and 'green' to be using a renewable, sustainable material, and predominantly oak. The only problem was that Britain no longer had a reserve of high-quality, mature, straight oak trees suitable for the purpose, but fortunately, just across the Channel, France did. For many years French foresters have been growing large crops of excellent oak trees, which by the time they are forty to sixty years old are ideal for construction work. In fact, about 98% of timber-frame oak is imported from France.

At this juncture I have to wonder if modern oak timber-framing has a legitimate place within the covers of this book. However, it can be viewed as an extension to a tradition firmly rooted in British woods and forests, quietly glossing over the fact that even 500 years ago timber was also being imported for such purposes from Europe and the Baltic.

The principles of timber-framing have changed little in the last 700 years, except that now we have the benefit of modern technology, engineering, and equipment for the design and construction. Essentially, the frame is the same as it always was, put together in two dimensions in a framing yard (a four- or five-bedroomed house takes three to four months to build all the components), disassembled and then erected on site, these days on a concrete plinth rather than straight on the earth (the above cited house taking roughly a week to erect). The spaces created within can then be studded or partitioned in whatever way suits the home-owner. Best practice shies away from using green wood or kiln-dried timber, and seasoning is by air-drying usually for about one year for every inch thickness of the wood. Modern membranes and insulation materials make the house warmer, drier and more resistant to adverse weather conditions.

On a more emotive level, as Tim Burrell of Carpenter Oak and Woodland avers, 'when you walk into a "normal" home you admire the soft furnishings or the decor, but when people enter a timber-framed home they immediately want to go to the exposed oak, to stroke it and invariably remark upon its beauty'. It seems to signify a reconnection with something we either lost or forgot about – the times when we all lived in wooden buildings carved out of the nearby woodland. Even more so, the significance of oak in particular seems to ignite a sense of national pride, an intimate association with all that is strong, dependable and enduring; no less than deep affection for our iconic British tree.

THE BOSCOBEL OAK

OPPOSITE: The Boscobel Oak
reinforced with two steel bands
to prevent it from collapsing,
with its young replacement to
the right, planted by Prince
Charles in 2001.

THE STORY OF THE BOSCOBEL OAK, and how King Charles II hid among its boughs to escape the Parliamentarian soldiers trying to capture him, is one of the most iconic episodes in British history. Children have been entranced by the story of pursuit, ingenious concealment and eventual escape to freedom.

In 1651, in the dying embers of the Civil War, Charles II made his last and unsuccessful stand at Worcester, but was no match for Cromwell's New Model Army. With defeat all but assured, the king fled north from the city with a few supporters, and in the early hours of 4 September they came to White Ladies Priory, not far from Boscobel House in Shropshire. The next day the king and Richard Penderel, a local farmer, made their way to the town of Madeley. They intended to cross the River Severn, but the crossings were well guarded so they were forced to return to the safety of Boscobel. The king later dictated his account of the following day to Samuel Pepys:

> *Careless* [variously captain, major or colonel in several versions] *told me it would be dangerous to stay in the house or to go into the wood. He suggested we climb into a great, so that we could see around us, for the enemy would search the wood. I approving, we (that is Careless and I) went and carried up with us some victuals for the whole day viz. bread, cheese, small beer and nothing else and got up into a great oak that had been lopt some three or four years before, and being grown out again very bushy and thick, could not be seen through and here we stayed all day.*

In his book *Boscobel* (1660), Thomas Blount describes more fully the scene in the tree:

> [Not only was there a] *cushion for His Majesty to sit on; the Colonel humbly desired His Majesty (who had taken little or no Rest the two preceding Nights) to seat himself as easily as he could in the Tree, and rest His Head on the Colonel's Lap, who was watchful that His Majesty might not fall. In this Oak they continued most Part of that Day; and in that Posture His Majesty slumbered away some Part of the Time, and bore all these Hardships and Afflictions with incomparable Patience.*

It is worth mentioning that the price on the king's head was £1,000 – a fortune to any man with less than royal affections. The penalty for aiding or harbouring the king was 'death with no mercy'.

Many people have written about the Boscobel or Royal Oak: In his 1706 edition of *Silva*, John Evelyn laments the fate of the original Boscobel Oak, 'which hid and protected our late Monarch from being discovered and taken by the rebel soldiers who were sent to find him, after his almost miraculous

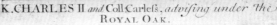

K.CHARLES II *and* Coll·Carless, *advising under the* ROYAL OAK.

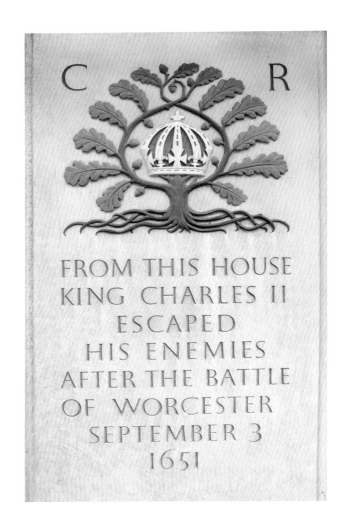

C   R

FROM THIS HOUSE
KING CHARLES II
ESCAPED
HIS ENEMIES
AFTER THE BATTLE
OF WORCESTER
SEPTEMBER 3
1651

ABOVE LEFT: *K. Charles II and Coll. Carless advising under the Royal Oak*, copper engraving, late eighteenth century. Carless appears to be encouraging the weary-looking monarch to flee to France on board one of the distant ships.

ABOVE RIGHT: A handsome relief-design plaque on King Charles House in New Street, Worcester, commemorates the fact that the king escaped through the house after his defeat at the Battle of Worcester, leaving by the back door as the Parliamentary forces pounded at the front door.

OPPOSITE: *The Royal Oak and Boscobel House*, copper engraving from *Arbores Mirabiles* by Joseph Taylor, 1812.

escape at the battle of Worcester.' Royalist souvenir hunters 'never left hacking of the boughs and bark till they killed the tree'.

Of the original oak's fate, Scottish botanist and horticulturalist John Claudius Loudon tells us that the original Royal Oak 'was prematurely destroyed by an ill-judged passion for relics; and a huge bulk of timber, consisting of many loads, was taken away in handfuls'. He continues:

> *Several saplings were raised, in different parts of the country, from its acorns, one of which grew near St. James's Palace, where Marlborough House now stands; and there was another in the Botanic Garden, Chelsea. The former has been long since felled; and of the latter even the recollection seems now almost lost.*

Doctor William Stukeley (1687–1765) provides a splendid account of the Boscobel Oak from his visit in 1712, where he lodged at an inn called Ivesey bank on the border between Staffordshire and Shropshire:

> *About a mile off, in a large wood, stands Boscobel House, where the Pendrils lived, who preserved King Charles the Second, after the battle of Worcester, and made famous by the royal oak... At a bow-shot from the house, just by a horse-track,*

passing through the wood, stood the oak, into which the king, and his companion, Colonel Careless, climbed, by means of a hen-roost ladder, when they judged it no longer safe in the house; the family reaching them victuals with a nut hook, during their continuance in that situation.

It happened, that whilst the king and the colonel were in the tree, a party of the enemy's horse, sent to search the house, came whistling and talking along the road. When they were just under the oak, an owl flew out of neighbouring tree, and hovered along the ground, as if her wings were broken, and the soldiers merrily pursued it, without making any circumspection.

The tree was enclosed within a brick wall, but had been severely damaged by travellers seeking souvenirs. Close to it stood another young oak planted from one of the acorns. The tree's acorns travelled even further afield: It was said that, 'the King, after the Restoration, reviewing that place, carried some of the acorns, and set them in St. James's Park, or garden, and used to water them himself'.

In his 1812 *Arbores Mirabiles*, Joseph Taylor observed that 'the present tree is fine and thrifty… and said to have originated from an acorn of the old oak'. At this time a brass plate was also affixed to the surrounding wall, which had been originally built in about 1680, and then restored in 1787 by Basil and Elizabeth Fitzherbert – who were both ardent royalists according to the tone of the inscription.

The Revd C. A. Johns attempts to establish exactly what had happened to the original oak and verify its authenticity in his 1847 *Forest Trees of Britain*. From the king's own account, the tree was clearly an old pollard. Johns was sure that the original tree had perished long ago. Local people remembered that the

last remnants were removed in around 1734. The tree Johns saw before him was therefore the second generation, but he notes with sadness that 'the present Royal Oak, however, is now rapidly following its predecessor to decay'. Around 1807 it seems an unseasonable snow storm had laden the tree's boughs so heavily that there was 'a terrific crashing and mangling of its limbs', which Johns believed signalled the start of the tree's decline. He was additionally of the opinion that by being protected within its sheltering wall for so many years, the tree had failed to acquire the hardness and toughness normally associated with the species.

While Johns made it sound as though the chips were down for this second Royal Oak, there does not appear to be any account of its final demise. Today, an oak still marks the sacred spot near Boscobel House, but it does look rather modest for a 300-year-old tree. Perhaps the trauma in the early nineteenth century set it back, and a close inspection of its bole would show some signs of that old storm damage. Maybe the tree had something of a renaissance or, alternatively, maybe it is a third-generation tree. Whatever the case, the elements were unkind once again in 2000 and the tree was struck by lightning, blasting a huge bough off one side. How long this tree will struggle on is anyone's guess, but in 2001 Prince Charles planted another sapling from an acorn of the present tree, thus ensuring a third (or perhaps fourth) generation Royal Oak.

ABOVE: The Boscobel Oak in 2001, before the bough on the left broke off. The tree had also recently been struck by lightning, blasting off the far side and destroying the iron railings.

THE MARTON OAK

W HILE MANY OF TODAY'S MOST FAMOUS OAKS GROW in the old parklands of the gentry (in other words simply a very large back garden), the Marton Oak grows in quite a small back garden in Marton, Cheshire.

The first mention of the tree seems to be in J.P. Earwaker's *East Cheshire Past and Present* (1877) when he recorded that 'not far from the Chapel is a very fine Oak, which, although but little known, is believed to be the largest in England'. At the time, its girth was measured at 43 feet at 4 feet above the ground. An engraving from this period shows that the old pollard was already hollow and the bole was beginning to fragment.

Several historical accounts reveal that in the past it has served as a bullpen and a pigsty. In fact a photograph from the 1890s shows its proximity to the nearby farm buildings, in recent years converted into a lovely house for the current owners of the tree. This old photograph reveals that the tree has changed very little in 120 years; if anything, the canopy today may be a little more luxuriant than it was then. The Marton Oak may look decrepit, but it seems to be in surprisingly good health. It still produces fine crops of acorns, many of which have been sold over the years to raise funds for the beautiful fourteenth-century, timber-framed village church.

This is a sessile oak and, even allowing for the substantial voids between its four remaining bole fragments, current girth measurement is about 44 feet, making in the biggest sessile oak in Britain. Its age is very difficult to estimate. One thousand years almost seems to go without saying, but 1,200, or even a little more, may not be out of the question.

The tree has been treasured by the village for many years. Previous owners once constructed a little Wendy house and wedged it inside the hollow bole for their children. This has now gone, and the present owners are deeply proud of their oak and very conscious of their duty of care for such a special tree. Remarkably, Earwaker's parting observation in his 1877 work reflects the same ethos as today's conservationists – 'It is much to be hoped that every care will be taken to preserve this tree.' To this day, so far so good.

OPPOSITE: The Marton Oak may look very decrepit today, little changed from the image below, made 140 years previously, but it is still in extremely good health.

BELOW: The Old Oak at Marton from Earwaker's *East Cheshire Past and Present*, 1877.

D. Parkes del. 1810.

Shelton Oak, near Shrewsbury.

OWEN GLENDOWER'S OAK

I T SEEMS STRANGE TO RELATE THAT AN OAK THAT WAS ONCE most
definitely rooted in the soil of England was celebrated as the great Welsh
patriot's tree. Long known as Owen Glendower's Oak, one wonders if the
anglicized title is more correct, since this is a Shropshire tree, but in deference
to the Welsh maybe it should more properly be Owain Glyndŵr's Oak. Several
other titles are on offer, including the Great Oak, the Grete Oak, Owen
Glendower's Observatory, or the Shelton Oak, for it grew in the grounds
of Shelton Priory.

On 21 July 1403, Shrewsbury became the focal point of the rancour between
Henry 'Hotspur' Percy and King Henry IV. Hotspur believed that his family had
not been justly rewarded for their services to the crown. In particular, they had
assisted in the struggle against Richard II in order to put Henry on the throne
in 1399, and had specifically helped to quell the Scots and oppose the Welsh
rebellion. After several years spent fighting the armies of Glendower in Wales
in the service of his king, Hotspur bizarrely reversed his allegiance and formed
an alliance with Owen Glendower and Edmund Mortimer. Together the new
alliance bid to usurp the crown from Henry and proclaim Mortimer, 5th Earl
of March, as rightful monarch. Henry, who, only a week or so earlier, had been
marching north to engage the Scots (in league with the Percys as he thought),
suddenly found Hotspur set against him. Henry and his army diverted westward
and won the race to Shrewsbury to put himself between Hotspur approaching
from the north and Glendower coming up from Wales.

Tradition relates that Glendower climbed the great oak to see the lie of the land
ahead. He realized that he would somehow have to ford the River Severn and fight
his way through Henry's considerable forces to join up with his ally Hotspur. He
also had word that the Earl of Northumberland (Hotspur's father) had not joined
his son. Assessing the situation to be highly disadvantageous, Glendower prudently
withdrew with his 12,000 followers to Oswestry. For a battle-hardened, formidable
leader like Glendower, this climbdown seems strange, but ultimately it was probably
a wise decision. The Battle of Shrewsbury was a fierce and bloody affair with
great losses on both sides, and is remembered as being the first conflict on
English soil in which massed ranks of archers with longbows were set against
each other. Hotspur was killed in the battle and, despite taking greater losses,
Henry won the day and thus put down the revolt of the Percy family.

Most authorities are convinced that Glendower's presence at Shrewsbury
is completely unfounded, as at the time of the battle he was fighting in

OPPOSITE: *Shelton Oak, near
Shrewsbury,* copper engraving
from *The Gentleman's
Magazine,* 1810.

The Gentleman's Magazine
of 14 August 1810 published
correspondence from one D.
Parker, who quoted Gough's
notice of the oak, and declared
the following:

*This tree is now in a complete
state of decay, and hollow, even
the larger ramifications. It is
visited by many people, from the
above tradition. A gentleman
whom I accompanied was so
charmed with the old tree, that
he gave it the name of Owen
Glendwr's Observatory.*
This is perfectly reflected in the
accompanying wood engraving.

Carmarthenshire, unaware of Hotspur's actions and, indeed, his plight.

It is difficult to explain how this oak gained its apocryphal association with Glendower. According to J. G. Strutt, the earliest reference to the tree appears to come from 1543 in a title deed appertaining to one Adam Waring and his property. The deed contains a short description of the tree under the heading 'How the grette Oake at Shelton standeth on my ground.' No mention of Glendower appears.

English antiquarian Richard Gough (1735–1809) took sixteen years to produce his 1789 edition of William Camden's *Britannia* (1586), which included numerous additions and amendments to the original. Camden had not mentioned the oak in his manuscript, but Gough introduces 'the tradition that Owen Glendwr ascended this tree to reconnoitre'.

The Gentleman's Magazine of 14 August 1810 published correspondence from one D. Parker, who quoted Gough's notice of the oak, and declared the following:

This tree is now in a complete state of decay, and hollow, even the larger ramifications. It is visited by many people, from the above tradition. A gentleman whom I accompanied was so charmed with the old tree, that he gave it the name of Owen Glendwr's Observatory.

At this time the tree was 25 feet 1 inch in girth, at 5 feet from the ground. Mr Parker continued: 'Within the hollow of the tree, at the bottom, there is sufficient room for at least half a dozen to take a snug dinner.'

John F. M. Dovaston of Westfelton (owner of the famed pendulous yew) corresponded with J. C. Loudon about the oak in 1838, bemoaning the fact that it had recently been 'taken within the grounds of a very chastely ornamented house, built in the ancient fancy Gothic'. While Dovaston conceded that the overall effect of the new property on the appearance of Shelton was beneficial, he believed that there were…

… some who will think it [the oak] *has lost much of its grotesque and commanding wildness, now surrounded with shrubberies, dressed grass-plots, and gravel walks; since it towered with rude but majestic grandeur over groups of gipsies, cattle or casual figures, amid the furze, bushes, and wild-flowers of a rough uncultured heath.*

The harsh reality of the Glendower tradition is that the tree stood almost four miles from the battlefield, as the crow flies, which would have made a strategic overview of the situation well nigh impossible. The tree only just hobbled into the twentieth century, since Edwardian postcards picture it as a moribund hulk, wreathed in ivy. By 1940 it was said to be dead, and by the 1950s the old stump was removed to facilitate a road improvement scheme on the A5. An acorn collected from the old oak in the 1880s was planted in the Dingle in the Quarry, thus perpetuating the genetic line.

THE GOSPEL OAK AT GRENDON BISHOP

WHEN I FIRST HEARD ABOUT THIS TREE IN 2005 I was given no name; I was only told that it was an extremely large oak and that I would be well advised to go up and see it. A nearby tree surgeon, a man who must have seen many remarkable trees, told me of this impressive oak. Even though it is barely six miles from home, I still put off my visit. Part of this may boil down to living in Herefordshire for too long, where the oak is frequently dubbed 'The Herefordshire Weed'.

Then, one day, my octogenarian neighbour stopped me in the lane to tell me of a huge hollow oak on the farm where she grew up, and how she and her siblings used to play inside it when they were children. The penny dropped – this must surely be the same tree. She had always known it as 'The Gospel Oak'.

The following day found me striding down the fields of Newbury Farm with the owner. I knew instantly that this must surely be one of the largest oaks in Britain, and even though the massive hollow bole was effectively a craggy old wooden wall, it's overall vitality was undeniable. Together, we measured the tree's girth at chest height and discovered that it was 42 feet around! This made it the joint record holder as the largest English oak in Britain – indeed Europe – equal only to the famous Bowthorpe Oak in Lincolnshire. The owner was astounded, and said, 'It's just always been there, simply a well-loved member of the family; we had no idea of its significance.' The Gospel Oak has managed itself very well for perhaps 1,000 years, maybe more. The only assistance it has received was the occasional pollarding. The big question now is whether or not to pollard again. Oaks that have not been touched for a hundred years or more can be traumatised by this, so if this is the chosen route, it will have to be a gradual process.

The shape of the Grendon Bishop Gospel Oak seems to lend itself perfectly to being a natural pulpit, from where a clergyman might ascend and preach to an assembled crowd. It would be fascinating to know whether local history records evidence of this event. One suspects that most clergy kept their feet firmly on the ground and simply preached beneath the tree.

When I first visited back in 2005 there was no recognised right of way for the public to access the tree, so for a few years I had to be slightly dark and mysterious about revealing its exact location. Happily, this has now changed and Jeremy has opened up a public bridleway right past the oak. The lesson I learned is that when someone tells you about a special tree, go and see it straight away; it may be 1,000 years old, but a gale might tear it asunder tomorrow.

OPPOSITE TOP: The Gospel Oak, Grendon Bishop, in winter.

OPPOSITE BOTTOM: The Gospel Oak bole with the author gives a sense of scale to this massive old tree.

JACK <u>of</u> KENT'S OAK

KENTCHURCH COURT IS THE HANDSOME ANCESTRAL HOME of the Scudamore family, owned by them for almost 1,000 years; situated close to the confluence of the Dore and Monnow rivers, and the Welsh border crossing between Hereford and Abergavenny. The origins of the house are eleventh century, but externally most of its appearance today is the result of extensive remodelling by John Nash at the turn of the eighteenth century. Originally, the parkland was a royal hunting ground owned by the Knights Templar, but the park was purchased by the family about 500 years ago from the Knights Hospitallers of Dinmore. Since that time, the park has changed very little. Stretching eastwards to the foot of Garway Hill, it presents open lawns for the fallow deer (around 250 of them at present) to graze, interspersed with dense covert clumps of old and gnarled hawthorns, as well as some stupendous open-grown field maples, sweet chestnuts and oaks – notably the famous Jack of Kent or Jackie Kemp's Oak.

There are also many individual large yew trees dotted across the park, some almost certainly in excess of 1,000 years old. A long-standing superstition on the estate is that it bodes extremely bad luck to fell a yew, holding a threat of instant dismissal. Almost certainly these trees are remnants of the woodland cover from which the park was carved out many centuries ago. Step outside the park perimeter and many more fine oaks are encountered and, as one climbs the hill, negotiating old quarries, from which the very stones of the house must have been cut, there are some stupendous old small-leaved limes clinging to the rock faces.

One of the largest oaks in the land stands sentinel on the lip of the southern escarpment that sweeps down into the centre of the park. Jack of Kent's Oak has a massive bulk, girthing at a little over 37 feet, is stag headed, but with a very healthy crown, and has been estimated to be about 950 years old. Its location might make it quite vulnerable to the elements, but it is so broad, with big buttressing roots grabbing the hillside and such a low centre of gravity, that it would take a titanic force to topple this tree.

Who was Jack of Kent? Sometimes called Jack o' Kent or Jack-a-Kent, he appears in various folk guises along the Welsh borders – sometimes described as a wild-eyed priest, sometimes a wizard, he takes on the Devil with many different deals or tasks, but always manages to outwit him. One local story describes how Jack asked the Devil to help him build a bridge over the River Monnow to Kentchurch in one night, and in return the Devil could have the soul of the first one to cross the bridge. Once completed, Jack threw a bone across the bridge and a hungry dog rushed over after it, thus sparing a human life. Another tale tells how Jack

OPPOSITE: The author and Jack of Kent's Oak.

BELOW: An oil painting portrait, dated *c.*1400, reputed to be Sion Cent (Jack of Kent). It is said to have been painted by Flemish master Jan Van Eyck (1385–1441). Other suggestions for the subject have been Sir John Oldcastle, Sir John Scudamore or even Owain Glyndŵr. Where was the ruined castle on the hill and the fortified house in the middle distance, and is there a significance to the sapling? Much mystery surrounds this painting, but for now it holds the association with Jack of Kent.

ABOVE: Medieval deer park
at Kentchurch Court, with an
abundance of old hawthorn for
game cover. Jack of Kent's Oak
stands on the ridge in the
middle distance.

OPPOSITE: Jack of Kent's Oak
on a chilly winter morning in
Kentchurch deer park. I see a
face deep-set within the burry
old bole; perhaps the spirit of
the great old tree watching
over the estate and the family.

formed a pact with the Devil to tend his crops. Jack would plant the crop and the Devil would make sure plenty of sun and rain would help it grow. Jack asked the Devil what share of the crop he wanted – tops or butts? The Devil chose the tops, thinking he would get all the grain and Jack would be left with the straw. Jack planted turnips and the Devil got the leaves. The following year the Devil tried to outwit Jack and chose butts, but this time Jack planted wheat and the Devil lost out again. Essentially, this is the story of good triumphing over evil, albeit in a rather crafty manner. At Kentchurch Court, a tradition persisted for many years that Jack of Kent supposedly kept 'magic horses' in the cellars in case the need should ever arise for a quick getaway from the Devil.

The alternative name for the tree is Jackie (or Jack) Kemp's (or Kent's) Oak. Unravelling who this person might actually have been is something of a conundrum, for in the fifteenth century many educated men with remarkably similar names come to light, but it is most likely to have been a corruption of Siôn Cent, a Welsh-language poet (c.1400–1435). An oil painting from this period, of a middle-aged man in monkish robes, resides at Kentchurch. Could he be Siôn Cent? Nobody seems to know for sure. Siôn Cent was said to have been a chaplain to the Scudamores and a tutor to their children, travelled abroad, been highly educated, translated the Bible into Welsh, and spent much time beneath the great oak tree writing his poetry.

THE MONARCH

F EW WILL HAVE HEARD OF THE MONARCH, although the term Monarch Oak has been often used as a generic, even poetic term to denote the majestic stature of our national tree. Tucked away in a corner of the old deer park at Holme Lacy, this Monarch Oak might have been considered a 'lost' great oak until a few years back.

Ploughing through the transactions of the Woolhope Naturalists' Field Club, a Hereford society made up of historians, geologists, archaeologists, and naturalists and established in 1851, revealed that a comprehensive survey of the county's remarkable trees had been undertaken in around 1870. Mr Ladmore & Son had been engaged as official photographers for the survey, to provide a visual record of many of the trees for posterity. In several annual volumes of the transactions, albumen prints were tipped into the pages, leaving a superb, accurate record.

The Scudamore family first acquired the Holme Lacy Estate through marriage in 1354. The deer park here probably pre-dates John Scudamore's construction of the first mansion in the early sixteenth century (the present house, now a hotel, was built in 1672). Although Christopher Saxton's (c.1540–1610) map of 1577 shows a park, certainly the oldest trees encountered today are well in excess of 450 years old. Most of the remaining oaks are out-grown pollards, so clearly a wood-pasture regime must once have prevailed here, whether as a park or part of a hunting forest.

Among the Woolhope transactions is a reference and photograph of 'The Monarch', which is described as a 'noble, well-balanced tree [that] stands on the ridge of Holme Lacy Park'. The entry continued to describe the tree in great detail:

The circumference of the bole at 5 feet from the ground is 21 ft. 10 in. The exact height, by Mr Well's Clinometer, is 97 ft. 6 in., and the diametric spread of its foliage is, north and south 102 ft., and east and west 97 ft. The tree is now rather past its prime. A swarm of bees has located itself in one place; fungus appears here and there on the trunk; and two or three small boughs are broken off.

In the photograph two members of the club strike a formal pose beneath the Monarch. One assumes that this name already appertained to the tree, but it is also possible that the club created the name.

I set out one evening to investigate the tree for myself. To my joy, there it was! The ramification of the boughs was conclusive. There, on the highest point of ground, stood the superb sessile oak, with a fine spreading crown and seemingly in the best of health. This Monarch will rule the park for a good while longer.

SHIPBUILDING

'The particular, and most valued qualities of the oak, are hardiness and toughness… it is supposed that no species of wood, at least no species of timber, is possessed of both these qualities together in so great a degree, as British oak. Almost all arts and manufactures are indebted to it; but in ship-building, and bearing burdens, its elasticity, and strength are applied to most advantage… it is not the erect, stately tree, that is always the most useful in ship-building; but more often the crooked one, forming short turns, and elbows, which the shipwrights and carpenters commonly call knee-timber.'

WILLIAM GILPIN, 1791

THE LATE EIGHTEENTH CENTURY WAS A PERIOD of unprecedented imperial expansion – Britain required ever more trading vessels that were large and capable enough to travel around the world. There was also a need to maintain a powerful navy to defend our mercantile interests as well as protect our sovereignty. Oliver Rackham's claim that about half of the timber ships ever built in Britain were constructed between 1800 and 1860 relays the intensity of shipbuilding around this time. Thereafter, a rapid decline in the use of timber with increased production of ironclad vessels.

For 4,000 years, oak has been used around the coast of Britain to build seafaring vessels of all types and sizes. It was always quite simply the best wood available for the purpose. Records indicate that many small dugout boats have been found throughout Britain, but the earliest vessels constructed of oak planks come from a group of three boats discovered at North Ferriby in East Yorkshire in the mid-twentieth century, the oldest of which has been carbon dated to 2030–1780 BC. These boats were built with cleft oak boards that were stitched together with yew withies. Gaps were caulked with moss and capped with oak laths to make the boats watertight. A replica of the first and most complete of these boats, made using three large oak trees, Bronze Age techniques, and replica tools, was built by the National Maritime Museum Cornwall, and successfully launched in Falmouth in March 2013. Another Bronze Age boat of similar construction was discovered during road-building work in Dover in 1992, and is on display in Dover Museum. It would seem that this technique of boat building continued relatively unchanged for a couple of thousand years.

OPPOSITE: The *Cutty Sark* at Greenwich in 1978. Designed for speed, she was built in 1869 as a tea clipper for the trade with China. By this time marine design was advancing apace with the increased use of iron hulls and the advent of steam power. The *Cutty Sark* has an iron internal frame and timber construction is principally of East India teak and American rock elm, but English oak was still deemed to be the best choice for the ship's rudder.

ABOVE: The replica of a Bronze Age boat, based on those found at North Ferriby in the mid-twentieth century, being built by volunteers at the National Maritime Museum Cornwall.

Even though construction appeared rudimentary, and the boats would have been propelled by paddle rather than sail, it is believed that these boats were perfectly capable of making long sea crossings. Ships with sails are believed to have arisen some time around 250 BC in northern Europe.

Roman merchant ships excavated in the Thames have shown that by the second century, ship construction consisted of oak boards laid edge to edge (known as carvel construction), and nailed to a frame. This technique was predominantly Middle Eastern in origin and had obviously filtered through the Mediterranean into the Roman Empire. As opposed to the clinker-built (boards overlapping) vessels that were favoured by the Vikings and the Anglo-Saxons, carvel-built vessels were stronger, could be built on a larger scale, and could carry greater loads, and were thus much better suited to long ocean voyages.

In 1418, the *Grace Dieu* was completed for Henry V as his flagship. She was the largest ship of that period, a remarkable 218 feet long, with a keel of 112 feet, still clinker-built with three overlapping layers. After the two years that it had taken to build her, she put to sea only once, in 1420. The assumption must be that such a large clinker-built ship was unseaworthy. The ship lay moored in the River Hamble until 1439, when she was burnt after a lightning strike. By the time the *Mary Rose*, an English carrack, a purpose-built warship, was launched in 1511, the lessons had been learnt. Although she accidentally sank during an engagement with the French in the Solent in 1545, she was salvaged by the Mary Rose Trust in 1982. We now have first-hand evidence of her construction: carvel-planked, with oak boards fastened to the oak frames with wooden treenails. The treenails or trenails, which are wooden pins or dowels, swell in water to make a tight fit. Some of these pins were of impressive proportions, as large as 36 inches long and 2 inches in diameter. Great skill was required to drill the right-sized hole and then drive the trenail through.

Around this time, the first cannon were being cast by the ironworks in the Sussex Weald, which created a conflict of interest around the supply of oak. The iron masters ordered up vast quantities of oak wood charcoal, while the shipbuilders demanded larger oaks for their purposes. In 1543, Henry VIII instituted his Statute of Woods, which commanded woodland owners to retain twelve standard oaks in every acre. The concern about the availability of oak for shipbuilding soon became a problem. In 1562 Thomas Tusser complained that 'men were more studious to cut down than to plant'. Queen Elizabeth tried to place restrictions on the use of oak for charcoal by banning the felling of oak trees of more than a foot in diameter within fourteen miles of the coast.

As the seventeenth and eighteenth centuries progressed, ships became larger, faster, more manoeuvrable, and capable of carrying greater firepower. A plethora of treatises concerned with the planting and management of oak trees to produce timber suitable for the naval demand began to appear in print. A bewildering

assortment of claims for the acreage of oak woods required to yield a certain tonnage of timber to satisfy the needs of building specific types of vessels also started to emerge.

Two particular kinds of oak were required to build a ship, as Prideaux John Selby (1842) asserts:

> *Timber for naval purposes is not confined to planking, or that portion of the tree produced by a long straight trunk; the knees and bends formed by the angles the side branches and limbs make with the main stem of the tree, are also of paramount importance in naval architecture, and these are always procured in the greatest perfection from trees that have grown in their natural and expansive form, and hence it is that hedge-row Oak in general affords so large a supply of this valuable denomination of timber.*

The natural ramification of English oak seems to have been better suited to the custom pieces required for ship frames, leading to the erroneous belief that the quality of English oak was preferred to that of sessile. It was simply that the English oak grew naturally in the necessary forms. The act of pollarding also encouraged oaks to regenerate with the desired types of boughs. Some landowners in the late eighteenth and early nineteenth centuries even experimented with training young oaks into the shapes that might be required of them in the future. The shipyard buyers were constantly out scouring the land for the right sort of oaks.

Felling trees for use in shipbuilding had to be done with extreme care in order not to injure the crooks in the branches. South describes the felling of the Langley Oak, in the New Forest in 1758, as such:

The knees and crooks were cut off, one by one, whilst the tree was standing, and lowered by tackles, to prevent their breaking. The two largest arms were sawed off at such distances from the bole as to make first rate knees; scaffolds were then erected, and two saw-pits being braced together, the body was first cut across, half through, at the bottom, and then sawed down the middle, perpendicularly, between the two stumps of arms that had been left, at the end of one of which stood a perpendicular bough, bigger than most timber trees. To prevent this being injured, a bed was made of some hundred faggots, to catch it when it fell.

The Stuart period (1603–1714) saw a gradual decline in the stocks of large oaks. This was largely due to the monarchs' demands for funds, which meant that many woods and forests were simply sold off. No concerted effort to replant took place and, during the Commonwealth, the government simply took whatever oak it needed from royal forests and the estates of sympathisers. It was then hardly surprising that shortly after the Restoration of Charles II, another round of despair at the state of the nation's oak reserves, and worries about the threat to naval supplies, spawned what is considered to be one of the most iconic books about Britain's trees. In 1660, John Evelyn had been a founding member of the Royal Society, and in 1662 he delivered his paper 'Sylva, or a Discourse of Forest-Trees and the Propagation of Timber in His Majesty's Dominion' in an attempt to stimulate awareness of Britain's looming plight and encourage landowners to plant trees. The first edition of *Sylva* was published in 1664, and would go to twelve editions by 1825. One assumes that every time the title was rolled out, a surge of tree planting resulted.

From the very beginning of his text, Evelyn comes straight to the point:

Since there is nothing which seems more fatally to threaten a weakening, if not a dissolution, of the strength of this famous and flourishing nation, than the sensible and notorious decay of her wooden walls, when, either through time, negligence, or other accident, the present navy shall be worn out and impaired; it has been a very worthy and seasonable advertisement in the honourable the principal Officers and Commissioners, what they have lately suggested to this illustrious Society for the timely prevention and redress of this intolerable defect.

Leading by example, in 1669 Charles II issued a royal mandate to plant 300 acres of the New Forest with oak. This seems to have encouraged a nationwide effort to plant trees, which was endorsed by Evelyn in his address to the king in 1678:

I need not acquaint your Majesty how many millions of timber-trees, beside infinite others, have been propagated and planted throughout your vast dominions, at the instigation, and by the sole direction of this work.

MR. LAIRD'S SHIP-BUILDING YARD, LIVERPOOL.

One must remember that planting oaks that are required to build very large ships is far from a speedy process. It takes something like 120 years before a tree can be considered for this purpose and, after felling, the timber must be allowed to season. It didn't help the shipbuilding supply when catastrophic events like the Great Fire of London resulted in a high demand for oak timber to rebuild the city. Add to this natural disasters like the great storm of 1703, which lasted a whole week (not just the single night, like 1987) and took out many thousands of mature oaks, as well as the lives of 8,000 people. The eighteenth century was littered with continual problems, not just because of the scarcity of larger-scale timber, but because the use of unseasoned, green oak and timber that included sapwood meant that ships began to rot in the water, and had very short working lives. With smaller vessels this was not so much of an issue, as smaller trees could still provide enough heartwood to make sturdy ships.

The logistics of transporting the largest oak timbers to the shipyards could be something of a nightmare and, where possible, timbers were floated downriver and by sea to their destination. Overland journeys were lengthy and added to the expense of the timber. Depending on how passable the roads were due to the weather, the biggest timbers often took two or three years to reach the shipyard, which seems inconceivable in today's high-speed world.

Perhaps the widespread initiative to plant trees, and oaks in particular, was misplaced, or maybe the huge increase in demand for oak simply outstripped

ABOVE: Mr Laird's ship-building yard, Liverpool, 1856. Lots of activity in the yard with several vessels, seemingly of timber construction, in view and good stocks of timber in the foreground. From about this period shipbuilding moved into the new era of iron and steel, and Lairds was no exception. Early images of shipyards at work are difficult to find, which makes this wood engraving from *The Illustrated London News* rather special.

ABOVE: *The Fowey River at Mixtow* by James Valentine, *c.*1885, with sailing ships moored in the river. The relatively slow shutter speeds of Victorian cameras meant that such photographs of ships were more successful than those taken of them at sea. The artists could still steal a march on the photographers.

available supplies. Whatever the case, by 1776 Dr Hunter expresses another round of concern in the notes to his own edition of Evelyn's *Silva*:

> ... *the cutting down of all kinds of wood is become so general, that unless some effectual remedy be soon applied, it is more probable that very little full-grown timber will be left in this island for the use of the shipbuilder. The simple apprehension that this nation will, at some distant period, feel this great calamity, cannot but occasion some uneasiness in the minds of those who wish well to their country.*

As the eighteenth century progressed, so did the demands of the merchant shipping fleets, notably the East India Company, who were building ships almost as big as the Royal Navy. This put them in direct competition for the largest and best oak timber. The scarcity of good compass timber meant that experiments were made with steaming timber into the required knee shape. This was certainly a better alternative to cutting them out of straight timber, which meant exposing the grain. By the end of the century, it was plainly evident that other commercial pressures were in serious competition for oak wood. Many trees did not grow to maturity because of the demand for tan bark and charcoal, so coppice provided quicker returns to owners. As the price of corn rose, so many landowners converted woodland into arable land and, as a consequence, many hedgerows and their useful oaks were grubbed out to enlarge these fields.

Several accounts reveal the prodigious amount of timber required for a single warship. *The Report of the Commissioners of Land Revenue* respecting timber, published by the House of Commons in 1812, states that it required 'three thousand loads of timber or two thousand well-grown oak trees to build a seventy-four-gun ship'. If we work on the principle of forty mature oaks to the acre (a liberal estimate, assuming the trees are all fit for shipbuilding), then it would take fifty acres of oak grown over at least a century to make a single seventy-four. However, Rackham states that the main problem for the navy was not accessibility to good oak, but the lack of funds to purchase it. He also questions the massive quantities of timber that were entering the yards, as this hardly reconciles with the amount used in the finished vessels. His calculations reveal that about two-thirds of the timber went back out of the yards as a longstanding perquisite for the shipwrights; known as 'chips', these were the offcuts that remained after the main pieces had been cut.

Probably the most famous ship of all time is Nelson's flagship, HMS *Victory*. Admiralty records have left us with an extremely detailed description of her construction and the costs involved. Chatham Dockyard received the warrant to build the ship in 1759, she was launched in 1765, and commissioned for action in 1778. It took the timber of 6,000 trees to build her, and roughly 90 per cent of this was oak. Other timbers included elm, almost certainly for the keel, fir, pine, and spruce for the masts and yards. She cost £63,176 to build, which equates to a value of about £10 million today. The *Victory* is 226 feet long and 52 feet wide, and during her thirty-two years in service was renowned as one of the fastest first-rate ships of the line, with excellent handling. As a tourist attraction today, it's difficult to imagine the ship in the heat of battle at Trafalgar in 1805. Naval engagements were brutal affairs, and at Trafalgar the casualties on this ship alone amounted to fifty-seven killed and 102 wounded out of a complement of about 800 men. The *Victory* is now in a decidedly fragile state and recent estimates suggest that she will need about £50 million spent in restoration over the next fifteen years.

Although numerous treatises and manuals of forestry were published in the eighteenth and early nineteenth centuries, often enjoining landowners with a patriotic conscience to plant and tend oaks for the future, they could have little notion that by the mid-nineteenth century, the tide would turn decisively in favour of iron and steel construction.

As the nineteenth century progressed, different timbers – including imports – came into play in maritime construction. At the beginning of the century, the 4th Duke of Atholl had commissioned a fine brig, constructed of larch timber from his estate. Named the *Larch*, she was a great success; so much so that between 1816 and 1820, a frigate of twenty-eight guns was laid down at Woolwich, the first British warship constructed entirely of larch and named the *Athole*. It's a mystery why larch was not used more often, as it did not corrode iron fittings (as oak eventually does), it was less prone to shrinkage (thus requiring less caulking maintenance), and did not splinter under cannon fire (thus reducing casualties).

OPPOSITE: Lord Nelson's flagship HMS *Victory* in dry dock at Portsmouth.

BELOW: *Fishing boats off Penzance* by James Valentine, c.1885.

On many other vessels, pitch pine was often used for the planking and exotic timbers such as teak and mahogany were also used; the remarkable density of these woods making them virtually impervious to water. A restoration project observed at Bristol Docks in the 1980s used teak planking sawn from salvaged timber that had lain beneath the Irish Sea since 1914. Less than one-quarter of an inch from the surface, it was still perfect. If these alternative timbers had been tried or introduced earlier, perhaps the perennial scare about the scarcity of oak could have been allayed.

By the end of the nineteenth century, wooden shipbuilding was in serious decline, although oak was still used for small fishing vessels, barges, and pleasure craft. One of the very last large ships to be built substantially of oak was Captain Scott's *Discovery*, which was used for his first expedition to the Antarctic between 1901 and 1904. Built in Dundee at the only shipyard that could be found at the time with the necessary skills, the choice of a wooden ship in an age of iron and steel surprised many, but Scott firmly believed that it would perform better in the pack ice, and his choice was a wise one since *Discovery* withstood two years locked in the ice before bringing everyone safely home. Today she is moored in her home port of Dundee, reminding everyone of the indomitable spirit of one of our greatest explorers and the fine craftsmanship of the shipbuilders of yore.

WITHIN THE TRUNK OF THIS VENERABLE OAK (ACCORDING TO WELCH TRADITION) THE BODY OF HOWEL SELE,
A POWERFUL CHIEFTAIN, RESIDING AT NANNAU, IN MERIONETHSHIRE, WAS IMMURED, BY ORDER OF HIS RIVAL
OWEN GLYNDWR.—See *PENNANT, Vol. I. p.* 348.

THE ORIGINAL SKETCH FROM WHICH THIS ETCHING IS MADE, WAS DRAWN FROM NATURE ON THE 27TH DAY
OF JULY, 1813, BY SIR RICHARD COLT HOARE, Bart. AND ON THE SAME NIGHT, THIS AGED TREE FELL TO THE
GROUND. IT WAS SITUATED WITHIN THE KITCHEN GARDEN WALLS OF SIR ROBERT WILLIAMS VAUGHAN, Bart.
AT NANNAU, NEAR DOLGELLE.

THE NANNAU OAK, THE SPIRIT'S BLASTED TREE

OPPOSITE: A fine etching made of the Nannau Oak, after the original sketch by Sir Richard Colt Hoare, shortly after it fell in 1813.

FEW TREES IN THE LAND CAN EVOKE such bloodthirsty and terrifying images as the infamous Nannau Oak, which once grew on the wild hills of the Nannau Estate near Dolgellau in Gwynedd. It is exactly 200 years since the old tree fell, and yet it has retained a prominent place in Welsh folklore ever since.

There are many mentions of the tree in early nineteenth-century books. William Hone provides what is perhaps the most comprehensive gathering of references to the tree's inauspicious past in his *The Every-Day Book* (1830), including a dramatic stanza from the writings of Mrs Radcliffe, who sets the scene:

> *It stood alone, a wither'd oak*
> *Its shadow fled, its branches broke;*
> *Its riven trunk was knotted round,*
> *Its gnarled roots o'erspread the ground*
> *Honours that were from tempests won,*
> *In generations long since gone,*
> *A scanty foliage yet was seen,*
> *Wreathing its hoary brows with green,*
> *Like to a crown of victory*
> *On some old warrior's forehead grey,*
> *And, as it stood, it seem'd to speak*
> *To winter winds in murmurs weak,*
> *Of times that long had passed it by*
> *And left it desolate, to sigh*
> *Of what it was, and seem'd to wail,*
> *A shadeless spectre, shapeless, pale.*

The tree's gruesome history stems from a bitter enmity between Owain Glyndŵr and his cousin Howel Sele, Lord of Nannau. Glyndŵr, who laid claim to the throne of Wales, was passionately opposed to the invading armies of Henry IV, and knew that Howel Sele, if not blatantly in league with the House of Lancaster, had leanings towards the English monarchy. This infuriated Glyndŵr, and in 1402 (or 1404, dates vary) he made it his business to visit Nannau to thrash out their differences. It is said that the Abbot of Cymmer brought the two men together in hope of reconciliation and, with peace apparently brokered, the two men vowed to hunt together, but all was not well. It is said that Owain spied a doe feeding and remarked to Howel that this should be a fine mark for him. Howel bent his bow, aimed at the doe, but at the last moment turned and let fly his arrow at Owain's breast. Fortunately the armour beneath his clothes saved him from harm, but enraged by this treachery, Glyndŵr slew Howel Sele and burnt his house. With the assistance of his companion Madoc, Glyndŵr then concealed the body in the hollow oak. They then hurried away from Nannau, as they knew that Howel Sele's family would soon send out a search party. Search they did, but nothing was found of their slain lord.

Accounts vary concerning the discovery of Howel Sele's body. Some say that ten years later, Glyndŵr beseeched Madoc from his deathbed to return to Nannau to reveal the fate of Howel Sele to his family. Another conclusion to the story relates how, thirty years later, one of Howel's retainers was out hunting when he spied a heron perched atop the old oak. He levelled his crossbow and the heron fell transfixed into the hollow trunk. The hunter climbed down inside the tree to retrieve his quarry, only to make the alarming discovery of the skeleton of his erstwhile master. A long poem entitled 'The Spirit's Blasted Tree' (author unknown) relates the whole tragic tale, as if narrated by Madoc:

> *I marked a broad and blasted oak,*
> *Scorched by the lightning's livid glare*
> *Hollow its stem from branch to root,*
> *And all its shrivelled arms were bare.*
>
> *Be this, I cried, his proper grave! –*
> *(The thought in me was deadly sin.)*
> *Aloft we raised the hapless chief,*
> *And dropped his bleeding corpse within.*

Upon his return to Nannau, Madoc takes Howel Sele's horror-struck wife and her retinue to the fateful resting place:

> *He led them near the blasted oak,*
> *Then, conscious, from the scene withdrew;*
> *Te peasant's work with trembling haste,*
> *And lay the whitened bones to view! –*
>
> *Back they recoiled! – the right hand still,*
> *Contracted, grasped a rusty sword;*
> *Which erst in many a battle gleamed,*
> *And proudly decked their slaughtered lord.*

Stark and horrendous images such as those depicted in 'The Spirit's Blasted Tree' helped to lend the oak its ghastly, haunted reputation. The traveller Thomas Pennant, visiting in the late eighteenth century, described it with eloquence:

On the road side is a venerable oak in its last stage of decay, and pierced by age into the form of a gothic arch; yet its present growth is twenty-seven feet and a half. The name is very classical, 'Derwen Ceubren yr Ellyll,' 'the hollow oak, the haunt of demons.' How often has not warm fancy seen the fairy tribe revel round its trunk! Or may not the visionary eye have seen the Hamadryad burst from the bark of its coeval tree.

Remarkably, there is a detailed account relating how the old oak finally fell on the night of 27–28 July 1813, immediately after the artist Sir Richard Colt Hoare had completed his sketch of the venerable tree. Colt Hoare recalled the following:

During a visit to Sir Robert Vaughan, in the year 1813, this aged tree, mentioned by Mr. Pennant, attracted my notice; and, on the morning of the 27ᵗʰ July I made a drawing of it, in one of the most sultry days I ever felt; the succeeding night was equally hot, and on the same night this venerable oak fell to the ground.

The original watercolour, framed in the wood of the fallen tree, is still on display at Colt Hoare's family home of Stourhead, Wiltshire. Various etchings and engravings, mainly derived from this image, were published of the old tree, versions of which appear as prints and illustrations in several books of the period.

The fall of the tree was not the end of the story, for the timber was taken and crafted into numerous beautiful items such as tables, cabinets, and drinking vessels. Among these is a set of six superb silver-mounted acorn-shaped cups (hallmarked London 1816) inscribed 'Ceubren yr Ellyll a Syrthiodd I lawr yr 28 ain O Orphenaf 1813' (The Hollow Tree of the Demon which fell on the 28ᵗʰ of July 1813), as well as a superb silver-mounted oak table seal (London 1817) and many snuffboxes, which were 'distributed among the Baronet's friends, and highly are they valued by their fortunate posessors' [sic]. The cups were reputedly used as part of the celebrations for the coming-of-age of Robert Williames Vaughan of Nannau, a direct descendant of Howel Sele, on 25 June 1824. These, and several other items of treen, were eventually acquired by the National Museum of Wales, where they reside to this day.

The Nannau Estate exists to this day, and a recent CADW report reveals that a pillar in the old kitchen garden is supposed to mark the spot where the tree once stood. On a map of 1889 a sundial marked the spot, but that has now gone. Images from antiquity and the vivid accounts of its sad story will forever keep this tree alive in Welsh folklore.

THE PONTFADOG OAK

NTIL 18 APRIL 2013, WHAT HAD FOR OVER A CENTURY been renowned as the largest and oldest oak in Wales, stood behind a hillside farmhouse above the village of Pontfadog in the Ceiriog Valley. A sessile oak, this great old stager was considered by some to be about 1,200 years old. It must have already been a substantial tree in 1165, when tradition asserts that a Welsh army raised by Owain Gwynedd (and an alliance of Welsh princes) in response to Henry II's invading army, gathered beneath this tree before the Battle of Crogen further down the valley. There is no way of verifying this claim, but the tree had certainly long served as a historic and patriotic rallying point.

In 1850, the owner of the tree discovered two gold chisels that had been hidden in the trunk. They were apparently on view locally in 1880, but their subsequent fate is unknown. It seems strange to craft a chisel out of such a soft metal, but perhaps these served some symbolic importance. At the turn of the century the fashion for sending postcards brought forth a delightful image of a little lad standing beneath the great tree, from which it appears that the tree's trunk has now reduced quite considerably in volume. Whether this was down to pollarding, or boughs simply falling off or rotting away is unknown.

The present owner recalls that, as a girl in 1963, she heard a loud noise one night. She thought that the chimney had fallen over on the farmhouse, but discovered in the morning that a large limb had broken off the tree and fallen on to the roof. Since then the tree has been in a gradual state of deterioration. On 18 April 2013, fate intervened in the form of 80 mph gusts of wind. When the crushed and shattered corpse of the tree was examined, a remarkable lack of live root connection was discovered – it had been a miracle that the tree had stood and lived for so long.

An Edwardian postcard claimed the Pontfadog Oak to be 'the largest oak in the United Kingdom, 17 yards around', a measurement probably taken at ground level. In truth, the sessile oak at Marton in Cheshire probably just pips this tree to the record post, but before it fell it was certainly still the largest oak in Wales, based on its girth measurement of 42 feet 5 inches, at 5 feet above ground.

The image of the tree was adopted as a logo for Pontfadog Primary School, the local children always starting their annual Easter egg hunt from the tree, looking for eggs hidden in its numerous nooks and crannies. Even the local Brownies used to recite their promise beneath it. Its loss will be sadly borne by the village and the family who owned it for five generations.

OPPOSITE: The Pontfadog Oak in November 2012, less than six months before it fell.

BELOW: The crumpled bole of the Pontfadog Oak, blown down in April 2013.

THE GOLYNOS OAK

THE GREAT GOLYNOS (OR GELONOS) OAK sadly no longer stands. A detailed account of its felling during an era when oak timber was prized for shipbuilding, and oak bark, used for tanning, was often more valuable than the wood itself, gives a fascinating insight into the timber trade of 200 years ago.

The ubiquitous J. C. Loudon provides a detailed account of the tree's felling and conversion in his *Arboretum et Fruticetum Britannicum* of 1838:

> The Gelonos Oak, felled in Monmouthshire, A.D. 1810, has been often cited as an example of vast ligneous production. The bark was sold by the merchant for the scarcely credible sum of £200. This oak was purchased by Mr. Thomas Harrison for 100 guineas, under the apprehension of its being unsound; but Burnet tells us that it was resold, while still standing, for £405; and that the cost of converting it was £82; amounting altogether to £487: it was subsequently resold for £675. There were at least 400 rings or traces of annual growth, within its mighty trunk.
>
> The Gelonos Oak, which was cut down in 1810, grew about four miles from Newport, in Monmouthshire. The main trunk was 10 ft. long, and produced 450 cubic feet of timber; 1 limb, 355 ft.; 1 ditto, 472 ft.; 1 ditto, 113 ft; and 6 other limbs, of inferior size, averaged 93 ft. each; making a total of 2426 cubic feet of convertible timber. The bark was estimated at 6 tons; but, as some of the very heavy body bark was stolen out of the barge at Newport, the exact weight is not known. Five men were 20 days stripping and cutting down this tree; and two sawyers were 5 months converting it, without losing a day, Sundays excepted.

Edward Jesse expands on the felling in his *Gleanings in Natural History* (1834):

> It was felled in separate parts, and stages were erected for the workmen to stand on to cut down the valuable limbs. Previous to being felled it was divested of its brushwood, which was placed as a bed, to prevent the timber from bursting in falling. The main trunk was nine feet and a half in diameter, and consequently no saw could be found long enough to cut it down; two saws were therefore brazed together.

Much of the larger timber, itemised by Jesse in knees and futtocks, went to the Royal Navy Dockyard at Plymouth, while lesser timber was converted into cooper's staves. The tree was obviously something of a celebrity before it was felled, as several fine engravings and lithographs from the period attest; but it is uncertain whether anything over and above its great size attracted this notability.

OPPOSITE: The Golynos Oak drawn by Peter De Wint *c.*1800. Note the artist at work in the distance.

THE GOLYNOS OAK.

THE BUTTINGTON OAK

A SHORT WALK NORTH FROM THE VILLAGE OF BUTTINGTON, near Welshpool, along the eastern banks of the River Severn, will bring you to one of the most impressive oak trees in Wales. There are many oaks dotted around the fields hereabouts, but this behemoth outstrips them all; its massive, burry bole squatting resolutely in isolated splendour on the old water meadows.

Absolutely nothing has endowed this tree with any colourful associations: it does not appear in any archives or publications, and no mention is made of it in local hearsay or tradition. Suffice to say, the Buttington Oak is a huge English oak tree (*Quercus robur*). In the wake of the recent demise of the Pontfadog Oak, at 36 feet 2 inches, it is the second largest oak in Wales.

The Buttington Oak grows fairly close to the projected alignment of Offa's Dyke and may once have performed a role as a boundary tree although, quite clearly, even with a guesstimated age of around 1,000 years, it would not have existed in the eighth century when King Offa ordered the construction of the dyke. There are no obvious physical remains of Offa's Dyke at this particular location, and the boundaries between England and Wales will have moved back and forth over the centuries, making it difficult to determine with any certainty whether the tree was once an actual boundary tree. The present-day boundary is only a couple of miles to the east, and in the past the River Severn has performed boundary duties, so it would seem quite credible that the oak was at the very least a significant landmark.

It was only as recently as 2009 that the tree was recognised for its extreme size and antiquity by Veronica Henry, who logged her discovery with the Woodland Trust's Ancient Tree Hunt. A critical examination of the tree reveals it to be in the pink of health, although some might say the severe trampling around the base by livestock could eventually lead to deleterious consequences due to compaction. While this eventuality is possible, the tree has already survived many centuries, almost certainly serving as shade and protection for livestock during much of that time, with no visible signs of distress.

Ancient oak pollards like this raise the issue of how best to care for such trees. Clearly, well over a century ago the tree would have been pollarded on a regular basis, perhaps every twenty or thirty years, and this would have kept the tree in good health and a state of continual renewal. Conservationists are now hotly debating the best way forward for the management of such oaks.

OPPOSITE TOP: Highly valued by farmers for the shade and protection of their livestock, huge oaks such as this have an enduring role to play in the countryside.

OPPOSITE BOTTOM: The Buttington Oak in early morning mists along the River Severn.

OAK CRAFTS AND INDUSTRIES

Oak has been the ubiquitous provider to so many branches of industry that one could fill a book of this size with examples. I will try to cast a net across just a few of the principal strands in this chapter. Shipbuilding and building construction have traditionally been seen as the most important uses of oak (aspects which are addressed in separate chapters), but there are three other particularly important historical uses: The management of pigs by putting them out to pannage in the autumn months; the stripping of oak bark for use in the tanning industry; and the making of charcoal. All three are virtually redundant today. Most pigs are factory farmed, tanners rely on synthetic chemicals, and huge quantities of cheap charcoal are imported. Even so, a few people still believe in the pursuit of these traditional methods of production.

PANNAGE

There is a long, well-documented history of domestic pigs being turned out to forage in the woods for acorns and beech mast. This custom and right is known as pannage, and dates from a time well before the Norman Conquest. In his *The Oak* (1910), Charles Mosley states that 'during the seventh century King Ina enacted the Pannage Laws for the preservation of the forest, and regulating the right to keep swine therein'. The OED reveals that the word is late Middle English, from the Old French *pasnage*, from medieval Latin *pastionaticum*, from *pastio*, which means pasturing. In his *Treatise of the Forest Laws* (1717), John Manwood claims that pannage is derived from the Latin *pannagium*, more properly a gathering of money, or profits of the fruits of trees. The more commonly held current understanding is that pannage refers to the process of autumn foraging, rather than the financial settlement.

Pannage was usually a right that is exercised on common ground or sometimes in royal forests. The New Forest is one of the last places where this can be seen in operation today, and it is referred to as 'Common of mast'. In the nineteenth century, 'pannage month' used to last for about six weeks, and involved around 6,000 pigs in the forest. These days the period is usually around sixty days, but can be longer,

OPPOSITE TOP: *Forest swine* from Sir T. D. Lauder's edition of *Remarks on Forest Scenery* by William Gilpin, 1834.

OPPOSITE BOTTOM: Gathering acorns to plant, for human consumption or for livestock. A glorious wood engraving from 1868.

and is a period decreed by the Court of Verderers to coincide with variations in the seasonal fall of acorns. Usually there are around 200–600 pigs at pannage.

In his *Remarks on Forest Scenery* (1791), William Gilpin provides a detailed account of pannage undertaken close to his Boldrewood home in the New Forest. He observes how 'the method of treating hogs at this season of migration, and of reducing a large herd of these unmanageable brutes to perfect obedience and good government, is curious'. In effect, it would appear that the swineherds of the period had mastered a method of conditioning the pigs by first providing them with plentiful mast in an enclosure accompanied by the sound of his horn, so that they would then return each night to the safe haven, associating the summoning horn with food. Once they were trained to come in at the end of each day, the swineherd 'throws his sty open, and leaves them to cater for themselves; and from henceforward has little more trouble with them during the whole time of their migration'.

A few lines from the poet Robert Bloomfield (1766–1823) capture the start of the pannage season:

From oak to oak they run with eager haste,
And, wrangling, share the first delicious taste
Of fallen acorns; yet but thinly found,
Till the strong gale has shook them to the ground.

Acorns, particularly when they are still green, are actually harmful to deer, cattle, and horses and, in extreme cases can lead to death, so pigs provide a valuable service by scooping these up before other animals find them.

We know from frequent references in the Domesday Book (1086), that woodland was often measured in relation to the number of pigs it would fatten at pannage. Typical entries might include Mildetone (in the parish of Dorking, Surrey), where 'the wood yields nine hogs for pannage, and ten hogs for herbage', or Tandridge, where 'the wood yields forty hogs for pannage, and eleven for herbage'. The latter wood contained many more oaks, which explained the greater number of beasts at pannage, while the grazing rights, which were very similar between the two, might indicate roughly the same size of wood. Even tiny woods 'of one hog' get a mention in the Domesday Book. It was also a common custom for either a pig or a fee per head to be given to the lord of the manor as payment for the use of the wood.

Early illustrated manuscripts show images of men knocking down acorns for their pigs – typically the Queen Mary Psalter from the fourteenth century. In his *Sylva* (1664), John Evelyn avers that 'a peck of acorns a day, with a little bran, will make a hog, 'tis said, increase a pound weight per diem for two months together'.

There is also strong evidence to suggest that thousands of years back, humans used the acorn as a food source. Acorns are high in tannin, and thus rather bitter to the taste, but leaching them in water for a while disperses the concentration of tannins and makes them far more palatable. Records for 1116 show that times were extremely dire. The year was 'so wanting in mast that there was never heard such in all this land'. When crops failed as well, both livestock and the populace faced starvation. Times of hardship were not uncommon. Geoffrey Chaucer (1343–1400) mentions some who 'weren wonte lightlie to slaken his hunger at even with akehornes of okes'. Starvation overcomes such reservations of taste, as Charles Mosley indicates: 'Acorns as an article of human diet can scarce be said to have much temptation about them, but rather the reverse, from their austere and bitter taste.' A bizarre snippet from Evelyn's discourse about the oak, however, claims 'that those small young acorns which we find in the stock-doves craws are a delicious fare'. One wonders who might have been the first experiment with these delicate morsels!

In his *Oak – The Frame of Civilization* (2005), the American arborist and author William Bryant Logan embarks on a mission to trace the history of human consumption of acorns worldwide, using the generic term balanoculture to describe human subsistence from nuts. Accounts of dubious authenticity have repeated for almost 3,000 years that acorns were a staple of human consumption, but much myth and legend is interwoven with these tales. The universal frequency with which accounts of acorn consumption recur, however, convinces Logan of their importance and drives him to culinary experimentation. He concludes that food made from the flour ground from acorns, while tasting of next to nothing in its own right, imparts an excellent sense of constitutional well-being; an assuaging of hunger not to be ignored in a society that was staring at the spectre of starvation. Logan looks around the world and finds that acorns, while no longer a staple element, retain a place in the diet of many different cultures.

Usually ground into flour that would have been made into a bread, the nuts were also baked or roasted before grinding and used to adulterate coffee. As roasted snacks, along the lines of the peanut, acorns were consumed in southern Europe, but it is assumed that these were different species to our native oaks, which were somewhat sweeter and more palatable on their own. Oak leaves are also known to have been mixed with tea and tobacco. In *Rambles with Nature Students* (1899), Mrs Eliza Brightwen reveals:

> When dried, roasted, and ground into flour, a not unpalatable kind of coffee can be made of acorn kernels… I cannot say it had the aroma or flavour of coffee, but it made a fair substitute for it, and it is believed to be wholesome and strengthening.

TAN BARK

It is thought that the use of tannin or tannic acid to cure animal hides may go back to the Neolithic period. More detail about the use of bark in the process of tanning leather comes from the medieval period; the words tan, tanning, and tawny are all derived from Medieval Latin *tannare*, meaning 'to convert into leather'.

The rise in demand was slow, and for a long time bark was essentially a minor by-product of woodland produce. By the late eighteenth century the leather industry moved into a boom period that would last until about 1860. Although in the past the bark of several different trees has been used for tanning, including alder, birch, sweet chestnut, rowan, willow, spruce, larch, and hemlock, by far the most superior is that of oak, as it has the highest tannin content.

During the early nineteenth century, vast areas of coppiced oak woods became more valuable for bark production than for any other use of their timber. In fact, so lucrative was this market that many landowners planted oaks purely for coppice.

Stools were usually cut on a 20–30-year rotation, and the active period for harvesting was generally late April to mid-June or, more specifically, that period of spring when the concentration of tannin in the bark is at its highest and the sap is rising so that the bark peels more easily from the cut poles. The tannin is found on the inside of the peeled bark, while the outer side, known as the 'krap', is relatively valueless. Could this be the origin of the word that has successfully entered the English vernacular?

An account of how the teams of barkers worked was published in *The Penny Magazine* in 1835. The extract below describes women stripping a large felled oak:

A number of women called 'barkers' are each furnished with light short-handled mallets made of hard wood, about eight or nine inches long, three inches square at the face, and the other end sharpened like a wedge, in order the more easily to make an incision in the bark, which is done all along the side of the tree which happens to be uppermost, in a straight line; and as two barkers generally work together, it is proper that whilst one is employed in making an incision with the mallet, the other, being furnished with a pointed instrument called the 'barking-bill,' cuts the bark across the tree in lengths of from two feet six inches to three feet, and then, by forcing a shovel-shaped instrument called a 'peeling-iron' between the bark and the wood, easily separates the former, and peels it from the timber in entire pieces… The bark, when peeled, is carefully dried for two or three weeks, and then piled in stacks of about eight feet square by fifteen feet in height, and sold to the tanner.

By 1894, James Brown's woodland-management manual *The Forester* bemoaned that age-old problem of cheap foreign imports of tan bark and the depression it was causing to the home market. Brown gives calculations for bark yields from coppice and how to recruit the correct workforce, 'in order to strip one ton of bark each day, including all the necessary operations pertaining thereto':

1 lad stripping lower parts of stems, at 1/6 per day	*£0/1/6*
1 man 'laying in' these, at 3/- per day	*£0/3/0*
2 cutters, at 3/- per day	*£0/6/0*
2 pruners of trees, at 2/6 per day	*£0/5/0*
3 lads pruning branches, at 1/6 per day	*£0/4/6*
2 boys carrying branches, at 1/- per day	*£0/2/0*
1 man putting up stages, and attending to bark on them, at 2/6 per day	*£0/2/6*
2 lads carrying bark to stages, at 1/6 per day	*£0/3/0*
12 women or boys stripping, at 1/6 per day	*£0/18/0*
Total Wages Bill	*£2/5/6*

There seems to have been two principal methods of harvesting. Some foresters believed that barking the tree while it was still standing, a practise that was particularly common in the Forest of Dean, was the best way. There was also a theory that debarked, large standing oaks would then develop greater strength

in the timber as they died. This system had its critics, who refuted this assertion. More often, smaller trees and coppice poles were used for tan bark. It was claimed that the tannin concentration was higher in the bark of these younger trees.

By 1842, in his *British Forest-Trees*, Selby was scathing about anyone bothering to grow coppice oak for its bark, as the market had already collapsed to a point where it was worth less than £7 per ton – less than half of its value during the Napoleonic Wars (1803–1815). The demand for oak bark waned further after about 1860, as various chemicals from vegetable and mineral sources displaced oak bark tannin, and the industry's requirements gradually diminished into the twentieth century. However, accounts of the industry from 1926 still firmly assert that oak-bark tanned leather was of superior quality.

The days are gone when whole teams of perhaps thirty or forty wood cutters and bark peelers, men, women, and children all with their jobs to do, camped out in the forest to harvest bark. Today, there are only a handful of isolated bark peelers dotted around the country, all supplying one solitary tannery in Devon. J. & F. J. Baker, at Colyton, are the very last company who still believe that oak tan bark makes the very best quality leather, and proudly proclaim that they can trace the roots of their tannery back to the Roman period.

One of the few bark suppliers left today is Paul Jackson, who runs a small business with his father and son in the Wyre Forest in Worcestershire. When Paul started out, he served his apprenticeship with Bill Doolittle and his wife Gerry, learning how to coppice, to strip the bark, and then to use the stripped poles

(known as black poles – although, strangely, they are quite white) to make rustic furniture, garden arbours, and fencing. When Bill retired, Paul picked up the reins. Each year Paul negotiates with the Forestry Commission, who own much of the forest, to cut various compartments of oak coppice. He then trucks the poles back to his yard for peeling. Apart from the chainsaws to cut the poles, exactly the same tools that might have been found in the nineteenth century are used today. The coppicing is good for the woodland, which allows the ground flora and shrub layer to flourish and helps to maintain the biodiversity for associated wildlife. Paul is intent on making a respectable living from his physically demanding business, but also seems to take pride in keeping alive a very old tradition.

ABOVE: Building the charcoal heap or stack. An air-tight layer of turf covers the wood to stop it bursting into flames. This is a demonstration 'burn' in the Forest of Dean, so is a relatively small stack compared to those that would have been built in the nineteenth-century heyday of charcoal burning. Modern charcoal burners use cylindrical steel kilns.

CHARCOAL

In the past, many smaller poles or cordwood would have been converted into charcoal. Although a variety of native hardwoods have been used for this, there has always been a preference for the high-grade quality of oak charcoal, as oak retains 20 per cent of its weight after conversion to charcoal, making it particularly good for glass making and iron smelting. The use of charcoal can be traced as far back as the Bronze Age, but it was the Roman settlers who used great quantities of oak charcoal for their iron-smelting operations in the Kent and Sussex Weald, and the Forest of Dean. Huge tracts of woodland were given over to charcoal production, the scale of which is evident in the Forest of Dean, which boasts the remains of over 2,000 charcoal hearths. It was only in the eighteenth century,

with the discovery of how to make coke from coal, that a replacement was found for charcoal. With a decline in the demand for charcoal for fuel, filtration, insulation, and other chemical processes, the whole industry seemed doomed by the mid-twentieth century. A side effect was the downturn in coppicing, which heralded problems for the vitality and diversity of many woods.

To a certain degree this trend has been reversed over the last twenty or thirty years. Both woodsmen with a living to be found and amateurs with a love for the revitalization of woodland have taken to making charcoal once again. Admittedly, production is not destined for high-volume use in heavy industry, but often seen more as a challenge to the sometimes less than ecologically sound barbecue charcoal imports from various corners of the globe. Knowing that we still import more than 90 per cent of our barbecue charcoal is something of a travesty when we have so much redundant coppice woodland that could be productive again. Since 1995, the Bioregional Charcoal Company has co-ordinated a network of producers who are making it possible to fulfil large contracts to major retail outlets.

BASKETS AND BARRELS, FOOD AND FURNITURE

Another very specialized use of oak is the weaving of oak spale, spelk, or swill baskets, a long-standing traditional craft that once thrived in the southern part of Cumbria, often known as Furness. They were also made in Shropshire, where the baskets were called whiskets, and in Derbyshire, where they were known as skeps. The oak required for weaving is cut from coppice woods. Cleft billets of oak cordwood are first boiled to make the wood more pliable and then riven into thinner strips suitable for weaving baskets. Each piece is smoothed with draw knives on a shaving horse before it is used. The shorter, thicker strips are called 'spelks' and are used as ribs, while the longer, thinner strips are called 'taws', and are woven through the spelks. The whole assembly is attached to a steamed hazel rod, a 'bool' or 'bow', bent into the characteristic oval shape.

BELOW: Owen Jones
makes an oak swill basket
in his workshop in Cumbria.

These handsome baskets were once part of the workaday scene in mines, mills, factories, and farms, and had many uses in the home. Manufacture took place on the level of cottage industry, and was usually handed down within families, with the expectation that a skilled worker could produce about six 22-inch baskets in a working day. In 1922 the piece rate for each of these was two shillings (10 pence). Many old men in the trade complained that young boys were not interested in learning the trade as 'there's too much work in it for them', which was another way of saying that there was not enough monetary return for the time they invested in learning. This was probably the reason so many country crafts declined and disappeared. In post-war Britain, particularly with the rise of plastic utensils, basketry went into the doldrums. Recent years have seen a widespread revival in many types of basketry, and one full-time woodsman in Cumbria, Owen Jones, has made something of a speciality out of reviving the craft of swill making.

Barrels and casks have been made for the storage and transportation of all manner of dry and wet goods for hundreds of years. Whether it was herrings, flour, beer, or whisky, the barrel provided a durable, leakproof container in a variety of sizes: hogshead (54 gallons), barrel (36 gallons), kilderkin (18 gallons), firkin (9 gallons), pin (4 gallons). Thankfully, even with the massive use of plastics and steel, there is still a place for the oak barrel today; most particularly in the drinks industry, where the use of oak imparts a certain character to the wines and whiskies that are stored in them to mature.

The manufacture of barrels has changed little down the years. Construction is divided into four main processes, namely dressing, raising, heading, and gathering. Dressing is the preparation of the cask staves, which involves taking seasoned pieces of oak and precision planing them so that they butt perfectly together. Raising the cask is the assembly of the staves in the familiar shape, held in place by ash trusses. A small fire is placed inside the cask so that the staves yield to the trusses, bending and contracting into a tight fit. Heading is the making of the cask ends, which fit into pre-cut slots. Gathering is the final steel hooping and finishing of the cask, including the creation of the important bunghole.

The drinks industry aside, oak has found uses in food production. Various fish, meats, and cheeses have been traditionally smoked using oak chips. The village of Crastor on the Northumbrian coast has long been famed for oak smoking herring in order to make the finest kippers. Oak is also used along with beech wood to produce Arbroath Smokies from haddock. The process imparts a very distinctive flavour, but also, in the past, would have been important as it prolonged the shelf life of food.

Oak has long held a place in the manufacture of furniture, its supreme durability along with its attractive figuring making it both functional and beautiful. It says much for the wood that many pieces dating back to the medieval period still exist. Very much like the oak-framed buildings in which they resided, early pieces of furniture were held together with wooden pegs or dowels. Given the more refined manufacturing methods and the use of

sophisticated tools and techniques today, these pieces may look primitive in style and rugged in execution, but they must be viewed in the context of the period in which they were made. Early pieces of oak furniture have acquired a remarkable patina through years of enduring smoky rooms, as well as the rubs, scuffs, and knocks of everyday use, the natural oils absorbed from their users and, latterly, layers of polish.

The Suffolk firm of Titchmarsh & Goodwin (T&G) are one of several companies who have developed something of a speciality in fine oak furniture, inspired by the rich legacy of pieces stretching back over the last 500 years. They are a family company who can trace their roots back to 1770, when Samuel Goodwin, a Woodbridge carpenter, sent his son George to apprentice with a London cabinetmaker. George later returned to his native Suffolk, by now a highly skilled craftsman, and the rest (as they say) is history. In its modern incarnation, T&G dates back to 1920. The company not only have their own mill to saw the timber, but also own the woods where they nurture the high-quality oak required for the business. The company is also proud to employ some of Britain's finest wood turners, carvers, cabinetmakers, and French polishers, as well as a gilder, a glazier, and even a lacquer artist. Their catalogue of oak furniture is a sumptuous celebration of the beauty of Britain's most important hardwood tree.

Another celebrated manufacturer of traditional oak furniture in Britain is the North Yorkshire firm Robert Thompson's Craftsmen Ltd. Born in 1876 in Kilburn,

Robert Thompson was the son of the village carpenter, joiner, and wheelwright, and worked alongside his father until he died, taking over the business in 1895. The process of building the business and his reputation was gradual. Inspired by the legacy of medieval craftsmen and the burgeoning Arts and Crafts Movement, Thompson soon developed his own distinctive style. He accepted one of his most prestigious projects in 1919, when nearby Ampleforth Abbey commissioned furniture and fittings. At this time, in a casual conversation with a colleague, Thompson muttered about how they were all still poor as church mice, which led to the first tiny mouse being carved on a section of church screen. The tradition persisted, and since then almost every piece of Thompson furniture has borne the trademark mouse – the Mouseman's distinctive signature. Robert died in 1955, but had built up a thriving business for his successors. The company is still in the village of Kilburn, and continues to go from strength to strength. Each craftsman builds a single piece of furniture, from the selection of the timber in the mill to the application of the final coat of wax polish, and each individual carves their own subtly distinctive version of the mouse on their work.

I was exposed to the Mouseman tradition as a little lad, when my grandma took us to the twelfth-century church at Hubberholme in Upper Wharfedale, and challenged my brother and I to count all the mice on the oak choir stall and pews that Thompson had crafted in 1934. I remember scurrying around, looking high and low, but whether we found them all, I still don't know.

ABOVE LEFT: This *c.*1600 oak court cupboard has acquired that wonderful rich patina and dark colouring usually associated with oak furniture from this period. It has a castellated cornice above a guilloche carved frieze, the gadrooned columns are centred by a pair of doors bearing a Tudor rose design, and the lower section with lozenge-carved doors stands on stile feet.

ABOVE RIGHT: The Norfolk Press from the Epicormic Oak range by Titchmarsh & Goodwin.

THE BOWTHORPE OAK

A VISIT TO THE MIGHTY BOWTHORPE OAK, near Bourne in Lincolnshire, is a bit like meeting a famous celebrity. The tree has been renowned for the last thirty years as the greatest girthed English oak in the whole of Europe and, until a few years ago, at a remarkable 42 feet in girth, no other tree stood a chance of stealing this title. However, a relatively recent discovery in Herefordshire may bring the two into a closely contested 'measure-off' for the true title holder.

With an oak tree of such massive proportions, the burning question for most people is working out exactly how many centuries it has been around. This is always far from easy with a craggy old pollard that has been hollowing out for perhaps the last 500 years. There is no heartwood left to measure rings, so one simply has to extrapolate from sound oaks with known ages or planting dates. Dating trees is not an exact science, but best guesstimates put this oak at around 1,200 years old (give or take a century).

Today the tree sits in a small paddock behind Bowthorpe Park Farm, but the name is the clue to its historic background, for the land was once a deer park belonging to a long-lost manor house. There were, no doubt, other oaks of a similar vintage here. Charles Mosley's *The Oak* (1910) asserts that the earliest account of the tree comes down from a Lincolnshire farmer's diary of 1763:

Visited Bourne and stopped at Bowthorpe Park to see the celebrated oak-tree there. The lower part was used as a feeding-place for calves, the upper as a pigeon-house. The hollow trunk measured 48 feet in circumference [assumed to be at the base].

Five years later the diary tells us that:

It was neatly fitted up inside with tables and seats, and could contain a 'tea-drinking' party of sixteen persons. When the tables and chairs were removed there was standing room for twenty-eight people.

Another account, in 1884, revealed that it was the owner, George Pauncefort, who installed the accommodation in 1768, 'and a door of entrance: frequently twelve persons have dined in it with ease'. The tales of how many people attended tea parties and dinners in the tree seem to fluctuate at whim, but perhaps the most ambitious claim was that thirty-nine people once stood together inside the tree. I have been there, and frankly this seems highly unlikely and must have

OPPOSITE TOP: The Bowthorpe Oak, copper engraving, drawn by J. C. Nattes, 1804.

OPPOSITE BOTTOM: The huge bole of the Bowthorpe Oak.

been an early version of the 1960s game of 'how many students can you cram in a Mini or a phonebox'!

In 1805 a fine engraving of the tree was made for a Lincolnshire history and this clearly shows the door in the tree as well as the farmhouse behind. At this date, it was said that the tree had 'been in the same state of decay since the memory of the older inhabitants and their ancestors'.

In the 1820s John Clare (1793–1864) was moved to write of the tree in the sonnet 'Burthorp Oak' (this was the form of Bowthorpe until the end of the sixteenth century):

> OLD noted oak! I saw thee in a mood
>   Of vague indifference; and yet with me
> Thy memory, like thy fate, hath lingering stood
>   For years, thou hermit, in the lonely sea
> Of grass that waves around thee!—Solitude
>   Paints not a lonelier picture to the view,
> Burthorp! than thy one melancholy tree,
>   Age-rent, and shattered to a stump. Yet new
> Leaves come upon each rift and broken limb
>   With every spring; and Poesy's visions swim
> Around it, of old days, and chivalry;
>   And desolate fancies bid the eyes grow dim
> With feelings, that Earth's grandeur should decay,
> And all its olden memories pass away.

With the exception of the above sonnet by Clare, the old tree appears to slip from awareness for the rest of the nineteenth century, only surfacing again in Mosley's 1910 book and a few Edwardian postcards, before submerging once again into anonymity until Alan Mitchell refers to it in 1982.

Over the last thirty years the tree has maintained a very high profile. Thomas Pakenham's *Meetings with Remarkable Trees* (1996), both book and television, brought the tree to an audience of millions. Subsequently, the family who own the tree, and have tended it through many generations, decided to open it to the public, making a small charge for the privilege. One can only imagine their distress when, in 2002, gales blew off one of the tree's huge limbs, which amounted to about a quarter of the whole crown. Eleven years later, the tree is still very much in the best of health and the crown has closed over so completely that it's difficult to see where the loss occurred. In truth, this 'pollarding by storm' might have helped the tree, for by reducing the size of the crown it has reduced the size of the structure that the root system now has to support. Recent years have seen the tree featured in several heritage tree books, cementing its fame as one of the nation's greatest trees.

THE OAKS OF SHERWOOD

IT IS A RATHER REMARKABLE OCCURRENCE THAT A SINGLE OAK TREE has harboured such great affection in the hearts of British people for over 200 years. The Major Oak stands proud, yet propped, in its own little clearing in the middle of Sherwood Forest. While there are many other equally, if not more impressive ancient oaks throughout Britain, it seems strange that this tree's fame and fascination has endured. One of the reasons for this must surely be the long-held association that the forest enjoys with folk hero Robin Hood. Debate has raged for centuries about whether or not Robin or Robert Hood really existed, bolstered in no small measure by a rich folk tradition. Various accounts set him in the late twelfth or early thirteenth centuries, but the continual reworking of the legend, particularly in the Victorian era, was undoubtedly some of the best tourism promotion one could imagine. Romantic tales of the renegade, the benevolent outlaw, and his faithful band of followers, have excited and intrigued ever since.

The much-celebrated Major Oak is found in an area of Sherwood Forest known as Birkland (or Birchland, as Rooke knew it), a 447-acre remnant of the once vast forest that stretched from Nottingham to Mansfield. As the name implies, this was once largely a birch wood and, even today, birch soon infiltrates any space vacated by the fall of an ancient oak. Many of the oak pollards that are still here could certainly date back 400–500 years, which would seem to indicate that a regime of wood-pasture once prevailed. Writing in the late sixteenth century, the topographer and historian William Camden reported on the state of the ancient Forest of Sherwood, or Shirewood:

> [The forest is] *anciently thick set with trees, whose entangled branches were so twisted together, that they hardly left room for a single person to pass. At present, it is much thinner, but still breeds an infinite number of deer and stags with lofty antlers.*

With plentiful deer in the woods at that time, pollarding would have been vital if the oaks were to survive.

The first reference to the Major Oak comes from a wonderful book entitled *Remarkable Oaks in the Park at Welbeck* (1790), by Major Hayman Rooke. The book provides a superb description of the oaks on the Duke of Portland's estate, along with a portfolio of nine copper engravings of the trees by W. Ellis. Most of the oaks Rooke describes had already gained names of distinction. The Duke's

OPPOSITE: A rare albumen print of the Major Oak, *c.*1890, shows the tree with its venerable guardian sitting proudly at the foot of the tree. At this time the tree appears to have stood in isolated splendour, unlike today, surrounded as it is by mature trees.

'The Major Oak is guarded by a man who told me that he had recently superseded a fellow villager who was now "breaking up". "He is getting old", said he, "and could not come any longer."
"How old are you?" I asked.
"I am eighty-four", said he. What age then must have been the man whom he replaced, and who was only beginning to get old? Perhaps the people hereabouts measure life by the duration of oak trees. My friend of eighty-four evidently looked upon himself as a mere juvenile.'

From *Rambles Among the Hills in the Peak of Derbyshire, and the South Downs* (1880) by Louis J. Jennings.

PREVIOUS PAGE: The Major
Oak in spring, arguably the
most famous oak in Britain.

BELOW: The earliest known
image of the Major Oak,
described in the title of Major
Hayman Rooke's *Remarkable
Oaks in the Park at Welbeck* as
'An Ancient Oak in Birchland
Wood'. Copper engraving
by W. Ellis from Rooke's
drawing, 1790.

Walking-stick was clearly an impressive timber tree: a tall, straight oak some 111 feet high, it had no branches before 70 feet. Then there were The Porters, 'having [been] once a gate between them', two impressive trees, 90 feet in height and 23 and 20 feet in girth. The Seven Sisters was a huge, multiple-stemmed oak (perhaps an old coppice stool) that, by 1790, had been reduced from seven to six stems. The Green Dale Oak, which was mentioned a lot during the eighteenth century, had a less than auspicious fate thanks to a large hole that was cut right through the middle of its ample bole to satisfy a wager (of which more anon). It was a tree with no name, simply titled 'An Ancient Oak in Birchland Wood', that moved Rooke to remark:

I think no one can behold this majestic ruin without pronouncing it to be of very remote antiquity; and might venture to say, that it cannot be much less than a thousand years old.

Of course, by the very nature of its huge, hollow trunk it is very difficult to age, but best estimates today put the Major Oak at 800–1,000 years old, and yet with a girth of 35 feet and a height of 52 feet, it is by no means the biggest or oldest oak in Britain. If it had existed in the twelfth century, there is no chance that Robin Hood would have been able to hide inside it. The tree has long been a local landmark, and was known as the Cock-pen Tree in the eighteenth century, as its hollow trunk was used as a roost for fighting cocks. A map of Sherwood Forest in 1791, found in Nottingham Archives, actually shows the tree marked as Major Rooke – the first evidence of the tree being named. However, few, if any, of the tree and forestry books of the nineteenth century then refer to it again by name. Certainly by the end of the nineteenth century, it had become known as the Major Oak, or Major's Oak, or even the Major, in deference to Major Rooke, although it was also referred to as the Queen or the Queen's Oak, which simply reflected its size or status, as there is no known royal connection.

In the late nineteenth century, several of the large travel photography publishers, as well as some of the local practitioners, made albumen prints to be sold to tourists. This was swiftly followed, from about 1900 onwards, by a plethora of different postcard views of the tree. The incredible number of cards of this one tree, vastly outnumbering images of any other ancient oak in Britain, reveals the tree's unrivalled popularity.

In Edwardian times, concerns for the tree's structure led to the first round of chains and braces in the crown and wooden props beneath some of the larger boughs. By the 1970s, further concerns were raised about the old tree's health. Huge numbers of visitors were starting to cause compaction problems beneath the tree and undue

die-back was starting to occur in the crown. A perimeter fence was erected to keep people at a distance, and a bark mulch laid down to encourage worm activity and promote aeration of the root system, with the aim of improving water and nutrient absorption. Putting fences between trees and people can be a little sad, but with more than 600,000 annual visitors from all over the world, it is for the best in this instance.

Although Sherwood Forest amounts to far more than a single famous denizen, the artist and writer Joseph Rodgers encapsulates the affection held for the Major Oak in his late-nineteenth-century *Scenery of Sherwood Forest*:

What memories of happy hours spent in its leafy shade does the name of this tree bring to thousands! Old men in distant cities tell with what pleasure in their youthful days they climbed the Major's great branches, or hid themselves within his hollow trunk; and that when years had sped away and their climbing days were over, these excursions were still remembered as the happiest of the year; and no journey to the forest could ever be made without a call upon the Major, where, reclining on his ancient roots in company with life-long friends, time passed too quickly away.

ABOVE: A wonderful Edwardian postcard featuring a large group of men beneath the Major Oak. What are they doing? Two of them appear to have taken off their jackets, perhaps for some contest. Was this an impromptu boxing or wrestling bout? The gentleman with hands authoritatively on his lapels in the small group to the right has the air of a referee.

Within Sherwood there once stood several other notable oaks that were of sufficient interest to be incorporated into the early twentieth-century postcard boom. One tree that certainly did look old enough and big enough to have been a hiding place was a crumbling old pollard called Robin Hood's Larder, the Butcher's Shambles Oak, or simply Shambles Oak. It is here that Robin Hood is reputed to have hidden venison poached from the king's deer. The correlation of butchers to shambles is that the latter was once the term used for an open-air slaughterhouse or meat market, thought to be derived from the Anglo-Saxon word *fleshammels*, or flesh shelves (where butchers displayed their meat). Travel writer Louis John Jennings, recorded his visit to the tree in 1880. When he questioned one of the forest keepers about the burnt-out state of the oak, he was told that:

In the summer of 1878 a 'Party of Sheffielders' came over, and amused themselves by setting fire to this venerable tree, which a band of savages would have respected. What pleasure there can be in wantonly destroying an object like this it is very hard for the ordinary mind to conjecture, but there stands the charred remnant of the tree a mark of the gentle instincts which inspire some people when they are out for a holiday.

Jennings's rueful observation, his heart-felt sarcasm, is somehow timeless. Vandalism is not just a modern phenomenon! One saving grace was that

Jennings was able to report that the tree was still pushing out new foliage in the May of his visit. In 1913, the tree was once again damaged by a fire that was started by a group of picnickers boiling a kettle inside the old bole. Still the oak survived, but in 1962 strong gales finally saw off what was left of it.

On the edge of Sherwood, right next to the Mansfield to Edwinstowe road, stands the precarious remains of the Parliament Oak. The tree is reputedly 1,000–1,200 years old, which is perhaps a little generous given its girth of 29 feet (at the end of the nineteenth century), but it has been a landmark tree for many centuries. Its fragmented state today, and for at least the last 200 years, probably indicates that it has grown very little in that time. Compared to the decrepit state of the tree in the nineteenth century, it has, however, had something of a resurgence in recent times.

The tree was a boundary marker for Clipstone Royal Deer Park, which was enclosed in 1180. Now completely hollowed out, the old boundary runs right through the gap in between the two remnant parts of the bole. The name derives from two accounts of kings who supposedly held court beneath its boughs. In 1212, while King John was hunting at Clipstone, he was informed of a Welsh revolt and an insurrection in the north of England. He called his council together beneath the tree to plan his response; his first barbarous act was reputedly to hang 28 Welsh boys, aged 12–14, who had been held in Nottingham Castle. History also relates how Edward I convened a Parliament at Clipstone Palace in 1290, there being two sessions in the autumn of that year. Whether they actually met beneath the tree must be left to conjecture. Judging by its size, it would seem more likely that the tree was planted to commemorate Edward's visits in 1290.

In 2008, the Sherwood Forest Trust took this tree under their protective custody. They have since done much to raise a new awareness of the historic significance and special nature of this ancient oak, including some much-needed restoration and tidying up of the surrounding area.

Perhaps the most extraordinary tale of use – if not abuse – of an ancient oak comes down from the Duke of Portland's estate of Welbeck Park. One evening in 1724, while the 1st Duke was entertaining a group of dinner guests, the wine clearly having flowed freely, he claimed there was an oak so big in the park that a coach and six might drive right through the middle of it. Incredulous, one of

The Shambles Oak, Sherwood Forest. No. 897.

ABOVE: The Shambles Oak in around 1900. Sadly, we don't know who these two gentlemen are, although they might appear to have some significance to or association with the forest.

ABOVE: The Greendale Oak
which grew on the Duke of
Portland's estate and no longer
survives.

his guests challenged the duke to a wager. That night a team of woodsmen set about the Greendale Oak, cutting a massive arch, over 10 feet high and 6 feet wide, through the base of the old bole. Next morning, the guest was obliged to witness the duke's smallest coach duly driven through the aperture. One wonders how much the wager was for – surely not an insignificant sum to warrant such a radical remodelling of a fine oak. George Vertue was the first of many artists to render this strangely modified tree; Rooke included it in his 1790 work; Grimm made detailed views from both sides for Hunter's edition of Evelyn's *Silva*; and Strutt included it in *Sylva Britannica*. A tradition was for successive dukes to drive through the Greendale Oak arch when bringing their new brides home to Welbeck. The mutilated remains of the tree soldiered on, the crown slowly diminishing, but it seems that by the middle of the twentieth century it was all but dead. Certainly, nothing remains of it today.

EXTRAORDINARY OAKS

After more than twenty years on the quest for Britain's most remarkable and unusual trees, a beguiling array of oddities have emerged. It's not just oak trees; cast the net across all species, and bizarre forms and strange stories soon come to light. The famous oaks and their associated stories, so many of which feature in this book, are obvious subjects to explore, but it's the strange and often unexpected trees one finds, usually well off the beaten track, unnamed and unknown, that can be equally as exciting.

IN 2008, BRIAN WALKER FROM THE FORESTRY COMMISSION on the North York Moors sent me an email and snapshots to tell me all about some rather fine old oaks that he and his forestry colleagues had found along the fell sides above the tiny village of Ingleby Greenhow. One in particular, which they had dubbed the Medusa Oak, caught my imagination immediately. Here was an oak tree bursting forth from a great split in a boulder some 15 or 20 feet high and wide. I needed to see this for myself, but it would be a further five years before I found myself brushing through the undergrowth, squeezing beneath a dense plantation of spruce, and finally emerging into a small clearing, to be confronted by this very singular and dramatic oak. It seemed to prize the solid rock apart, frozen, almost certainly for several centuries, in the very act of escape. The folds of rough bark wrapped themselves, as if once molten, around the entrapping boulder. The serpentine boughs vigorously springing from the crown explained the Medusa synonym straight away, and I was transfixed. It was one of those trees that simply holds you in its power. My initial reaction was slight disappointment that the sunlight, which must have flooded the tree little more than an hour earlier, had moved around behind the conifers. However, the longer I stood and connected with this tree, the more the soft, subdued light and subtle tones seemed to impart the spirit of this old denizen of the rock.

One yearns to know how the tree has grown this way. How and why was it left to its own devices all these years? How come the foresters of a previous generation didn't simply grub it out to clear the way for a couple more conifers? It has most probably been cut over at some time in the distant past, but that will

OPPOSITE: The Medusa Oak discovered in its lair in hills above Ingleby Greenhow in North Yorkshire.

have kept it vibrant and alive. I took dozens of slightly different shots and was loath to leave. When I see something this special, a magnetic force holds me, and a fear that I might never see this tree again starts to creep in. Thank goodness Brian and his colleagues love it and will take steps to see that no harm comes to it. One hopes that this affection will endure with all who come after, for this oak is unique and irreplaceable.

Old tree books reveal many examples of anomalous oaks that captivated tree enthusiasts a century or two ago. As a result, a rich legacy of anecdote now accompanies such trees – one can even say that sometimes it's the stories that shade the trees. Take for example the ancient oak tree in Melbury Park, in Dorset. The tree has acquired the unusual name of Billy Wilkins. Nobody is exactly sure why, although it was very likely someone who lived and worked on the estate. One story, which is unsubstantiated, was that Wilkins was a bailiff on the estate, and was sent to warn his master, Sir John Strangeways (the owner, and a Royalist sympathiser) that Parliamentarian forces were approaching. Sadly, he was overtaken and killed by the Roundhead soldiers, and therefore never delivered his message. Whether the coup de grâce was delivered near the oak, or the tree was simply named as a tribute to this loyal servant is uncertain. J. C. Loudon mentions that the tree had a girth of 30 feet at the smallest part of the bole, and that it was 50 feet high, with a spread of 60 feet in 1838. In his *Dendrologia* (1827), Mitchell describes it 'as curly, surly, knotty an old monster as can be conceived'. It also receives a mention in Thomas Hardy's *The Woodlanders*, as 'Great Willy, the largest oak in the wood'. Elwes and Henry paid a visit to the old oak for their *Trees of Great Britain and Ireland* and included a beautiful photogravure plate of the tree. Elwes measured the girth, and by 1906 it had grown to 35 feet at chest height. It survives in good health to this day on the private estate.

The Remedy Oak is another Dorset tree with a strange history. In the very last throws of its considerable span, this oak in a hedgerow at Woodlands, near Verwood, has a plaque beneath which reveals that, 'according to tradition King Edward VI sat beneath this tree and touched for King's Evil'. The King's Evil was actually a skin disease known as scrofula, a swelling of the lymph nodes in the neck caused by tuberculosis. A popular belief was that the king had the God-given power to cure this condition simply by touching the person. In 1551, when the fifteen-year-old Edward VI visited Dorset, he spent much time on his travels touching and 'curing' people. There are no records of his success rate.

The massive old Damory's Oak also once stood in Dorset. Measuring 68 feet around at the base, it was surely one of the very largest oaks, and is mentioned by all of the nineteenth-century tree-book authors. Loudon relates that 'during the civil wars, and till after the Restoration, this cave was inhabited by an old man, who sold ale in it'. Severely damaged by storms in 1703, it finally had to be felled in 1755.

Back in 2003, I availed myself of the little ferry boat to cross the choppy waters of the Lake of Mentieth to visit the peaceful island retreat of Inchmahome. Here, the ruins of the thirteenth-century Augustinian Priory stand as a stark reminder of a monastic way of life that disappeared almost 500 years ago. Just

prior to the dissolution of this religious community in 1547, the infant Mary Queen of Scots, only four years old, was brought here by her mother, Mary of Guise, to seek sanctuary after the English victory at the Battle of Pinkie Cleugh. Not only is the island famous for its ancient monument, but it also boasts three enormous sweet chestnut trees of great antiquity.

Almost certainly in excess of 400 years old, it's conceivable that these trees might have been young saplings when Mary sought refuge here. As I further explored the island, I came upon one of the strangest oaks I have ever found. Just above the shoreline, an oak lay tumbled amid the undergrowth, its massive root plate ripped from the sodden earth and turned into the air at right angles to the ground. It seems the event that caused the oak to topple took place many years ago, and the root system, which had not severed completely (in fact remaining very much alive), had subsequently grown bark, causing it to resemble an oaken wall. The horizontal tree was, in fact, thriving. Fallen trees that regenerate like this are known as phoenix trees and, although an unusual occurrence among oaks, are remarkable, beautiful, and a vivid reminder of the drive to survive.

ABOVE: Phoenix tree – a fallen oak on Inchmahome Island in the Lake of Menteith.

Oaks have the capacity to grow in very strange ways. A famous coupling of oak and beech once grew in the New Forest near the famous Rufus Stone, site of the demise of William Rufus in a hunting 'accident' back in 1100. Early twentieth-century postcards (of which many variations were published by numerous companies) show that they grew so close together that they appeared fused at the base. They are no more.

I discovered another cosy coupling in the woods of Ashridge Estate in Hertfordshire a few years back. This time a beech and an oak had grown up in such close proximity that they entwined with one another. Was this the result of some forester's joke? I have previously seen two beech trees with branches fused together and wondered at their origin. It can be a natural phenomenon known as inarching, which is usually caused by two boughs meeting, rubbing together for many years, before finally fusing in a kind of naturally occurring graft. Of course it is also possible for woodsmen to work their wacky ways with beech. The strange thing about the Ashridge trees is that one would expect to see two maturing trees, both seeking the sunlight, growing out and away from each other, rather than the embrace of what appeared to be entwined woodland lovers.

The upper Tywi Valley still has a great sense of remoteness. Small, intimate communities and farms snug-set among the hills have remained little changed for perhaps the last 400 years. Near the straggling settlement of Rhandirmwyn stands a mighty ancient oak that has found a very different role to play. Seeking the famous Rhandirmwyn Oak in the village doesn't take very long. It is such a splendid old stager and much bigger than any other oak for some distance, that everyone can point you in the right direction. It sits on the side of the lane that leads across the valley from the village centre, above Pwllpriddog Farm, on the road towards Cilycwm. Even though it has been there for 600–700 years, nobody can actually tell you why it is celebrated other than for its size, a very respectable 27 feet 6 inches. According to Rory Francis from the Woodland Trust, the oak had briefly become the scene of a musical performance that took place, not beneath its boughs – but inside the hollow trunk. Brothers Ynyr and Eurig Roberts, who hail from Snowdonia, and are known to their many fans as the band Brigyn (which, incidentally, means 'branch', reflecting their primary connection to trees and nature) were shown the oak by their friend Liz Fleming-Williams and, awestruck, they instantly thought it would be an amazing experience to perform a song inside the old tree. Having sought permission from the owner, they managed to wriggle inside and play their song 'Popeth yn ei le' (Everything in its Place); filming it as part of the promotional launch for their

ABOVE: A rare early photograph
from the 1860s, produced as a
carte de visite, shows a throng of
visitors around the Major Oak.

2005 album *Brigyn 2*. So now the tree has acquired a very modern – and perhaps
unique strand of fame – a film set and a recording studio!

Some oaks have consistently attracted more notice than the rest. The Major
Oak in Sherwood Forest has to be the most photographed individual oak in the
whole of Britain. Victorian tourists were lured by the romantic tales of Robin
Hood and his Merry Men and began to flock to Sherwood Forest. As it became
a tourist honeypot, local photographers began setting up studios in the field.
Here they could offer portraits taken with the tree; photographed, developed,
printed, and mounted for tourists to carry home for all to marvel at. By 1900
the postcard boom was churning out thousands of Major Oaks. Around the
same time another tree, much less impressive, begins to enter the best-sellers
list of tree postcards.

For ages the public has been captivated by superlatives, whether it be the
oldest, tallest, widest, or, in the case of the Lillington Oak, the tree that marks
the very centre of England. Lillington is a suburb of Leamington Spa, and the
numerous early twentieth-century postcards of the oak depict a tree that does
not appear to be of any great antiquity – perhaps 150–200 years old. Nobody
knows if the 'centre of England' tree was planted with some preordained
knowledge, purpose, or calculation, or whether at some point it became a
convenient landmark tree to fill the role. It survived until 1970, a neglected
monument and occasionally a maltreated billboard. When a large bough
dropped off, exposing a rotting interior, the end was nigh and the tree was

soon felled, although a replacement tree was planted not long afterwards.
Various other places in the Midlands have claimed this central status. Meriden
in Warwickshire has perhaps the strongest claim, since a medieval cross on the
village green has traditionally been thought to mark the spot. However, in 2002
the Ordnance Survey defined the geographical centre of England as being a point
on Lindley Hall Farm, at Fenny Drayton in Leicestershire, some 25 miles north
of Lillington. Perhaps an oak should be planted there.

The important role that oaks have consistently played in the nation's cultural
history, due to historical associations, landmark significance or simply their great
size or longevity, has provided an enduring focal point for communities to the
present day, as many of the individual tree biographies elsewhere in this book
vividly illustrate. A strange tale attends the occurrence of 'double-oaks' in an old
green lane near the village of Wichenford in Worcestershire. An account from a
2003 issue of *The Countryman* magazine recalls a local inhabitant encountering
a returning traveller in the green lane near his home. The conversation turned
to the visitor's reason for seeking out this spot. The traveller explained that many
years ago, when he lived on the road, his family had been camped there, during
which time his baby daughter had sadly died. She was apparently buried on the
edge of the lane, in the old gypsy tradition of burying a child with an acorn in
each hand so that the oak(s) that grow mark the spot for family to return
periodically to pay respects. Whether there is any substance to this story
is debatable, but so many double-oaks along this one stretch does seem
a remarkable coincidence.

Arguably among the most unusual sporting prizes to ever be awarded were distributed at the 1936 Olympic Games, when Adolf Hitler decided to present oak saplings in pots to all of the 130 gold-medal winners. He hoped that German oaks, albeit ironically *Quercus robur,* the English oak, would end up being planted the world over, thus achieving colonization by tree stealth. It's not hard to understand why many of the trees were hacked down in the wake of the Second World War. Four of these oaks came back to England, but only one now survives. The fate of two is a mystery. One, brought back by long-distance walker Harold Whitlock, was planted at his old school in north London. For seventy years it thrived at Hendon School, until 2007 when it was diagnosed with a fungal disease, declared to be unsound and, for safety reasons, had to be felled. The fourth tree came back with yachtsman Christopher Boardman and was planted at his home, How Hill, in Ludham, Norfolk. It took quite a battering from the great storm of 1987, and by April 2013 it was in danger of collapse. The How Hill Trust, who now care for the oak, commissioned some remedial pollarding to be undertaken with the hope that this will stabilise the tree and enable it to regenerate. There is much pleasure to be taken in the thought that one of the four oaks that Hitler presented to Jessie Owens (a photograph exists of Owens with his teammates and the potted oaks) is still thriving in Cleveland, Ohio.

Collecting historical images of oaks, some still extant, others long departed, provides a fascinating window into not just the physical attributes of the oaks that were around in the past, but also their cultural significance. Engravings exist of many famous trees prior to the middle of the nineteenth century; usually these are fairly prosaic, but now and again an indication of a tree's social or cultural significance is revealed. The great Caeryder Oak in the lower Usk Valley, for example, may now only be a bleached, bare-bone hulk, but in 1837 it stood proudly above the villagers as they celebrated the coronation of Queen Victoria.

With photography in full swing by the end of the century, the postcard publishers provide the most comprehensive archive of tree images. Many of these signify very local associations, delineating trees that might have otherwise gone unrecorded. Some of the most charming images include small family groups, enthusiastic village gatherings, or simply a couple of naughty children. An oak in Shropshire featured as a postbox for many years. 'Eve' (survivor of 'Adam & Eve' Oaks) at Moreton-on-Lugg in Herefordshire was initially a navvy's hut when the railway was being built in the early 1850s. It later briefly served as the stationmaster's residence and office, and subsequently went on to become a lamp room on the railway. Bulls have been penned inside oaks, cattle and horses have been stuck in them, and sheep have given birth in them; and then there are countless tales of packing as many people as possible inside, whether that be standing, sitting down to dine, or playing a merry tune.

Just as so many people today (myself included) are intrigued by the anthropomorphic aspects of oaks – human faces, lion heads, dragons, and demons – so

ABOVE: Unexplained
phenomenon to the right of
the Elfin Oak. Elves at work?

OPPOSITE: Edwardian
postcard of the Lassington
Oak in Gloucestershire,
photographed with two
(or is it three?) ladies.

were the Edwardians, and a few postcards record these strange manifestations. Even more bizarre are the occasional images of trees that leave one wondering if the photographer had visualized a strange occurrence, or whether this is just the prerogative of the viewer with a fertile imagination. Stare into the flames of a fire, or alternatively, cloud gaze, and each and every one of us will see something unique, so why should trees be any different?

Back in 1996, when I visited the Elfin Oak in Kensington Gardens (see p.76), I took about a dozen photographs of the tree in its little iron enclosure. Afterwards, as I studied the transparencies, a strange and unexplained will-o'-the-wisp was seen on just one of the frames. This is quite clearly not a manufacturing or processing fault and the shutter speed of the camera was too fast for it to have been the blur of a bird in flight. I have never worked out what it was, but perhaps the 'little people' of the stump had wrought their magic!

One of the most recent oak stories involves part of the 2012 London Olympic legacy. In 1890, Baron Pierre de Coubertin, founder of the modern Olympic movement, visited Much Wenlock in Shropshire to observe the Olympian Games (as they were then known) devised by Dr William Penny Brookes, who believed (quite rightly) that health and spiritual well-being were promoted through exercise. After this, de Coubertin was inspired to hold the first modern Olympic Games in Athens in 1896. In celebration of his visit to Much Wenlock, an English oak cultivar 'Concordia' was planted on Linden Field, in the town. In 2004, acorns were collected from the original tree by local school children, grown on at Kew Gardens, and then 40 saplings were planted out at various sites, in a ribbon between Much Wenlock and the Olympic Park in London. If the Olympic Games comes round to London in another 64 years, it will be interesting to see how our commemorative oaks are getting along.

Lassington Oak, Gloucester.

Brooke, Gloucester Copyright

Strutt

THE COWTHORPE OAK

THE COWTHORPE
OAK

I F EVER THERE WAS AN OAK OF TRULY HUMUNGOUS PROPORTIONS then it has to have been the mighty Cowthorpe Oak, which once grew close to the church at Cowthorpe, near Wetherby, in Yorkshire. From the mid-eighteenth century onwards, virtually every writer on trees refers to the incomparable bulk of this monstrous English oak. In his edition of John Evelyn's *Silva* (1776), Alexander Hunter notably claims that the Cowthorpe Oak outshines any of the fine oaks that Evelyn referred to more than a century before:

> *The dimensions are almost incredible. Within three feet of the surface it measures sixteen yards, and close by the ground twenty-six yards. It's height in its present and ruinous state (1776) is about eighty-five feet, and its principal limb extends sixteen yards from the bole. Throughout the whole tree, the foliage is extremely thin, so that the anatomy of the antient branches may be distinctly seen in the height of summer. When compared to this, all other trees are but Children of the Forest.*

The accompanying plate by John Miller (aka Johann Sebastian Mueller) does the tree more than ample justice.

The name of the village manifests in numerous different guises – Calthorpe (Strutt), Cawthorpe (First Hunter edition of Evelyn's *Silva*, and Ablett), Coltsthorpe (Lauder), Cowthorp (*The Gentleman's Magazine*), and Cowthope (an 1804 engraving).

A plethora of lyrical accounts and a rich archive of early representations of the tree chart its progress through senility, but continually reinforce the veneration that was felt for this champion of oaks. An illuminating snippet from *Langdale's Topographical Dictionary of Yorkshire* (1822) vividly describes the declining state of the tree: 'The intermixture of foliage among the dead branches, show how sternly this giant struggles for life, and how reluctantly it surrenders to all conquering time.'

The artist J. G. Strutt visited Yorkshire in 1822 to sketch its distinctive frame, later providing J. C. Loudon with a copy for his *Arboretum et Fruticetum Britannicum* (1838). Strangely, Loudon managed to reproduce the image reversed, but, of course, still complete with the slightly bizarre presence of a peacock sitting on one of the boughs. Loudon furnishes the reader with an account of the tree sent to him in 1829. By this date the girth of the tree had remained the same for fifty years, indicating that it was well and truly in a state of decline. Its height was now estimated at 56 feet and 'three of the living branches are propped by

OPPOSITE: Cowthorpe Oak from Sir T. D. Lauder's edition of *Remarks on Forest Scenery* by William Gilpin, 1834. The plate appears to be credited to J. G. Strutt, although etched by Kidd, yet the image is reversed from Strutt's rendition in his *Sylva Britannica*.

substantial poles, resting upon stone pedestals'. However, also in 1829, the
Revd Thomas Jessop, whose account Strutt offers in his 1830 edition of *Sylva
Britannica*, records reduced dimensions of the girths, several feet smaller than
Loudon, and the height as only 45 feet. It is difficult to know how girths were
measured (with or without burring) and how heights were estimated. With
ancient trees there is always a margin of error by the very nature of their forms.

Jessop recalls the following:

> *It is said by the inhabitants of the village, that seventy persons at one time got within
> the hollow of the trunk; but on enquiry, I found many of these were children; and, as
> the tree is hollow throughout to the top, I suppose they sat on each other's shoulders;
> yet, without exaggeration, I believe the hollow capable of containing forty men.*

It is amusing to see how often these tales of packing people into trees slowly
escalate in magnitude, the fanciful nature of the legend leading inexorably to
epic – if not ridiculously impossible – computations.

In Sir T. D. Lauder's edition of William Gilpin's *Remarks on Forest Scenery*
(1834), another delicate engraving of the tree appears and, although remarkably
similar to Strutt's rendition, again the image is reversed as in Loudon (although
by now the peacock has flown). The strange occurrences of the image reversal
cannot immediately be explained; for if an artist or engraver copies a form as
distinctive and well known as this oak, then such a basic error seems a mystery.

In 1835 an article about the tree in *The Mirror of Literature, Amusement, and
Instruction* (vol. 25) plunders much of the foregoing accounts and then rounds
off with a reference to the local tourism:

> *Cowthorpe being so short a distance from the celebrated watering-place –
> Harrowgate* [sic], *it is often visited by the company for the purpose of inspecting
> this 'Giant of the Forests;' and, I think I can safely say, a visitor never returns,
> after seeing this noble and ancient tree, without being highly gratified.*

The great oak soon became a star attraction of any tour of the North Country,
satisfying the Victorian fascination with romantic landscapes, enhanced by the
superlatives of the natural world.

H. J. Elwes visited the tree in July 1906, and seems to have been less than
impressed with what he found, going so far as to suggest that the oak might have
been somewhat overrated: 'No oak in England has probably been the subject
of so much writing as the Cowthorpe Oak, near Wetherby, which perhaps never
was such a great tree as has been supposed, and is now a mere wreck.' Elwes
remarks that since a large part of one side of the bole had caved in, it was almost
impossible to take an accurate measurement of the girth. He dismissed the claim
of John Clayton, who had found the tree to be smaller in 1893 than when it was
recorded by Marsham in 1768, Clayton surmising that this must be because the
roots had lately rotted and the tree sunk into the ground. Elwes viewed this
claim with palpable derision. Still, he noted that 'the few living branches still
bear acorns, from which some seedlings were raised in 1905 by Messrs. Kent

and Brydon, nurserymen of Darlington'. Where these younger trees ended up would be fascinating to know.

However, the whereabouts of one documented descendant of the Cowthorpe Oak is known. During the 1870s, Captain James Runciman is reported to have taken one of the acorns right across the globe to New Zealand, where he planted it on his farm at Drury, South Auckland. With its girth of 16 feet 5 inches, it has put on remarkable growth in 140 years, possibly because of the very favourable climate. It survives to this day, although is now beginning to show signs of decline. Yet more acorns have been taken from this tree in a bid to keep the line going into the future.

A wide variety of ages were credited to this tree. In the nineteenth century, Professor Burnet considered that it could have been 1,600 years old. Since it had already been hollow for several centuries, there was no way of telling the age when it finally fell. However, with today's knowledge of age and size relations in oak a little more refined, it would be quite acceptable to suggest an age of 1,200 years, give or take a century. Obtaining a definitive date for the final demise of the tree has proved difficult, but suffice to say that by about 1950 it had finally given up the struggle. It will be interesting to see in the future whether any of our biggest oaks ever match the remarkable magnitude of the Cowthorpe Oak.

THE SHIRE OAK, OR SKYRACK

OPPOSITE: A romantic drawing of Skyrack in 1854 by the artist Thomas Sutcliffe (1828–71), who lived at this time in Far Headingley. The artist and his wife and child are depicted at the foot of the tree. The child was Frank Meadow Sutcliffe who, when the family moved to Whitby, gained fame for his photographs of local scenes. Drawing given to the Thoresby Society by Thomas Sutcliffe's widow in 1902.

I WAS BROUGHT UP IN YORKSHIRE, AND STILL HAVE A VIVID childhood memory of my parents talking about taking buses to go shopping in Leeds and 'changing at the Skyrack'. What on earth was this thing, I wondered? A 'skyrack' sounded like some sort of aerial stacking system for planes or something built for the space race, so I was surprised to hear that it was 'just a pub'.

Since then, the name cropped up again when I bought an old postcard of Headingley featuring the Skyrack pub. Just across the road from the pub was a massive, but clearly moribund, stump of an oak tree in its own little iron-railed enclosure. The more I looked, the more of these Edwardian images came to light. Clearly the remains of this old giant were celebrated and deemed eminently saleable by numerous postcard publishers.

Eveleigh Bradford of the Thoresby Society has researched the history of the tree most thoroughly. According to Bradford, there would appear to have once been a landmark oak tree signifying the site of a wapentake (the Norse name for an administrative area and meaning 'a taking of weapons'). Known as 'Siraches' in the Domesday Book of 1086, the Old English spelling comes down as 'Scir-ac', meaning Shire Oak. Writing in 1715, the Leeds antiquarian Ralph Thoresby referred to it as 'Skire-ack', which certainly has a Norse resonance, but still means 'Shire Oak'. As early as 1529 it was referred to as 'Skyrack'. A recent, alternative meaning of the name suggests that it derives from Anglo-Saxon, and means 'Bright Oak'.

If only because of its imposing stature (perhaps bigger than anything else in the vicinity), the oak seems to have been firmly endorsed in Thoresby's time as the self-same ancient tree that had shaded the great tribal gatherings for maybe 1,000 years. While this sounds optimistic and romantic today, in the nineteenth century little more was required to convince the Victorians. Early in the nineteenth century a notice nailed to the tree claimed that it was 'The Original Oak from which the Wapentake is named Skyrack'. Capitalizing on the tree's fame, the two nearby public houses were, and still are, the Original Oak and the Skyrack.

Until the 1890s, the oak stood in the garden of an adjacent cottage, but with the introduction of trams the road needed to be widened and overhead electric wires had to be installed. These adjustments meant that suddenly the tree was sitting in the middle of the pavement, and had now to be protected with a small stone plinth and iron railings. Although the oak doesn't feature in any nineteenth-century books about trees, it does get a brief mention in Charles Mosley's *The Oak* (1910):

Plate XI.—THE SKYRACK OAK, HEADINGLEY.

The Old Oak, Headingley

An old oak which marks the meeting-place of one of the shire moots or open-air courts… At these shire moots every freeman was supposed to have a right to attend and vote.

However, in his *Annals of Leeds*, Mr Edward Parsons suggests the following:

This remarkable tree has been conjectured to have witnessed the horrible religious rites of the Ancient Britons, and in fact to have formed part of a Druidical grove.

Such an assertion is surely a flight of fancy, with no concrete evidence, but again it would have appealed to the romantics!

Up until the early twentieth century, the oak was still just about alive, although the end was clearly in sight. In postcards of the late Edwardian period, it looks most definitely dead. An acorn from the tree had been planted nearby and grew well until 1921, when it was decided that the tree was growing in the perfect spot for a Great War memorial (surely a fine English oak would have made an excellent memorial itself!). The tree was uprooted (sadly, without an attempt to replant it) and one of its acorns was planted in the churchyard. This 'grandson' of the original oak unfortunately died.

Although the tree was merely a hulk, it remained in its roadside enclosure until 1941 when it finally collapsed. The tree's final fall was reported with an amusing cricketing analogy in the *Yorkshire Post* of 28 May:

Headingley [then, as now, a regular venue for test cricket] *is accustomed to collapse. Has not even England collapsed there before now, when the Australian bowling proved too deadly? But a collapse took place yesterday which even the most hardened Headingleyite could not see without a pang…*

The pubs live on and the name Skyrack survives to puzzle and confuse another generation of children; well, outside Headingley anyway.

THE ALLERTON OAK

OPPOSITE: The Allerton Oak in the middle of Calderstones Park.

CALDERSTONES, OR MORE PROPERLY CALDER STONES, is one of the finest green spaces in Liverpool, but its existence today owes much to several visionary Victorian owners of the estate. Prior to 1828, in what was essentially an area of open farmland and countryside, after many years of neglect, the eponymous 'Stones' from what was the original Neolithic burial site were dismantled and redistributed, thus the integrity of what today would be considered a hugely important historic monument was lost. A quote from Samuel Lewis's *A Topographical Dictionary of England* (1831) records the actions of amateur archaeologists: 'Adjoining the farm on which stands the famous Allerton oak there is a supposed Druidical monument, called Calder Stones, in digging around which, about sixty years ago, urns of the coarsest clay, containing human bones, were found.'

While the stones may have been rolled away, the Allerton Oak, the great oak that Lewis mentions, would come to acquire an even stronger significance than the ancient stones. A long-standing tradition asserts that what were then known as 'hundred courts' were held within the shade of the tree from the medieval period onwards. These gatherings, pitched somewhat higher than parish level, but lower than county level, were regular judicial meetings intended to solve disputes, mete out fines or punishment, or muster men to arms. A 'hundred' was usually described as an area that supported a hundred homesteads.

Various parties continued to desecrate what must once have been a sacred burial site, until Joseph Need Walker purchased the estate in 1828. Realising the importance of the stones on his land, he took the trouble to gather them together and secure them within iron railings, where they remained for the next 125 years. Need Walker also built himself the handsome mansion and eventually bought more land, naming the estate 'Calderstones' and effectively creating the park that exists today.

A dramatic event occurred on the night of 16 January 1864, at Woodside Ferry on the River Mersey. The *Lottie Sleigh*, laden with eleven tons of gunpowder, was waiting for the morning tide before departing for Africa. As one of the local ferries passed by, the crew of the *Lottie Sleigh* frantically hailed it over, demanding to be speedily taken off the ship. The evacuation was at 6 p.m.; at 7.30 p.m. the whole ship blew sky high in a spectacular yet terrifying catastrophe. All the windows were shattered for a mile inland along both sides of the river, including Caldertones; shards of timbers and lumps of ironwork rained down all around. It was a miracle that nobody was killed. The cause was a simple mishap. While a steward was filling an oil lamp it was upset, dropping burning oil down into the hold near the gunpowder. When the fire could not be brought under control, the crew quite understandably abandoned ship.

The Famous Old Oak, Calderstone Park.   Liverpool.

The Wavertree Series.   No. 104

Reports indicated that the Allerton Oak was struck by some of the debris, shattering several branches, which eventually had to be removed. Other, perhaps fanciful, accounts of the event relay that something approaching a mini earthquake caused the tree to split down the middle, even though the tree stood three miles from the explosion. While this is a good yarn, it's about as likely as the popular myth that the Allerton Oak is 1,000 years old. Its girth of 18 feet simply doesn't put it in that league, but 500–600 years might be nearer the mark. Given this timeframe, the tree's significance in medieval times then becomes debatable. It could be a replacement for a much older oak at the same site.

Calderstones was sold on to Charles MacIver in 1873, a man of considerable means. It was, after all, Charles and his brother David, along with Samuel Cunard in America, who established the famous shipping company Cunard Line. They, in turn, sold the estate on to Liverpool Corporation in 1902, whereupon they began the process of transforming a private working estate into a public park, which was opened to visitors in 1905.

Throughout these times of change the Allerton Oak has survived. This is possibly because the Edwardians thought it prudent, given its decrepit state and split bole, to provide the old timer with numerous props to steady its aging boughs. During the Second World War, lots of seedlings were grown from Allerton Oak acorns to ensure the genetic continuity of the tree (in case a stray bomb should do its worst). Today, it is still one of the focal points of the park, and much loved by all who know it. As for the famous Calder Stones, they are now safely indoors, in one of the old Harthill greenhouses, where they were placed in 1964 after worries that air pollution was eroding their strange carved symbols.

OPPOSITE TOP: An Edwardian postcard of the Allerton Oak with its many props but no surrounding railings as yet.

OPPOSITE BOTTOM: The Allerton Oak in Calderstones Park. This Edwardian postcard, much like the one above it, shows little sign of the great split that is supposed to have riven the tree in two after the *Lottie Sleigh* explosion. However, it would appear that it may well have lost a few boughs.

ABOVE: The tree photographed from the other side clearly shows how the split now goes all the way through the tree, and yet it still appears to be in good health.

THE HENRY VI OAK

NORTH OF ESKDALE, ON THE COAST OF CUMBRIA, on the lawn in front
of Irton Hall, stands the Henry VI Oak, or Irton Oak. It is reputedly 1,000
years old, although its relatively unspectacular girth of a little over 17 feet makes
this assertion rather unlikely. A more realistic assessment of the tree's age might
be 400–500 years old, so this could be a classic example of one oak tree taking
on the mantle of a far more esteemed forerunner.

In 1461, in the aftermath of the Wars of the Roses' Battle of Towton, reputedly
the largest and bloodiest battle on English soil, Henry VI and his retinue, fleeing
from York, sought shelter at Irton Hall. The Hall being a Yorkist house, they were
denied entry. One account relates how the king spent the night beneath the great
oak in front of the house before heading south over the fells to Muncaster Castle
where Sir John Pennington, a loyal Lancastrian, welcomed in his monarch to be
fed and sheltered. Another account states that the king hid inside the hollow
tree, and was secretly brought food by a loyal servant from the Hall. The servant
was later exposed and beheaded for his treachery to the Lord of Irton.

OPPOSITE TOP: The Henry VI
Oak in front of Irton Hall.

OPPOSITE BOTTOM: An
Edwardian postcard of the
Henry VI Oak at Irton Hall,
Cumbria.

BELOW: Henry VI, steel
engraving from a painting at
Kensington Palace, c.1850.

In gratitude to Sir John, Henry presented him
with a glass drinking bowl with the prayer that the
Pennington family would prosper as long as the
bowl remained unbroken. This bowl, known as 'The
Luck of Muncaster', remains intact to this day and
is proudly displayed in the castle. There is also a
painting in the castle of Henry VI kneeling at the
altar with the bowl in his right hand.

The tree today seems to be in pretty good shape,
albeit hollow and, at some relatively recent date,
filled with concrete to stabilize it. Few experts today
would recommend this strategy for tree conservation,
but there are several examples of this practice
elsewhere, notably the ancient yew at Tisbury in
Wiltshire, which is still soldiering on with its great
hollow trunk cavity full of concrete.

OAK PESTS
AND DISEASES

In a book which is essentially a celebration of the oak, it might seem to be a rather negative departure to introduce the topic of pests and diseases, but most people are unaware that our oak trees are under threat from a variety of sources.

THE GREY SQUIRREL

While watching people feeding grey squirrels in public parks or putting food out for them in their gardens, I can't help but wonder whether they would persist if they knew about the darker side of these bushy-tailed tree rats. Not only do they steal birds' eggs and even nestlings, dig up bulbs and corms, plunder fruit, vegetables, nuts, flowers, and buds, but worst of all for foresters and lovers of oaks (and many other trees), they strip bark, thereby killing thousands of trees every year and costing the forestry industry millions of pounds. Why do they strip bark? Different theories have been espoused. Some say that squirrels seek the sweet sap beneath the bark, while others believe that this is a territorially fuelled display that occurs when too many squirrels are living in close quarters. The period of the year in which this occurs matches the time when juvenile squirrels start to seek their own patches.

In areas of high-density squirrel populations, the peak period of bark-stripping activity is late April to July, and they can strip great quantities of young trees very quickly. Trees most at risk are in the 10–40-year age bracket. Younger and they won't support the weight of the animal, older and the bark is too thick and tough to peel. If the tree is completely ring-barked, then the supply of sap is cut off to the crown above the girdling, causing that part of the tree to inevitably die. Partial barking puts the tree under stress, risks ingress of disease and fungal attack, and disfigures the tree for the purpose of timber production. Admittedly, much squirrel damage occurs in plantation woodland, which is to some degree already a manufactured ecosystem, but where it occurs in natural or semi-natural woodland it has the capacity to completely alter the ecological balance

and biodiversity. Over and above this, when trees are affected in amenity woods or public parks, the partially dead trees can present hazards to the public, with dead or diseased branches falling.

It may not be a popular move with people who see grey squirrels as cute, but as with other introduced species such as deer, which have few natural predators, culls must be invoked to keep populations under control. Another aspect of grey squirrel overpopulation is the threat to native red squirrels, not just through competition but also because the greys carry the deadly squirrel pox virus, to which they are immune, but to the reds it proves fatal. In fairness, it must be said that the red squirrel will also strip bark, but there simply aren't high enough concentrations of this animal to have a significant impact. Other concerns about grey squirrels are the eggs and fledglings they will take from nests, as well as the serious damage they can inflict on peoples' homes. Total eradication of any animal seems unreasonable, after all, domestic cats take millions of birds from our gardens every year and we wouldn't contemplate a widespread cat cull, but grey squirrels present a problem that has to be addressed.

Until I paid a visit to the Forest of Dean a couple of years back, and was directed by foresters to areas that had suffered particularly bad squirrel depredation, I had no idea how much damage they could cause. Whole stands of young oak and beech stood gaunt and leafless, their dead branches rattling together in the breeze.

MICE, DEER, AND MOTHS

In 1838, forty years before the arrival of the grey squirrel, it was field mice that were taking a massive toll on oak seedlings and saplings, and arousing the foresters' wrath in the Forest of Dean. Mr Billington provides a detailed account of how acorns were eaten and saplings were bitten off at the base. All manner of attempts were made to catch the mice, by 'cats, dogs, owls, poison, traps, baits, etc.', but to no avail. In the end they hit upon the idea of small pits next to the trees into which the mice fell and could not escape. Two men who were paid to dig the pits and collect and dispatch the mice were paid by the dozen and they 'soon caught upwards of 30,000'. Mice can still be a problem today, but modern tree guards reduce their impact to a minimum.

Oak trees attract some of the tiniest pests, to some of the largest in the British countryside – deer. Travelling around the country, one might not think there were many wild deer around, but though they may appear to be shy creatures there are plenty of them in the depths of much of our woodland, and they take a heavy toll on our broadleaf trees, browsing new shoots, saplings, and seedlings. As they have no natural predators, since wolves and bears have long disappeared, measures have to be taken to control the number of deer, as well as the time and money to protect trees.

It's not often that something that attacks trees also turns out to be harmful to human beings. In 2006, an alien species of moth arrived in Britain in a consignment of oaks from Tuscany, brought into a housing development near the Royal Botanic

ABOVE LEFT: The green oak tortrix moth (*Tortrix viridana*).

ABOVE RIGHT: Deer may look sweet, but they take a massive toll on all British trees, not just oak.

Gardens at Kew. The moth soon spread into gardens; somewhat ironic given that Kew, so long associated with scientific and horticultural excellence in trees and plants, unwittingly became host to a new scourge of oak trees in Britain.

The oak processionary moth (*Thaumetopea processionea*) can reproduce in vast numbers and its larvae (caterpillars), which march in nose-to-tail processions, giving the species its common name, have the capacity to strip oaks bare of foliage. This is a species that until recently was confined to central and southern Europe, one assumes because of climate. It would seem that conditions now suit the processionary moth in northern Europe and Britain as well, or, if we deny any recent climate change, it has simply adapted to a new climate. In southern Europe the moth does have natural predators, which keep numbers at bay, but in the north it multiplies unchecked. At present, the moth is mostly confined to an area around southwest London, but since its arrival its range has been rapidly expanding. Recent sightings include Berkshire and throughout south London, as far east as Bromley in Kent.

The larvae will feed on both native oak species as well as turkey oak, and they have also been found on hornbeam, hazel, beech, sweet chestnut, and birch, but usually where trees are close to oak. The extremely hairy larvae congregate in nests of densely woven silk that are usually about the size of a tennis ball, on the trunks or beneath the boughs of oaks, and march out of these in columns to feed. The larvae have clumps of long white hairs growing all along the body, but it is the thousands of much smaller, barely visible shorter hairs, particularly on the older

larvae, that create problems for human beings. These contain a toxin that upon contact or inhalation can cause painful skin irritation, allergic reactions, and even respiratory problems. Bearing in mind that the moth has so far occurred most frequently in public parks and amenity woods, the threat to health is a big concern.

Like so many other pests and diseases, once they have a toehold, control is a difficult, uncertain, and expensive process. Only the early stages of larvae (of which there are six) can be treated with insecticides. Once they are more than a centimetre long, this form of treatment is ineffective. The colonies are also well protected by their silk nests. Complete defoliation of trees is serious, yet healthy oaks can often weather the storm and put out a second flush of leaf in late July or early August, known as Lammas growth. This should sustain the trees, and as long as they aren't repeatedly denuded year after year, one suspects they will survive. At present it seems the concerns about human health are far more worrying. Given the high costs of control, which cash-strapped councils will find increasingly hard to find, anything less than total eradication will not be sustainable. The combination of a moth that can fly anywhere and ubiquitous host trees makes it difficult to see how this pest can be stopped. At present, the oak processionary moth is limited to the south-east quarter of the country, but controlling its spread could only be achieved by total eradication, and this is virtually impossible. Now that the genie moth has escaped from the bottle, it will be very difficult to usher him back inside.

While the oak processionary moth must be the most serious threat to oak foliage, several other species are also known for large-scale defoliation: green oak tortrix, winter moth, and the mottled umber have long been known to depend on the oak. J. C. Loudon witnessed first-hand exactly what an infestation of moth larvae could do:

During the summer of 1827, we were told that an extraordinary blight had suddenly destroyed the leaves of all the trees in the Oak of Honour Wood, Kent. On going thither, we found the report but little exaggerated; for, though it was in the leafy month of June, there was scarcely a leaf to be seen on the oak trees, which constitute the greater portion of the wood. [They discovered that it was the work of green oak tortrix moths and deduced that] *the number, therefore, of these caterpillars must have been almost beyond conception.*

The life cycles of these moths are synchronized to coincide with the emergence of new leaves, which develop the high levels of tannin that make them unpalatable only as they age. A whole raft of invertebrates are keen to consume oak leaves – not just moths (many of which will eat the leaves of several other tree species), but also some chafers and beetles. Study almost any oak tree after the leaves have unfurled, and you will be hard-pressed to find many without holes. This makes one realize quite how many different creatures depend on oak leaves. It has been said that around one-fifth of all oaks suffer about 25 per cent defoliation. This sounds quite serious, but the life force within the oak is strong, and they can survive these despoliations. Certainly if trees were denuded every year they would eventually die, so it is fortunate that population explosions very seldom happen in consecutive years. After all, it is counter-productive for any species to eradicate its own vital food source.

OAK MILDEW FUNGUS

Introduced into Europe from America in 1908, and still one of the most widespread and easily spotted adversaries of oak, is the oak mildew fungus (*Microsphaera alphitoides*). Many will have seen the white-coated leaves, most especially on new growth and often on coppice stools. While it doesn't appear to kill the trees, in Oliver Rackham's opinion this fungus has been the main contributor to the decline of the natural regeneration of oaks in woodland situations. Rackham calls this phenomenon the Oak Change. Certainly his observations have been corroborated by the fact that young oak seedlings have rarely prospered in dense woodland since 1908. Not only is English oak in particular very shade-sensitive, but the additional stress of oak mildew would appear to have made it even more intolerant to poor levels of light, which is understandable considering that leaves have to function through a screen of mildew.

OAK GALLS

With more than five hundred different invertebrates being completely or partially dependent on the oak, it is little surprise that their requirements for food, shelter, and breeding sites frequently leads to the depredation of the trees they depend on. That being said, as dendrologist John White points out, 'native invertebrates have lived in harmony with oak for ever; it's the human introductions that usually cause the problems'. Much damage or influence on the tree may go relatively unnoticed by the casual observer, as tiny invertebrates or invisible fungi work their way through leaf, bark, and root. Moth larvae defoliation will be very obvious when it occurs, but some of the most frequently observed signs

of insect influence on oak growth are the numerous different galls usually found
on leaves or stems, and sometimes roots, with more than forty different types
found on the two native oak species. These are mainly caused by the small gall
wasps *Cynipidae*, which lay their eggs by piercing the tissue of the tree with sharp
ovipositors. The tree reacts to this invasion by restricting the circulation of sap.
This in turn results in inflammation, which leads the tree to produce mutated
tissue (the gall) that is specific to each individual species of gall wasp.

The most commonly noticed galls, mainly because they are the largest, are
the oak apple and marble galls. The oak apple is a globular, slightly spongy gall,
sometimes two inches in diameter. Its green colour is often streaked with red,
obviously redolent of an apple. The protective oak apple contains many eggs,
which hatch in the second half of the insect's life cycle. The larvae then feed
off the gall contents and then emerge in late summer. These winged wasps
(*Biorhiza pallida*) then lay eggs on the oak roots, causing more galls (obviously,
rarely seen). In mid-winter, wingless adults crawl back up the tree to lay more
eggs in the leaf buds, and the cycle continues. The oak apple has given its name
to Oak Apple Day – 29 May – the celebration of the Restoration of Charles II in
1660, and indeed these galls would have been in their prime at this time of year.

Marble galls are smaller than oak apples, seldom bigger than an inch across,
and each gall supports just one developing wasp (*Andricus kollari*). These galls
are hard, smooth, and perfectly round – hence the reference to marbles in their

ABOVE: Marble galls on sessile oak.

name – and change from green to brown as they mature. One single hole in late summer denotes the successful departure of its denizen. This particular species of gall wasp was deliberately introduced into Devon from the Middle East during the 1830s, as the exceptionally high levels of tannin in the galls was prized for cloth dyes and for making ink.

A strange little gall called the artichoke gall is an absolute mimic of the considerably larger globe artichoke, with its tufts of overlapping scales. Sometimes also called the hop gall or pineapple gall, it is caused by *Andricus fecundator*. While none of these excrescences seem to have any deleterious effect on the host oaks, there is one gall, the knopper gall, which is caused by *Andricus quercuscalicis*, that distorts the acorn where the egg has been laid. Strangely, the sexual and parthenogenetic (all female) generations of this wasp's life cycle rely on the close proximity of two oak species – turkey oak and English oak. First recorded in Britain in Devon during the 1950s, these wasps were thought to have migrated naturally from Europe via the Channel Islands. The ribbed, roughly conical galls prevent the viability of the acorn, and the name is reputedly derived from the German word '*knoppe*', which is a distinctive seventeenth-century felt cap or helmet. It is said that squirrels are quite partial to the knopper gall – whether this is a blessing or not is debatable.

RIGHT: Two oaks in Staverton Park with dieback of foliage show typical symptoms of Acute Oak Decline.

RIGHT: Two oaks in Staverton Park with dieback of foliage show typical symptoms of Acute Oak Decline.

DISEASE

Since the disasterous onslaught of Dutch Elm Disease in the 1970s, disease seems to have been constantly stalking British trees. However, this is not a new phenomenon, as pollen records show that various tree species have been through numerous periods of decline in the past – sometimes due to disease, but also through unfavourable climatic conditions. In the 1990s, the dramatically named Sudden Oak Death (SOD) caused by the pathogen *Phytophthora ramorum* hit the news headlines in Britain and a mad panic ensued as everyone assumed that this was the death knell for our native oaks. As matters transpired, this was not to be the case.

Sudden Oak Death, which had first been detected in California and Oregon in 1995, turned out to be a disease that affected American oaks. Our two native species were immune, but the disease had reached southwest Britain and affected various other species, including holm oak, turkey oak, beech, sweet chestnut, and horse chestnut. Most victims appeared to come from the rhododendrons, azaleas, and camellias, which were probably brought in from European nurseries. The biggest threat with this pathogen is that it appears to be able to mutate its genetic make-up freely so that new strains insinuate themselves into a new range of hosts. In 2009, a huge concern for British forestry was the discovery of *Phytophthora ramorum* (widely dubbed Sudden Larch Death, or SLD) in vast tracts of Japanese larch – one of our principle commercial softwood trees. SLD was here, and the disease has now spread from southwest England, through Wales, and up into western Scotland. The abiding worry must be that if it has mutated into a strain that infects the larches, could it change again and eventually strike down the native oaks as well?

Of far more immediate concern is Acute Oak Decline (AOD), a bacterial disease that has already affected many thousands of native oaks across the Midlands, south-east England, and the Welsh borders. The symptoms are numerous black weeping legions from splits in the bark, which are often associated with the presence of the jewel beetle *Agrilus biguttatus*. The beetle is believed to be the carrier of the harmful bacterium, and as trees succumb there is much deterioration and dieback in the canopy. It is believed that the burrowing beetle larvae spread the bacterium through the galleries they excavate in the vascular tissue of the tree, in much the same way that Dutch Elm Disease was transported in elms. Strangely, the beetle has been around for a long time, being first recorded in 1874, but its role as a vector in this epidemic seems relatively new, but then, so is the bacterium *Gibbsiella quercinecans*, which appears, at present, to be the most likely culprit. However, scientists at Forest Research are trying to pin down a better understanding of the disease, how it spreads, and whether other factors are involved. At present no known cure is available, but what has been observed over the last couple of years is that although some trees have taken three to five years to die, some have clearly had the disease and weathered the storm, while others appear to have a natural resistance. Trees most at risk appear to be those of about fifty years old and more, and other stresses on the trees, such as drought, defoliation, or additional disease, makes them more susceptible. The potential for disaster is clear to everyone in the timber industry and all allied trades who rely on a steady stream of high-quality British oak, and yet the government seems incredibly tardy about funding more research.

At present, most high-profile activity targeting tree disease seems to be aimed at the problem of ash dieback (*Chalara fraxinea*) – a futile cause, it is in Britain and will take its course. At this stage one can only hope that the great diversity of both the ash and oak gene pools will see the nation through these difficult times, for realistically there is no practical way at present of preventing either of these diseases from progressing. One might expect to learn from past events brought on by such diseases, and be more proactive at a much earlier stage in future, but it seems that bureaucracy simply can't react quickly. The loss – whether total or partial – of our principal native hardwood tree, our national icon and – perish the thought – some of the nationally important heritage oaks in this book, would be a massive catastrophe.

THE FUTURE OF THE BRITISH OAK

Given the number of pests and diseases that exist today, how rosy does the future seem for Britain's oaks? Although some people appear to be in denial, most would agree that our climate is changing. It's the speed of change that has occurred in the last twenty years that causes concern and debate about the future of the British oak. For perhaps the last hundred years, our remorseless burning of fossil fuels for domestic and industrial purposes has shaped the climate we are now inheriting. If you link this to an accelerated plundering of the world's forest trees, those green lungs that absorb the prodigious levels of carbon dioxide generated by human activity, problematic imbalances seem inevitable.

If global warming increases, then the oak will have to adapt to change, but it's been doing that already for thousands of years through many other climatic vicissitudes. Our native oaks are effectively at the northern limit of their natural range, so if they can survive in southern Europe, then they should be fine in Britain for the foreseeable future. Weather patterns that will put trees at risk include prolonged periods of drought, of which we've had several in recent years, unseasonal frosts, and powerful storms. The Great Storm of 1987, with its gusts of 120 mph, came in mid-October, before leaf fall. This unfortunate timing was the main reason for the extensive damage to trees. Since then, violent storms appear to be occurring with more frequency.

The surrounding environment and attendant wildlife will also have an impact on the oaks. A warming climate may well affect the types of pathogens to which the oaks are susceptible, ordaining the various species and concentrations of invertebrate pests. Fungi, many of which develop important myccorhizal relationships with oaks, may be affected by excessive rainfall, drought, management regimes, or of course pollution. The symbiotic relationship that these fungi establish with the oak is critical, as they aid the transfer of nutrients from the soil to the tree, while the tree provides the fungi with sugars for energy. Other fungi, known as saprotrophic, obtain their nutrients from rotting or decaying wood, and a smaller group of parasitic fungi, a notably aggressive example being honey fungus (*Armillaria mellea*), actively attack living trees. A complex ecosystem, not only of fungi, but also of mosses, lichens, ferns, and liverworts, comprise the various manifestations of oak woodlands. Similarly rich assemblages attend the ancient and veteran oaks in parkland, creating a balance that has taken many centuries to evolve.

Oak conservation, whether of individual trees or woodland, needs to be guided by the specific history of the sites and a sensitivity to influences, both natural and human, that make them so special. Most of the management of ancient oak woodland has traditionally been coppice with standards, and a return to this regime has been adopted by many woodland owners today; reclaiming the biodiversity that was greatly diminished when woods were left neglected and unmanaged. Large, old oak pollards have survived several centuries longer than the natural span of most maiden oaks, but boughs have grown long and cumbersome and the risk is that such trees will eventually split apart. It wasn't neglect, but simply a lack of purpose for the cut poles, that led to the cessation of regular pollarding. The conundrum now is whether or not to leave these ancient pollards to keep growing out, or to try to cut once again and keep them alive and sound for a few more centuries. The staff at Epping Forest and Burnham Beeches have experimented with pollarding ancient oaks and beeches. Their conclusion is that when trees have remained untouched for so long, they need trimming back a little at a time on a regular basis, until the whole tree has been pollarded after perhaps five to ten years. If they are cut back all in one go, such trees are easily traumatized and die. Ultimately, if pollard oaks are to become the veterans of the future, we need to think about pollarding relatively young trees now.

There are a few, seemingly obvious, tree-management strategies that can be implemented to save damage to large oaks. Deep ploughing close to oaks can potentially cause serious root damage, as many people underestimate the true extent of a mature tree's root system, which often extends well beyond the drip line of the canopy, with about 90 per cent of the roots in the top 3 feet of the soil. Excessive land drainage schemes that drastically alter the water table will also cause old oaks to struggle. Proof of this is evident in the decline of many of the old oaks in Sherwood Forest. Estimates show that a single mature oak will require about 40,000 litres of water in one summer. Unbelievably, incidents of people lighting fires next to oak trees and, sadly, even inside the hollow shells of ancient oaks (see Strathleven House Oak, p.290) have caused massive damage or total destruction. It's a problem that goes back centuries – the famous Fairlop Oak was probably projected into its final phase of decline because of a fire, although the Major Oak, probably as close as we have to a national tree monument at present, also fell prey to such vandalism but has managed to survive.

Over the last twenty years, increasing numbers of people have become fascinated and involved with the nation's ancient trees. Witness the success of the Woodland Trust's Ancient Tree Hunt, for example, that encouraged so many people to get out and about in order to record the biggest and best trees that they could find. Britain can boast about 80 per cent of all of northern Europe's ancient trees, and a large proportion of these are oaks. The data has been gathered (although new discoveries are constantly coming to light) and we are learning more about ancient trees and their care. However, a concerted Green Monuments campaign, supported by government legislation, the provision of information, protection, advice, and financial support for trees and their concerned communities and private owners, would be a massive boost to a secure future for Britain's most important heritage trees.

OVERLEAF: Late-evening sunlight briefly illuminates a familiar oak on the edge of Bromyard, close to the author's home.

THE LOCHWOOD OAKS

A FEW VERY SINGULAR SITES IN SCOTLAND have developed, largely through neglect rather than active management, into oak woods with a decidedly ancient character. One of the finest examples is Lochwood Oaks, near Moffat, in Dumfries and Galloway. In the shadow of Lochwood Tower, the ruinous residence of the Clan Johnstone, lies an oak wood of a most extraordinary nature. A glorious community of knobbly, veteran sessile oak pollards, bedecked with mosses, lichens, and ferns crouch amid a sea of bracken. The wood is a combination of the kind of ancient oaks that you might expect to find in a forest such as Sherwood, or a deer park such as Windsor, combined with the rich bryophite colonies you would see in the Atlantic oak woods of the west coast. The only reason that these trees have survived so long is because they were pollarded over hundreds of years in a wood-pasture regime.

There is little historic information about such woods, but the presence of nearby Lochwood Tower may offer clues. The first mention of the house is in 1476, so a mid- to late-fifteenth-century building date has been assumed. As the main residence of the Johnstones, it appears to have had a precarious existence, being captured by the English in 1547, who promptly burned it down as they left in 1550. Rebuilt, it was yet again burned down in 1585 by the rival Maxwell family. The castle was rebuilt once more, but by the early eighteenth century must have been considered outmoded, for it was then abandoned by the Earl of Annandale. The proximity of the wood with its pollards would seem to indicate a small deer park, or at least some sort of enclosure where animals grazed. Dr Walker wrote of the wood in his *Essays* in 1773 and again, in 1836, Hope Johnstone, Esq. corresponded with J. C. Loudon about the largest oak in the wood:

> *This tree stands in a wood of oaks, in which the Castle of Lochwood (the original residence of the Johnstone family) is situated. It is quite vigorous; but most of the other trees are in a state of decay. There are the remains of larger oaks, the diameter of the trunk of one is 6 ft.; but little of its head remains.*

Selby also briefly mentions Lockwood [sic] in 1842. A reasonable guesstimate of the age of some of the older oaks would be in the 400–500-year range. However, in fairly recent times, that guess has been converted into hard fact.

In the mid-1970s, Lochwood was chosen, as one of a very select group of sites in Scotland, for a study of annual growth rings, otherwise known as

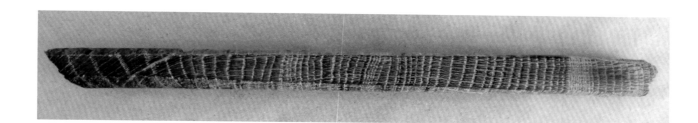

dendrochronology. Every year a tree lays down a new layer of cambium, which shows as an annual ring. Depending on the prevailing climatic conditions, these rings may be narrow in unfavourable years (particularly drought) and wider in favourable years. Each ring consists of a less dense and more dense layer of cells, which corresponds to the spring and summer growth. The contrasting light and dark tones make each annual ring discernable. In 1973 and 1975, Dr Mike Baillie, from Queen's University Belfast, took core samples from the oaks at Lochwood, and by cross-matching sixteen samples he obtained a chronology for the site, which established a range from 1571–1975. By 1977 this study, along with others in lowland Scotland and Northern Ireland and core samples from a variety of timbers from historic buildings, built a master chronology that extended from AD 946–1975. Subsequently, over the last thirty years, with access to even older timber artefacts and bog oak, this chronology has been extended to 7,000 years. In practicality, a spread of annual rings in a piece of oak timber can now be matched to some point along this master map to establish age and, if there is the presence of sapwood, a felling date can be established too. This information is of huge significance to archeologists, architects, conservators and climatologists, and has also provided an invaluable cross-reference for carbon dating.

In recent history, Lochwood has been unfenced and open, which must have put any natural regeneration of the oaks under serious pressure, what with roe and fallow deer in abundance, and probably grazing sheep and cattle in the past as well. Recently, deer fences have been erected around a large section of the wood, so it will be interesting to see what happens on the woodland floor. Spaces for sunlight to penetrate are there, although some bracken control will probably have to be instigated to open up the ground for young trees.

It is actually very fortunate that the oaks have survived so well here, since beech wood is encroaching from the northern end, and stands of conifer forestry overlap with the woodland margins. Its continuing survival is a testament to the great good sense of the present Earl of Annandale. You can admire the wood from the narrow lane, which weaves through it. Simply to stand among these grand old trees, wondering by whom and exactly when they were last pollarded, and imagining the sights they've witnessed over the last 450 years or more in this turbulent border region, is an unforgettable experience.

OPPOSITE: A wild and windy day in Lochwood Oaks; one of the ancient trees festooned in mosses, lichens and ferns.

ABOVE: This oak core, just over 6 inches long and displaying 82 annual rings, was taken from an old cruck timber in a Herefordshire house. Dendrochronology has dated this span as 1292–1373. Evidence of sapwood suggests that the tree was felled in the spring of 1374. The three periods where the annual rings become very narrow probably relate to drought years.

THE CAPON TREE

THE CAPON TREE, A MASSIVE OLD, HOLLOW OAK, stands in Prior's Haugh, close by Jedwater, just a mile south of Jedburgh in the Scottish Borders, and is reputed to be one of the last great oaks of the ancient Jed Forest. The tree would appear to have grown up with two prominent leaders, although sadly one of these collapsed a little over a century ago and has since been borne aloft, albeit horizontally, by several large wooden props. Despite its semi-recumbent form, the tree is still in good health. Popular local opinion claims that it is at least 1,000 years old, but its size doesn't really vindicate this assertion. An age of 700–800 years would seem more likely.

One suggested origin of the name 'Capon' comes from the Scottish word '*kep*', which means 'meet' and so, as a clan rallying point, this seems quite a plausible option. Indeed, in his *Catalogue of Remarkable Trees in Scotland* (1808), Professor Walker of Edinburgh refers to this as the 'Kepping or Trysting Tree'. There is a map of 1838 with the tree actually marked as 'The Keppin Tree'. The name is unusual, but not unique in the North Country (two other Capon Trees once stood at Alnwick, Northumberland, and Brampton, near Carlisle). Surely 'Capon' in this instance couldn't be associated with the OED definition of 'a castrated edible cock'. Or could it? One account from 1880 by Robert Hutchison of Carlowrie acknowledges the fact that this was a trysting place, but goes on to surmise the following:

> From its name 'Capon' – and of which there are other trees similarly styled in different parts of Scotland – it served another purpose also, having probably been the selected spot, and under the shade of whose umbrageous head, the early border chieftain attended to receive the rents or tithes of his vassals, many of the lands being held of their superior by an annual payment of fowls, cattle, corn, &c., and frequently we find the reddendo of a 'capon' was a common act of fealty.

Another reference from George Tancred's *Rulewater and its People* (1907) mentions a Jedforest roll of 1669 in which rent was described as being paid in 'money, capons, chickens, trees and services.'

Another suggested connection derives from the shape of the tree resembling the hood or '*capuchon*' of the monks of nearby Jedburgh Abbey, who also may have sheltered beneath its boughs. This seems a tenuous association, however, and difficult to substantiate. It is noted that the French word '*capuchon*' has never entered the Scottish vernacular. So, the overwhelming opinion seems firmly set towards the association with domestic fowl.

As recently as 1947, a local committee of Jedburgh worthies decided that there should be an extension to the customary (since 1853) Jedburgh Border

OPPOSITE: The Capon Tree, in Prior's Haugh, near Jedburgh.

OPPOSITE TOP: The Capon Tree, Jedburgh. This Edwardian postcard actually includes two small children, one by the gate and another, barely visible, at the foot of the tree.

OPPOSITE BOTTOM: This image of the Capon Tree dates to around 1900 and is printed from an original glass-plate negative, photographer unknown. Spotted on the internet, it was untitled, but was instantly recognisable as the famous old oak.

BELOW: A delightful steel engraving of the Capon Tree by S. Williams, from Prideaux John Selby's *History of British Forest Trees*, 1842.

Games. They devised two preceding weeks of Rideouts from the town in memory of the famous Jethart Callant's ride to the Battle of Carter Bar in 1575, in which Callant bolstered the men of Liddesdale in their fight with the English. A rout of the English forces ensued. The final day of the Jethart Callant's Festival, in early July, incorporates a cavalcade to Ferniehirst Castle and thence to the nearby Capon Tree where 'The Callant' – a young man chosen each year to represent the town – has a small sprig of the oak pinned to his sash, before he rides back into the town. The oak tree thereby playing its part in the proceedings due to its significance as a traditional rallying point for the border clans during their frequent skirmishes with the English.

In 1838, J. C. Loudon published an account of the tree from a Mr Grainger, agent to the Marquess of Lothian, on whose estate the Capon Tree stands. At 2 feet from the ground, the girth was 24 feet 6 inches, the height was 56 feet, and the spread of the crown 92 feet, and yet he observes that, 'from being long neglected and ill pruned, the size has been for many years diminishing, though the marquess is now having every possible care taken to keep the tree alive'.

Despite this care, after a heavy snowstorm in 1882 the tree lost two large branches. This probably led to the partially collapsed shape of the tree as it appears on many turn-of-the-century postcards, and as it stands to this day. It is still thriving and revered as one of Scotland's most famous and beloved oaks.

THE WALLACE OAKS

OPPOSITE: *The Wallace Oak at Elderslie* from Sir T. D. Lauder's edition of *Remarks on Forest Scenery* by William Gilpin, 1834. As with the Cowthorpe Oak plate from this book, this also appears to credit J. G. Strutt. Whether Strutt actually executed these, or the etcher, Mr. Kidd, worked from Strutt's originals is uncertain.

TWO GREAT OAKS HAVE HISTORICALLY LAID CLAIM to the title 'Wallace Oak' in Scotland, and both probably had an equally legitimate claim to have sheltered the great patriot. Both trees are long gone, but their stories are as well documented as William Wallace himself.

After 1286, when King Alexander III died, Scotland had no clear choice of monarch, and so entered a rocky hiatus. Misguidedly, the Scottish lords called on Edward I to come north in order to arbitrate and in 1292, John Balliol was declared the strongest claimant to the Scottish throne. Edward perceived a weakness in Scotland that he was determined to exploit, with a view to stealing power. When John Balliol renounced homage to Edward in 1296, it sparked a sequence of battles and skirmishes. William Wallace entered the fray in 1297, most famously for his crushing victory of the English at the Battle of Stirling Bridge. He was knighted soon afterwards. Wallace's strategy was usually to raid and ambush, but in 1298 he was facing the English once more at the Battle of Falkirk. This time the outcome favoured the English, and Wallace was lucky to escape the field. He subsequently resigned as Guardian of Scotland in favour of Robert the Bruce.

William Wallace appears to have then spent several years keeping a low profile, but also seeking support from European powers in his struggle for Scottish independence. He had resumed his raids against the English by 1304, but in 1305 was finally betrayed, captured, and taken to London, where he was tried for 'treason and atrocities against civilians in war'. On 23 August, Wallace was stripped naked and dragged through the streets of the city behind a horse to Smithfield, where he was hanged, drawn, and quartered. His severed head was later displayed on London Bridge.

Since then, stories about Wallace have abounded throughout Scotland, but as Patrick Fraser Tytler avers in his *Lives of the Scottish Worthies* (1831):

Much, indeed, of all this is apocryphal; part decidedly untrue; but the admiration of his countrymen, which has thrown so rich a tint of the marvellous around his story, and transformed him from a patriot into a Paladin, has been favourable to the permanency of his reputation; for the bulk of mankind are ever more captivated by what is wonderful and romantic, than interested in the truth.

First mention of a Wallace Oak, or Wallace Tree, dates from 1687, when a contract was agreed for harvesting areas of the Torwood, near Falkirk, 'excepting [the] Wallace Tree'. In 1723, the tree was described as having a girth of 36 feet, still bearing leaves and acorns, and 'ever excepted from cutting when the wood was sold'. This is confirmed by a couple of other references from the late eighteenth century that note a diameter of 12 feet.

Strutt.   KM Etc.

THE WALLACE OAK
at Eldershe

OPPOSITE: The Wallace Statue, high above the Tweed Valley, near Dryburgh.

Writing in *On the Old and Remarkable Oaks in Scotland* (1880), Robert Hutchison provides a wealth of information:

Sir William Wallace's oak in Torwood near Stirling has been in the annals of Scotland immemorially held in veneration. In this ancient Torwood, it stood in a manner alone, there being no trees, nor even the ruined remains of any tree to be seen near it, or that could be said to be coeval with it. The tradition of its having afforded shelter and security to Wallace when he had lost a battle, and was escaping the pursuit of his enemies, probably served to secure its preservation, when the rest of the wood at different periods had been destroyed.

In fact, by 1771, when Dr Walker visited, and James Nasmyth executed his fine engraving, the tree was little more than a bifurcated stump. The larger part was 20 feet in height and 22 feet in girth, and as Dr Walker observed:

Whatever may be its age, it certainly has in its ruins the appearance of greater antiquity than what I have observed in any tree in Scotland ... it has been immemorially held in veneration and is still viewed in that light.

It would seem that no images exist of the tree when it was whole, and by 1820 the whole thing had been dug up and carried away, largely by souvenir hunters. The last bits of wood were made into snuff boxes and patch boxes, usually bearing a patriotic slogan or image of Wallace, and certifying that they were made from the old tree. A snuff box was even presented to George IV on his visit to Edinburgh in 1822 – one wonders what Wallace would have made of that!

Another famous Wallace Oak grew near the village of Elderslie in Renfrewshire, reputedly Wallace's birthplace. In 1825, the trunk of this oak measured 21 feet in circumference at the base, and 13 feet 2 inches at 5 feet from the ground. It was then 67 feet high, and the branches covered an area of 495 square yards. Hutchison recalls:

The tradition lending interest to this historical tree is, that Wallace and several followers on one occasion, when hotly pursued by the vindictive Southerns, found welcome shelter and safety among its umbrageous foliage.

However, like so many good stories, the scale of this oak's fame was sometimes over-exaggerated. In his *Continuation of Crawfurd's History of Renfrewshire* (1782), Semple recalled for example that, 'they say that Sir William Wallace and three hundred of his men hid themselves upon that tree, among the branches, from the English'. This is a strange claim considering that the tree only had a girth of 13 feet in 1825 – surely in around 1300 it would have been a mere sapling! This fact is vindicated by another claim that Wallace planted the Elderslie Oak while out riding with his uncle, which is much more plausible, one feels.

When J. G. Strutt made his sketch of the tree in 1830, there was still some life evident in the old oak, although he was somewhat scathing about the souvenir hunters who appeared to be hastening its demise:

The Wallace Oak seems destined, in sharing the fame of others of its brethren, who have been honoured by sheltering the hero Wallace, to share their fate likewise of despoliation: every year its branches pay tribute to its renown, and the western Highlanders, in particular, carry off relics from it in abundance which threatens extinction, at no very distant period, to the parent stem, unless it be protected from further violence by its present owner, Archibald Spiers, Esq. of Elderslie, M.P. who may not be quite aware of the extent to which ravages are committed upon it through the good feeling, though mistaken judgement, of the majority of its visitants.

By 1854 the tree was almost dead. A rare photograph taken around this time shows its stark form bereft of any foliage. A violent storm in 1856 was the final straw and the old tree keeled over. Probably, quite unaware that their previous ravages had damaged the old oak, Hutchison describes the scene as:

Hundreds of relic hunters in the district, hearing of Wallace's overthrow, hurried to the spot, and soon accomplished with bowie knife and gully a thorough dissection of the prostrate hero. Mr. Spiers of Elderslie, however, hastened to the rescue, and had the mangled and mutilated remains of the trunk conveyed and safely lodged in his residence at Renfrew, where they have since found a fitting resting-place. Several articles of furniture have since been converted out of portions of this tree by the proprietor of Elderslie and Houston, and when a few years ago the foundation stone of Houston parish church was laid, the mallet used on the occasion was made from a piece of Wallace's Oak. Two vigorous and thriving oaks in front of Houston mansion-house were reared from acorns of this famous tree, and so eager were the inhabitants of the district to secure some mementos of Scotland's liberator, that some of them even collected the sawdust in bottles for preservation when the stump was cut up!

Even today, as with the Torwood Oak, a variety of items made from the timber of the Elderslie Wallace Oak occasionally come on to the market. Typically snuff boxes, but in 2001 a pair of tables (perhaps commissioned by Mr Spiers) made from the tree came up for auction with an estimated value of £20,000–£30,000. The cachet of the Wallace association endures!

THE POKER TREE

OPPOSITE: A 1920s postcard
of the Poker Tree at Aberfoyle.
The poker appears to have
moved around different parts
of the tree over the years.

BELOW: This oak has changed
very little in the last hundred
years, although the poker
appears to come and go and
change its position on the tree.

IN THE MIDDLE OF ABERFOYLE IN THE TROSSACHS, Stirlingshire, stands an old oak, known since the nineteenth century as the Poker Tree and, sure enough, dangling by a chain from one of the boughs is a large iron poker. The naming of the tree has come down as a strange blend of fact and fiction.

Undoubtedly a famous Scottish folk hero and sometime outlaw, Rob Roy MacGregor (1671–1734) did exist. Records indicate that he was a sympathiser and activist in the Jacobite rebellion of 1715. Later in life when he had established himself as a respected farmer, an unfortunate turn of events led to him losing his herd of cattle and his money, throwing him into debt to the Duke of Montrose. The duke dispossessed Rob Roy of his lands, causing a bitter feud to erupt between the two men, which effectively cast Rob Roy as an outlaw. Many have called Rob Roy the Scottish Robin Hood, and that might have been why Sir Walter Scott adopted the character as part of his novel *Rob Roy*.

Scott published *Rob Roy* in 1817 to great acclaim, the first edition of 10,000 copies selling out in just two weeks. Scott's popularity was truly phenomenal. One suspects that, as with today's tourist industry, anywhere that could lay claim to a link with Scott in the nineteenth century milked it for all it was worth. A brief episode in *Rob Roy* describes how Bailie Nicol Jarvie, a kinsman of Rob Roy, and an expansive Glasgow magistrate and merchant, travels to Aberfoyle with Frank Osbaldistone, the novel's protagonist. Arriving at the inn in the Clachan of Aberfoyle, tired, cold, and hungry, they insist on entering despite the protestations of the landlady and her guests. A scuffle ensues, and one of the guests, a truculent Highlander, draws his sword and challenges them to a fight. The bailie attempts to draw his sword, but finds it rusted in its scabbard through lack of use. Looking around for something to defend himself, he grabs the poker from the fire, brandishes the red-hot tip, and catches his adversary's kilt, setting it ablaze. The Highlander flees, but later returns to acknowledge the bailie on his guile and mettle in combat.

Early photographs show a poker – clearly supposed to be 'the poker' – hanging from the oak, outside the Bailie Nicol Jarvie Hotel, in around 1900. Local concerns were raised in the 1990s when the poker, which had been removed for safe keeping, was thought to have been lost. Fortunately, it turned up, and a little piece of local folklore was restored to its rightful place.

THE COVENANTERS' OAK

THERE SEEMS A CERTAIN IRONY that a tree as proudly titled as an English oak can have been a historic rallying point for a group of Scottish people who held faith in a movement so diametrically opposed to the British monarch and his overbearing divine right to be considered the leader of their Church.

In the main avenue to Dalzell House, near Motherwell in North Lanarkshire, stands the famous Covenanters' Oak, a tree that was once a focal point for members of the Scottish Presbyterian Church. In 1638, when Charles I attempted to impose himself as head of the Church, the Presbyterians covenanted to defend their Church against this Sassenach interloper. The Hamilton family, who owned the Dalzell Estate, were sympathetic to the cause and offered safe haven to the Covenanters. This act risked the severest punitive measures. A monument erected in Greyfriar's churchyard in Edinburgh in 1707 claims that 18,000 were killed for the cause between 1661 and 1680.

One of the more outspoken leaders of the church was the Revd John Lauder, who is reputed to have preached to about 400 Covenanters beneath the great oak. These meetings, known as 'Conventicles', were conducted from 1638 to 1688.

The tree has a girth of 22 feet, and is rumoured to be about 800 years old, although this seems to be a generous estimate. If this is so, then it might tally with the belief that it was planted by King David I in the mid-twelfth century as part of a deer park, and would already have been impressive by the mid-seventeenth century.

Anne MacGregor's 2001 poem, 'The Covenanters' Oak', describes the oak:

The big oak stauns abin the wid
On Sunday morn' auld Lauder stid
Preachin' tae the true an' guid
Covenanters yin an' a'…

One Church elder, John Reardon, was heard to lament at a 2009 revival of the Conventicles, beneath the tree, 'what would our Covenanting forefathers think – that, what violence, bullying and persecution could not achieve, apathy is achieving today'. Fortunately John had the foresight to plant two saplings from the old tree in his garden, which will eventually be planted at other significant Covenanting sites, thus ensuring the continuity of the great oak's legacy.

OPPOSITE: The Covenanters' Oak in 2005.

BELOW: In 2005, when the tree was photographed for a book about Heritage Trees in Scotland, all was well, and author Donald Rodger described the tree as 'a fine old oak [that] stands to this day in good health'. Matters took a dire turn in February 2012, when one huge bough peeled away from the main tree, causing a horrible gash in the centre of the old bole that meant the crown had to be severely reduced to stabilise the tree and stop the rest of it splitting apart. Props have also been used.

THE STRATHLEVEN HOUSE OAK, OR THE BRUCE TREE

OPPOSITE: The mighty bole of the Strathleven House Oak hidden away within a plantation of conifers.

THE STRATHLEVEN HOUSE OAK, as it was originally dubbed back in 2002, was discovered as part of the Forestry Commission's 'Treefest Scotland' celebrations. It was found hidden away in a small woodland, barely 100 yards from the Palladian mansion of Strathleven House, between Alexandria and Dumbarton, north-west of Glasgow.

The fine mansion was built in 1700 for William Cochrane of Kilmarnock, 1st Earl of Dundonald and Commissioner to Parliament for Renfrew. It has been attributed to the renowned architect James Smith. The estate flourished for 250 years, owned by just two families in that time, but after the Second World War it was compulsorily purchased for redevelopment. The house fell into dereliction and became surrounded by an industrial estate. The glorious parkland around the house, its trees, and the great oak in particular (if anyone had recognized its significance) were left to fall into rack and ruin.

A late-eighteenth-century print of the property, then called Levenside House (it became Strathleven House in 1836) shows the building surrounded by clumps of trees. It is fascinating to think that within the grove, to the right of the house, the mighty Strathleven House Oak was already several hundred years old. The print also shows many other substantial broadleaf trees hard by the house.

Visiting the site in 2003 was initially somewhat underwhelming. The old mansion, so recently refurbished, stood proudly in a slightly denuded setting, still clearly surrounded by the neighbouring industrial estate. At first glance the location of the ancient oak, with its mighty girth of 29 feet (making it the largest and probably oldest English oak in Scotland), was not immediately obvious. A scramble though undergrowth into the little thicket opposite the front of the house revealed the old stager squatting in the gloom, hemmed in by a stand of larch. Craggy and heavily burred, the pollard had a distinctly brooding presence. One sensed this tree held secrets. Undoubtedly 600–800 years old, this was a tree from a lost landscape, its roots extending into a time that preceded the building of Strathleven House and the landscaping of its fine parkland.

In 2004 disaster struck. A group of children were playing inside the hollow oak and seem to have started a little campfire. Sadly their game went awry and the fire quickly flared up inside the tinder-dry 'giant chimney' of the hollow, and within seconds the whole structure was alight. Petrified, the children escaped,

OPPOSITE TOP: The charred
remains of the Strathleven
House Oak, June 2004 –
destroyed by fire, May 2004.

OPPOSITE BOTTOM: This
quaich (drinking bowl) is one
of many beautiful artefacts
made from the timber of the
fallen oak by the Strathleven
Artizans.

and the fire brigade were called, but by the time they arrived on the scene the great tree had collapsed and fallen. Hundreds of years of history wiped out in minutes. For several months the burnt-out shell of the oak lay forlornly in the wood, while decisions about its fate were considered.

A group of local enthusiasts called the Strathleven Artizans was formed in 2005 to promote the historical associations of King Robert the Bruce within their village of Renton and the nearby Strathleven estate, which was at one time owned by him. With a little creative imagination, it is just possible to believe that the Strathleven House Oak was growing in the early fourteenth century, and hence might have been known to the King of the Scots. Nobody will ever know for sure, but the possibility was good enough for the Artizans to rename the fallen oak the Bruce Tree in his honour. The group also sought permission to salvage the fallen tree with a view to carving and turning artefacts from the wood in memory of the tree and their hero – a fitting finale to a sad story. However, not all is entirely lost. The base of the old bole where the tree fractured and fell is still alive and throwing out fresh growth, proving that the root system still thrives. It is not impossible that in a few years' time another great oak will rise and perhaps live for a few more centuries.

The old mansion has been more fortunate. Acquired by the Scottish Historic Buildings Trust in 1986, it became their first major restoration project; work started in 1993, and was completed by 2000. It cost a hefty £2.4 million to restore the mansion to its former splendour, but it is now a splendid building, occupied once more, and filling a vital role in the local community, an architectural gem revived.

FAMOUS OAKS GAZETTEER

the roadside on the B1172, about half a mile south of Hethersett village, and is easily distinguished by its iron railings.

Page 92: Kett's Oak, Ryston
LOCATION: Ryston Hall, Norfolk
OWNER: Private Estate
ACCESS: By special permission only

Page 96: The Winfarthing Oak
(tree no longer stands)

Page 98: The Tea Party Oak
LOCATION: Ickworth Park, near Horringer, Bury St Edmunds, Suffolk
OWNER: National Trust
ACCESS: 7 a.m.–7 p.m. daily. The tree stands in the parkland, about 200 yards north of the main car park.

Page 112: Windsor Great Park Oaks
LOCATION: Windsor Great Park, Berkshire
OWNER: The Crown Estate
ACCESS: The park lies south of Windsor and most of it is open to the public at all times. To see Offa's Oak take Forest Road, north-west off the A332 (near the pink lodge). At the end of the long straight, at the first bend in the road, the tree is on the left. William the Conqueror's Oak is nothing more than a dead stump in dense woodland and is not easily found.

Page 118: Herne's Oak
(tree no longer stands)

Page 122: Goff's Oak
(tree no longer stands)

Page 124: Panshanger Oak
LOCATION: On the old Panshanger Park Estate, between Welwyn Garden City and Hertford
OWNER: Lafarge Tarmac
ACCESS: By special permission only

Page 140: Big Belly Oak
LOCATION: Savernake Forest, near Marlborough, Wiltshire
OWNER: Savernake Estate managed by Forestry Commission
ACCESS: The tree stands on the east side of the A346, about 3 miles south of Marlborough. You can't miss it!

Page 140: Duke's Vaunt Oak
LOCATION: Savernake Forest, near Marlborough, Wiltshire
OWNER: Savernake Estate managed by

Forestry Commission
ACCESS: Open at all times. The tree is in the middle of a dense plantation of conifers, and very difficult to find. Take Ashlade Firs Road northwards off the Grand Avenue, stopping where the road leaves the woods for open fields. The tree is 400 yards due east of this point.

Page 144: The Newland Oak
(original tree no longer stands)
LOCATION: Newland, Gloucestershire
OWNER: Private land
ACCESS: By special permission only. In the middle of a field, about 400 yards north-west of the village. Can be seen from a distance. (The replacement tree stands next to the dead stump of the original.)

Page 146: Gog and Magog Oaks
LOCATION: Wick, near Glastonbury, Somerset
OWNER: Unknown
ACCESS: Follow Stone Down Lane, from just north of Glastonbury Tor, down towards the village of Wick. After a little over half a mile, take the rough track or green lane to the left. The trees are located about 300 yards along this track and also back on to the caravan and campsite at Wick Farm.

Page 148: The Knightwood Oak
LOCATION: Near Lyndhurst, New Forest National Park, Hampshire
OWNER: New Forest National Park Authority
ACCESS: Open at all times. About 2 miles southwest of Lyndhurst on the A35, turn right along Boldrewood Ornamental Drive. The tree stands about 100 yards along, in the woods, to the right (carpark on left).

Page 152: The Silton Oak
LOCATION: Silton, Dorset
OWNER: Unknown
ACCESS: Open at all times. The tree stands in the middle of a large field to the east of the village church, on a public footpath.

Page 154: The Meavy Oak
LOCATION: Meavy, Devon
OWNER: In the public domain
ACCESS: At all times. The tree stands on the edge of the village green, near the church.

Page 168: The Boscobel Oak
LOCATION: Boscobel House, near Brewood, Staffordshire
OWNER: English Heritage
ACCESS: The tree is in the grounds of

the house. Opening times are April–October, Wednesday–Sunday, 10 a.m.–5 p.m. Admission charge applies.

Page 174: The Marton Oak
LOCATION: Marton, Cheshire
OWNER: Private owner
ACCESS: By special permission only. The tree is in a private garden

Page 176: Owen Glendower's Oak
(tree no longer stands)

Page 180: The Gospel Oak
LOCATION: Grendon Bishop, Herefordshire
OWNER: Private owner
ACCESS: Grendon Bishop is midway between Leominster and Bromyard on the A44. From Bromyard, look for the sign right to Hampton Charles, Bockleton and Hatfield. Turn left here up a small farm lane, after half a mile look for a steel-bar gate on the left, just before a bungalow. Go through this gate, down the side of the field, and the tree can be found in the middle of the second field. There is a parking place close to it. As this is a working farm, please be sure to close all gates behind you.

Page 182: Jack of Kent's Oak
LOCATION: Kentchurch Court, near Pontrilas, Herefordshire
OWNER: Private estate
ACCESS: By special permission only.

Page 186: The Monarch
LOCATION: Holme Lacy, Herefordshire
OWNER: Holme Lacy Estate
ACCESS: Open at all times. A public footpath passes close by the tree. Travelling westward along the B4399, pass Holme Lacy College on the right, a small tree on a grassy island on the left, and take the very next turning on the left, immediately past a black and white cottage. After 500 yards, park by a stone wall and continue walking up the farm track for another 500 yards (Holme Lacy House down on your left). At the top of the hill, look right. The biggest tree is the Monarch.

Page 198: The Nannau Oak
(tree no longer stands)

Page 202: The Pontfadog Oak
(tree no longer stands)

Page 204: The Golynos Oak
(tree no longer stands)

Page 206: The Buttington Oak
LOCATION: Buttington, near Welshpool, Powys
OWNER: Unknown
ACCESS: Open at all times. The tree stands in fields east of the River Severn and north of Buttington. Take the A458 towards Shrewsbury from Welshpool, and immediately after crossing the river bridge, park and walk through the very first gate on the left. A public footpath leads through fields for about half a mile to the tree.

Page 220: The Bowthorpe Oak
LOCATION: Bowthorpe, near Bourne, Lincolnshire
OWNER: Private owner
Access: On the A6121, heading south from Bourne, pass the Witham-on-the-Hill and Manthorpe crossroads, and after another half mile turn left into Bowthorpe Park Farm. Park in the farmyard. The tree is situated behind the farmhouse on the right. Visit at any reasonable time during the day. A small charge is made to see the tree.

Page 224: The Greendale Oak
(tree no longer stands)

Page 224: The Major Oak
LOCATION: Sherwood Forest Country Park & Visitor Centre
OWNER: Nottinghamshire County Council
ACCESS: Open at all times. The tree is signed along a broad path from the visitor centre (about a 15-minute walk).

Page 224: The Parliament Oak
LOCATION: Near Clipstone, Nottinghamshire
OWNER: Sherwood Forest Trust
ACCESS: Open at all times. The tree is in a little pull-in on the south side of the A6075, about 3 miles west of Edwinstowe.

Page 244: The Cowthorpe Oak
(tree no longer stands)

Page 250: The Shire Oak, or Skyrack
(tree no longer stands)

Page 254: The Allerton Oak
LOCATION: Calderstones Park, Allerton, Liverpool
OWNER: Liverpool City Council
ACCESS: Open at all times

Page 258: The Henry VI Oak
LOCATION: Irton Hall, near Santon Bridge, Cumbria

LEFT: Get close to our ancient oaks, give them a good old hug, and just remember that each of these grew from one tiny acorn. How amazing is that?

OWNER: Private owner
ACCESS: Open at all times. Irton Hall has b&b accommodation and a complex of self-catering holiday cottages.

Page 274: The Lochwood Oaks
LOCATION: Lochwood, south of Moffat, Dumfries, and Galloway
OWNER: The Earl of Annandale
ACCESS: Five miles south of Moffat, on the A701, turn left to Lochwood, and you enter the wood after about 1 mile. Since this is an SSSI, public access is limited, but you can drive through the middle of the wood and view many of the oaks.

Page 278: The Capon Tree
LOCATION: Jedburgh, Borders
OWNER: Marquess of Lothian
ACCESS: The tree stands on the banks of the River Jed, alongside the A68, about 2 miles south of Jedburgh. A 15-minute walk from the town centre, the tree is found after crossing the third bridge. Access granted to the oak with conditional warning that due to the nature of the ancient trees it is at your own risk.

Page 282: The Wallace Oaks
(trees no longer stand)

Page 286: The Poker Tree
LOCATION: Aberfoyle, Stirling
OWNER: Unknown
ACCESS: Open at all times. Enclosed by iron railings, the tree stands on the north side of the B829, at its junction with Manse Road in the middle of Aberfoyle.

Page 288: The Covenanters' Oak
LOCATION: Dalzell House, Motherwell, North Lanarkshire
OWNER: Managed by North Lanarkshire Council and RSPB Scotland
ACCESS: Open at all times. The tree is next to the main drive, 450 yards west of the house.

Page 290: The Strathleven House Oak, or the Bruce Tree
(tree no longer stands)

INDEX

Page numbers in *italics* indicate
   illustrations

ACKNOWLEDGEMENTS

First and foremost I have to thank Jan – my wonderful woman, my rock, who weathers my late-night poundings at the keyboard, the hideously early morning departures to photograph trees, as well as all the emotional and practical ups and downs of completing a book.

Special thanks go to Nick Robinson who loved the idea when I first suggested it, my commissioning editor Charlie Mounter, text editor Jenny Doubt, and all the team at Grade Design – Peter Dawson, Louise Evans and Joanna MacGregor, for creating such a beautiful book. Chris Bell for the index; William Smuts for the map; Gabriella Nemeth, proofreader; Gill Woolcott, production director; Katie Read, publicist.

To all those lovely folks who expressed faith in me and sponsored my work for this book (next page) I extend my personal thanks to: Peter and Sally Goodwin; Sir Henry Studholme; Jeremy and Roz Barrell and Mark Wadey; Lewis Scott and Belinda Moore; Virginia Hodge and Tim Hills.

Also: Rowan Miles; John White; John Plumptre; Mrs E. Clarke; Sarah Partridge at Orchard Barn; Clive Richards; Hamish Low and Lucy Kamall at Diamond Jubilee Fenland Black Oak Project; Monika Mann; Bettina Broadway-Mann; Annie Butterfield at Lafarge Aggregates; Keith Wade and The Sevenoaks Society; Clive Webb; Zilla Oddy at Hawick Museum; Dr Andy Gordon; Morag Embleton; Brian Walker of the Forestry Commission; Bill Cathcart; Claire Pinney at St Pancras Church, London; John Ridler; the Leighton Family; the Williams Family; Bill and Gerry Doolittle; Simon Thompson Cartwright of Robert Thompson's Craftsmen Ltd; Ralph Lloyd-Jones; Duncan Thomson of Strathleven Artizans; Sarah Riddle at National Maritime Museum Cornwall; Kerry-Anne Rookyard at European Squirrel Initiative; Tim Burrell of Carpenter Oak & Woodland; Jackie Simonini; Andrew Maxam; Jan Lucas-Scudamore; Owen Jones; Eveleigh Bradford and the Thoresby Society; David Alderman; Gary Battell; Dr Rosy Gray of Norfolk Museums and Archaeology Service; Michael McTague; Paul Weaver; All Saints, Weston Longville; the Pratt Family of Ryston Hall; Craig Thornber. If I have forgotten anyone, please forgive the omission. Thanks also to everyone who contributed with their pictures:

EXTRA PICTURE CREDITS
p.20 – The Diamond Jubilee Fenland Black Oak Project; p.49 – Laton Frewen; p.84 – Fownhope Heart of Oak Society archive; p.95 – Norfolk Museums and Archaeology Service (Norwich Castle Museum and Art Gallery); pp.102, 131 L – Courtesy Norman Blackburn; p.106 – Andrew Maxam Collection; p.190 – National Maritime Museum Cornwall; p.198 – National Library of Wales; p.201 – National Museum Wales; p.205 – Natural History Museum; p.219 R – Titchmarsh & Goodwin; p.228 – Nottinghamshire County Council; pp.251, 252 – The Thoresby Society; p.262 – Sarah McNeil (European Squirrel Initiative); p.263 L – Jon Stokes; p.264 – Tony Kirkham; p.277 – Robert Howard, Nottingham Tree-ring Dating Laboratory; p.289 – Donald Rodger; p.293 B – Strathleven Artizans.

BOOK SPONSORS

I wish to express my deep gratitude to the following companies and organisations who have kindly sponsored my work on this book, and hope that they are proud of their commitment and association with the project.

ARCHIE MILES, SEPTEMBER 2013.

WOODLAND HERITAGE
PATRON HRH THE PRINCE OF WALES

Woodland Heritage is a registered charity which seeks to join up the wood chain – a vehicle for tree growers, wood users and consumers to 'put something back' and contribute to the proper management of British trees and woodlands.

Woodlands are capable of growing high-quality timber while providing an environment that supports wildlife, but only if properly and continuously managed.

We seek to help by funding tree-planting projects, study bursaries, research grants, running educational courses and co-operating with other like-minded initiatives.

We are delighted to sponsor this stunning oak book, which is a fine tribute to our nation's iconic tree.
www.woodlandheritage.org.uk

TITCHMARSH & GOODWIN

Founded in 1920 by Gordon Goodwin, this small company has an international reputation for the finest cabinet making. They are probably unique in managing their own woodlands and having their own tree nursery while running their own specialised sawmill at nearby Witnesham. Their Ipswich workshops employ highly talented wood turners, carvers, machinists, cabinet makers and French polishers – not to mention a gilder and lacquer artist.

Titchmarsh & Goodwin specialise in using our native English oak. Their environmental policies lead them to co-found the Woodland Heritage charity which is renowned for its work with British foresters to ensure a sustainable future for our national tree.
www.titchmarsh-goodwin.co.uk

Many thanks also go to Peter and Sally Goodwin.

PHAUNOS TIMBER FUND

The Phaunos Timber Fund is a Guernsey-domiciled investment company. Their ordinary shares are listed on the Main Market of the London Stock Exchange. The company's investment objective is to provide shareholders with attractive long-term total returns through a diversified global portfolio of forestry and forestry-related investments. These are largely in Brazil, Uruguay, East Africa and New Zealand.

The company invests only in planted forests, which by providing a sustainable supply of timber, takes pressure off precious old-growth forests. Wherever possible and practicable, the forests are certified under Forest Stewardship Council guidelines, with 77% currently certified.
www.phaunostimber.com

THE CONSERVATION VOLUNTEERS

The Kent Heritage Trees Project is a five-year heritage lottery grant-funded project run by the Conservation Volunteers. The project aims to celebrate and promote the value of heritage trees and to inspire local communities about the wonder of their local heritage trees and woodlands.

To help us we are recruiting and training 330 volunteer Heritage Tree Surveyors; these volunteers will help us reach our goal of recording 10,000 heritage trees. We will also be helping communities create new woodlands by planting 23,000 new trees across Kent and running an education programme to inspire and teach the next generation about trees and the natural world.
www.tcv.org.uk/KentHeritageTrees

BARRELL TREE CONSULTANCY

Barrell Tree Consultancy (BTC) is a tree-advisory practice working all over the UK specializing in resolving planning and legal tree issues. That work inevitably brings them into contact with the very best of our heritage trees, many of them under threat from the pressures of modern development.

In 2008, alarmed by the losses of these irreplaceable natural assets, BTC began working on a formal method of assessing these unique trees. It is called TreeAH and it allows our top trees to be ranked, providing the status needed to justify their protection for future generations. Find out more at www.TreeAZ.com.
www.barrelltreecare.co.uk